THE COLLABORATIVE CITY

CONTEMPORARY URBAN AFFAIRS
VOLUME 8
GARLAND REFERENCE LIBRARY OF SOCIAL SCIENCE
VOLUME 1461

CONTEMPORARY URBAN AFFAIRS
RICHARD D. BINGHAM, *Series Editor*

THE COLLABORATIVE CITY
OPPORTUNITIES AND STRUGGLES FOR BLACKS AND LATINOS IN U.S. CITIES

EDITED BY
JOHN J. BETANCUR AND DOUGLAS C. GILLS

GARLAND PUBLISHING
A MEMBER OF THE TAYLOR & FRANCIS GROUP
NEW YORK AND LONDON
2000

Published in 2000 by
Garland Publishing Inc.
A Member of the Taylor & Francis Group
19 Union Square West
New York, NY 10003

10   9   8   7   6   5   4   3   2   1

Library of Congress Cataloging-in-Publication Data

The collaborative city : opportunities and struggles for Blacks and Latinos in
   U.S. cities / edited by John J. Betancur and Douglas C. Gills.
      p.   cm. — (Garland reference library of social science ; v. 1461.
   Contemporary urban affairs ; v. 8)
   Includes bibliographical references and index.
   ISBN 0–8153–3560–1 (acid-free paper)
      1. Afro-Americans—Social conditions—1975–   2. Hispanic Americans —
   social conditions.   3. Afro-Americans—Economic conditions.   4. Hispanic
   Americans—Economic conditions.   5. Afro-Americans—Politics and government.   6. Hispanic Americans—Politics and government.   7. Coalition (Social
   sciences).   8. Community development, Urban—United States.   9. Afro-
   Americans—Relations with Hispanic Americans.   10. United States—Ethnic
   relations.   I. Betancur, John Jairo.   II. Gills, Douglas C.   III. Series: Garland
   reference library of social science ; v. 1461.   IV. Series: Garland reference
   library of social science. Contemporary urban affairs ; v. 8.
      E185.86.C5816   1999
      305.89073—dc21   99–23665
                                                                              CIP
Printed on acid-free, 250-year-life paper
Manufactured in the United States of America

To Harold Washington and Rudy Lozano

Contents

Acknowledgments

This book started with an idea that everybody liked but only a few thought could be accomplished. First, we wished to create a forum for an open and candid dialogue and search between Latinos and African Americans about the possibilities of collaboration and the challenges of contention between the two communities in U.S. cities. Second, we sought to examine these possibilities in the context of restructuring/globalization and its impact on race/nationality-based policies and struggles. Third, we desired to conduct an analysis that integrated the national and the local, the general and the particular, the Latino and the Black perspectives, and the views of the activist, the politician and the academician. We were inspired by our belief that the destinies of these two communities in the future were tied together—particularly in cities— and that collaboration or contention between them would determine their possibilities of advancement. While our belief and the results of our efforts should be judged by the reader, we owe our gratitude to those who endured the process. We are grateful to those who supported us with their patience, encouragement, material support and inspiration. The list extends to our colleagues, assistants, editors, audiences, students, reviewers, families and critics. We can include only a few names here. Our gratitude, however, goes to each and all of them, in particular to the multiple participants in the discussions and actions behind these chapters.

The Great Cities Institute (GCI), the Center for Urban Economic Development (UICUED), the College of Urban Planning and Policy (CUPPA) and the Urban Planning and Policy program (UPP) of the University of Illinois at Chicago (UIC) were all home to our project at different stages. These and other units of the university provided magnificent support to our project through scholarships, assistantships and multiple other forms. Grants from the John D. and Catherine T. MacArthur Foundation, the Human Relations Foundation in Chicago and GCI helped organize conferences and dialogues around the chapters and topic and defray the costs of production of the book. Other institutions extending support or sponsorship were the Chicago Workshop on Economic Development (CWED), the Chicago Urban League, the Latino Institute, Instituto del Progreso Latino and Centro Sin Fronteras. We have been fortunate to receive the contributions of great scholars and activists for this book; not only did they bear with us the laborious process of producing each of the chapters, but they provided feedback to each other along the way. We owe our especial gratitude to the late Robert Mier, UPP professor, Wim Wiewel, Dean of CUPPA and Adriana Ballen and Susan Motley from the MacArthur Foundation.

We especially appreciate the support of David C. Ranney, UPP professor, Curtis Winkle, UPP director, Cedric Herring from the Institute for Research on Race and Public Policy at UIC, Otto Pikaza, Latin-American Studies professor at UIC, Jesus Garcia, Illinois State Senator, Johnny Cole, CWED policy director, Lauri Alpern from GCI and former Illinois State senator, Alice Palmer. We are indebted to the UPP staff: Charles Keys, Thelma Jackson, Sylvia Becerra and Jose Ayala. We are most grateful to our editor Penny Waterstone, to Esteletta Cameron and our assistants Michelle Story-Stewart, Patrick Riley, Jennifer Williams, Jaime Dominguez, Victor Alvarez and Cheryl Wilson. Special thanks to the series co-directors, David C. Perry and Sallie A. Marston, and to Catherine Rossbach from Sage. Without their continued support and guidance this book would have never come to light. Thanks also to Jeanne Shu, our production editor at Garland, and to Judy Ashkenaz, project manager at Stratford Publishing Services.

The encouragement of our families and friends was great; it carried us through hard times and sustained us through our daily routines. We want to acknowledge Scott, R.D., Wanda, Enrique, Rafael, Berenice, Aracelly, Dario, Margarita, Rodrigo, Angela, Hugo, Jose Maria, Olga Sofia, Maria Elena, Luis Fernando and William. While the book is finished, the dialogue and search are just beginning. This volume is dedicated very particularly to those who will continue this work for the advancement of our communities.

THE COLLABORATIVE CITY

CHAPTER 1

Introduction

JOHN J. BETANCUR
DOUGLAS C. GILLS

In 1982, African American and Latinos in Chicago organized as part of
an unprecedented grassroots movement and coalition that led to the election of Harold Washington as the first nonWhite mayor of that city. By
1989, this coalition had broken apart and the two communities were, in
fact, in contention with each other over multiple issues (see Chapter 4).
In 1989, after many failed attempts at unity in New York City, Latinos
and Blacks coalesced to elect David Dinkins the first Black mayor of the
city. After the defeat of Dinkins in 1993, their leadership parted company, suffering multiple losses in city political elections. This erosion
has had serious negative effects on local public policy for both groups
(see Chapter Three).

Even though both Chicago and New York are minority[1] majority
cities, Latinos and African Americans have been unable to consolidate
and sustain lasting political coalitions in these two places. While their
electoral successes demonstrate that they can translate their shared
power into significant improvements for their respective communities,
these experiences, as well as those of several other big city coalitions,
also reveal such coalitions' failures to create long-term, positive effects
on local public policy.

Blacks and Latinos have also engaged in joint actions of pressure,
protest and disruption in the nonelectoral arena (see Chapters 3, 4, 8 and
9). The 1992 Los Angeles riots are a clear example of the disruption and
chaos they can generate. Gains in education, housing and jobs, among
others, testify to the great power of these initiatives and communities
(see Chapter 3; also Mier 1993).

1

Regrettably, many initial gains have been lost during the implementation process or have been taken back, since these communities lack the institutional power and resources necessary to maintain them (Delgado 1994). Also, political conflicts between Latinos and Blacks, elites in particular—e.g., struggles for position or for control of public institutions, conflicts around distribution of goods and services—have set them back, often pitting one group against the other in the public and private arenas.

Thus, while success of grassroots coalitional activities demonstrates the power of minorities when acting together, the conflicts show that they can cancel each other's gains when acting in opposition.

As the system keeps failing these groups, the struggle for opportunity and resources needs to continue targeting the state very particularly. Ruled by a conservative ideology, the state is acting today to disclaim racism and the need for redress, while blaming Blacks and Latinos for their condition of underdevelopment. Thus, as both the private and the public sectors turn their backs on Blacks and Latinos, only self initiative keeps them going.

The situation calls for a new level of collective effort between African Americans and Latinos, and demands that they reassess opportunities and failures. Today, large and growing proportions of Blacks and Latinos are concentrated in the cities. Their majority in many of them provides the sociopolitical space for concerted action in both the electoral and non electoral arenas. Coalition around complementary agendas and policies can give them the political and community strength required to address their problems, at least locally.

This book explores Latino and Black and other relevant local experiences of collaboration and contention around policies and initiatives of advancement, in the context of recent global and national socioeconomic changes and changes in social policies. It examines these experiences to identify sources of success or failure, systemic inequities, possibilities of collaboration around common needs, and new approaches to common development problems. Moreover, aware of the contradictions that Latinos and Blacks confront—presumably resulting from the workings of the urban social system and its institutions—the book studies systemic and other sources of distress that can lead variously to unity or contention between them.

This work is important because Latinos and Blacks are unevenly incorporated in cities, yet are dominant populations within many of them. Collaboration may be the key to improving their condition. New policy approaches and organizing forms can make a difference for the majority who are low-income. At the same time, globalization poses challenges that need to be understood for effective strategizing (see Chapter 2). The place that these groups occupy within the global and urban political economy and the associations that they build may influence supranational and local politics and public policy formation. Certainly, this will have a bearing on the distribution of social resources, the substantive basis for most collective efforts in urban politics.

Searching for solutions together and participating in transformative dialogue[2] are critical because of the present deterioration of, or strain on, Black–Latino relations. Interactions among them have, perhaps, more impact on the politics and social policies of the nation and of selected cities than those of any other nationality groups. We need to learn about particular dynamics of the new political economy that bring Latinos and Blacks together or that set them apart. We must assess the capability of various strategies for community building, for facilitating collaboration, and for overcoming barriers to productive relations within and between these communities.

Three views of the difficulties of urban-based coalition efforts between Latinos and Blacks are explored here. First, separate cultural histories and racial or national differences explain their relative poor performances in the arena of sustained alliance building. Second, White elites are too dominant; their relative empowerment overwhelms efforts at change, especially when armed with the pervasive forces of racism and racial oppression. Third, activists and analysts have paid little attention to internal dynamics, such as class divergence, multi-nationality, and characteristics of the leadership strata, that emerge in political struggles and in collective efforts at reform. All these views highlight the roles played by racism and class dynamics, themes which are addressed in different ways by each of the chapters in this volume. The multiple analytical perspectives these chapters present are crucial for understanding Latino and Black relations and development possibilities and, thus, for developing strategies of action.

PURPOSES AND AIMS

This volume was triggered by recent local and national events such as the alleged split between Blacks and Latinos in cities like Chicago, New York and Miami; the elimination of government policies and programs of redress; and the condescending, racist national media projection given to Blacks and Latinos in the aftermath of the Rodney King police brutality trial verdict in Simi Valley and the riotous events in Los Angeles following the verdict. Not only have Blacks and Latinos been portrayed as *the problem* of the urban U.S.A., but rifts among them are being exploited to suggest new racial dynamics, in substitution for the majority–minority relationship.[3] Such events sounded the alarm that the editors used to initiate a dialogue and bring together Latinos and Blacks to identify and discuss their common fate in cities, to examine ways in which policies can be reinvented in response to economic and political restructuring, and to develop new approaches for resisting the accumulated effects of racism in an environment of denial. It is time for these groups to confront their differences and to search for common ground toward the solution of many of the problems that they confront together in cities. It is time for voices other than those of the majority elites and the media to be projected, including the voices of people closest to the ground.

We believe that Latino–Black rifts result more from the competition and contestation of middle class elites than from the actions of grassroots activists and ordinary citizens. They are promoted by an environment of renewed racial tension, social polarization, neoconservatism, opposition to minority immigrants, the attack on social welfare and other policies that may signal a coded attack on Blacks and Latinos. Much of it has to do with external forces pushing them to compete against each other for a fixed set of resources and opportunities. Restructuring is a case in point: it forces them to contend with each other and with other non-racial minorities and groups in need of assistance for a substantially reduced social wage.

METHODS AND APPROACHES IN THIS VOLUME

This book promotes and contributes to a new dialogue between Blacks and Latinos around the problems faced by them in cities, the ways in which they are being addressed and the possibilities of working together to overcome these problems. It has been built around a group of authors who are active in the search for solutions to the problems of these communities.

The book evokes a discussion of the future with a more inclusive audience than those who traditionally chart the course of social and political relations. This is done, in part, by removing the discussion from a purely academic discourse and from the exclusive purview of political elites and by starting the dialogue between Latinos and Blacks themselves. The legitimacy and success of searching together, we believe, requires the input of a broader audience of actors engaged in social action and applied social problem-solving. The articles in this volume are in the genre of *social action research.* They were written by people with organic connections to popular struggles and to activities of social, institutional and community change. The theme of consensus building and compromise is reflected in many of the contributions. The styles are intense and engaging. They manifest the dance between social action and scholarship where *meaningfulness* is an important ingredient (Mier 1993). While learning from the academic experiences of many of the authors, the chapters reflect the conviction and moral fervor of activists engaged in the struggle. It is as much a search for knowledge as the telling of insights and experiences gained in years of activism.[4] Generally, the contributors adhere to an approach that brings scholarship and social science research to *social problem solving.* The social problem solving approach is certainly not without method. It assumes that representatives are involved who are most affected by the extant social conditions.

The dialogue we wish to engender is symbolized by the team approach to writing in many of the chapters. The book brings together diverse elements of the communities who rarely intentionally speak with each other. The authors, in fact, engaged in dialogue and networking around the production of this book.[5] Most of the chapters are authored by teams of scholars, scholars and activists, scholar-activists, applied researchers and practitioners, and Blacks and Latinos mixed in multiple ways, at times with other individuals involved in the struggle.

The book brings together scholars and activists from across the country to share their experiences and research, exchange views, and to advance social action initiatives in cities like Chicago, New York, Philadelphia, Atlanta, San Diego, Boston, and Los Angeles. It is intended to inform the joint struggles of Blacks and Latinos in these cities and efforts as well as a broad audience of scholars, practitioners, activists, and their supporters.

GENERAL THEMES

The roots of the tenuous-to-estranged relations between Blacks and Latinos are deep, complex and intricately bound to the core relations of the overall society. These roots will not be untangled easily; nor will unity, no matter how strongly desired, be readily achieved without serious collective efforts. Such efforts require honest engagement and commitment of time and resources to identify ways to meet the challenges posed by unity-building. Frank dialogues, centered on the external and internal forces shaping their mutual and reciprocal relations are essential. All chapters explore changes and new opportunities or obstacles to development in Black and Latino communities. The analyses point to systemic and policy factors that define minority development in terms of competition or confrontation over externally controlled, limited allocations. The chapters suggest that both, objective and subjective factors need to be considered in proposals for collective action.

Several themes are explored or emerge from the chapters: (1) the reality and the pursuit of *diversity* and the collective effort to affirm cultural and social *difference*; (2) the manifold societal, institutional and individual acts of *racism*, as they operate within and among communities of color; (3) the pursuit of and struggle for social, community and human capacity *development* and related efforts to overcome the effects of uneven development; (4) collective initiatives and struggles to attain *democracy in public and civic life*, including access to decision making on the basis of equitableness; and (5) exposure of systemic inequities that preempt development in these communities.

The book advances the hypothesis that while current material and objective factors are conducive for alliance building, the most significant factors are subjective or qualitative. They include (1) the level of development of leadership; (2) its strategic vision of social change; (3) its orientation toward the involvement of ordinary citizens emerging in struggles in community and institutional settings; and (4) the need for both communities to interact and learn about each other as a trust-building foundation. These factors are explored in chapters five, six and ten.

Diversity, as it is presented here, is complex. It has dynamic social bases and is not simply shaped by individual volition or external dynamics. It has multiple aspects. There is the diversity of the issues that we examine and the diversity of the fields of engagement of the contributors. There is the diversity of racially defined groups and nationalities that is crucial for the building of social justice. And there is the diversity within our communities that may be as much a source of tension as are racial and nationality diversity.

There is considerable evidence of a growing class divergency *within* the Black and Latino political communities. That divergency is between the leadership elite and a more affluent class, on the one hand, and the working poor and dispossessed, on the other. Some authors see these internal sources of divergence as the central factor shaping Black and Latino politics in the near future (Chapters 3, 4, 5, 6 and 11). They argue that there are more possibilities for building united action and collaboration *from below*, among the masses, than between the affluent leadership of these groups. Developing a *culture of collaboration* requires more than willingness to conduct joint efforts (Chapters 4, 9, 11 and 12).

The second factor is the dynamic of *racism* and the meanings of *race* in the lives of Blacks and Latinos and in the reproduction of relations of oppression and privilege. The question is not whether racism is still significant in the experiences of Blacks and Latinos (Mier 1993; Jennings 1992, 1994; Webster 1992; Omi and Winant 1986; Winant 1994). It is how it articulates with *class* to determine their essential position in city politics. Some chapters (8, 9, and 12) argue that racism is still the defining factor shaping Latino and Black politics. Others suggest that racism is not merely a matter of prejudiced attitudes and misguided behaviors motivated by isolated, individual phobias or aggregated *personal* fears; but rather has strong social and material bases. Racism is pervasive and is allowed to fester because so many Whites derive collective, if not individual benefits from its marshaling.

Some analysts treat racism as primarily subjective (Rowan 1996), while others treat it as socially dynamic, with both subjective and objective aspects (Chapter 4). The distinction is important because the first views racism as a misguided policy that can be changed by educating White decision makers or replacing them, while the second sees it as a systemic factor with its own dynamic life that will require more than remediation of attitudes to rectify bad policies and practices (Chapters 4 and 5). A theory of coalition or collective action must come to terms with what racism is as well as identify the minimal conditions of unity required between urban minorities, the components of the coalition, and the forces upon which it is based.

The third theme, alluded to in most of the chapters, examines the *uneven economic and social development* of Blacks and Latinos at the community level. Objective conditions have improved for a few among them who have achieved mobility and access within the political-economic mainstream, aided by the windows opened by civil rights and economic opportunity legislation (Dawson 1994; Jennings 1992; Landry 1987). Some of these middle and upper-class Latinos and Blacks use their groups as stepping stones to individual power and opportunity. This motivation poses a serious social problem for the collective struggles of Blacks and Latinos when these persons gain control of decision-making positions in public and private institutions serving those communities[6] and use this power for their individual advancement.

In contrast, the relative position for the majority of Latinos and Blacks has deteriorated over the last three decades and may not improve in the coming decades, if present trends continue (Alkalimat, Gills, and Williams, 1995; Aronowitz and DiFazio 1994; Bean and Tienda 1987; Castells 1989; Kilson 1981; Ranney 1992; Ranney and Cecil 1993; Rifkin 1995). It is ironic that, at a time when the public discourse claims that racism is no longer a factor determining Black and Brown people's life chances, the socioeconomic gap is widening, relative to the majority of Whites (Jennings 1992; Morales and Bonilla 1993).

Simultaneously, social polarization is deepening between Latinos and Blacks—again, stirred by neoconservatism and competition promoted from the outside. They often differ on questions related to undocumented workers, access to the welfare system, bilingual education and African-centered curricula in majority Black public schools (Vigil 1994). In cities where one or the other group is larger, White elites court elites of the smaller group in attempts to form electoral majority coalitions. Despite these divergences, we see stellar examples of multinational cooperation between these groups.

The fourth theme addresses the struggles to attain and promote the extension of *democratic practice*, above and beyond the assertion of democratic ideals. An interesting sub theme, reflected in this book, is that when the popular forces within communities of color exercise initiative in struggles from the bottom, democratic rights are expanded for other sectors (Chapters 3, 4, 5 and 9). Moreover, the struggle for equality and justice has become more complex. Prominent policy framers now advance a political ideology based on *individual* claims to merit and personal character and a politics advocating the end of *group claims* to affirmative action, collective redress of discrimination, and social entitlement. This neoconservatism has distorted the issue of racial justice and reinterpreted the historic victories for economic and social security fought for and earned by all working Americans, as unmerited.

Federal devolution has brought additional problems. By giving more power and resources to the state and local government, devolution implies a greater assumption of social responsibility by these entities and ordinary citizens to determine the quantity and quality of public and social services in the cities where the poor are concentrated. Related to this, we are witnessing increases in *class* polarization with a *racial and nationality character*. One alternative would be for the poor, working people and sections of the fiscally challenged middle class to pressure the economic elites and the big corporations to pay their fair share of taxes by receiving fewer rebates in the form of tax incentives and exemptions. This alternative would require a broad-based, mass mobilization and an extensive new democratic movement for fiscal reform and the redirection of urban expenditures (Chapter 10).

Clearly, increased local empowerment, qualified by the assumption of greater social responsibilities by all residents and citizens, might be appropriately viewed as a desirable "benefit or good" (Dawson 1996). However, the tradeoffs are not likely to be considered acceptable or even tolerable by most poor and working people, regardless of their racial nationality identity (Alkalimat, Gills, and Williams 1995).

Finally, a fifth theme identifies systemic inequities that perpetuate the condition of underdevelopment of these two groups. Some are class-related (hence affecting Blacks and Latinos disproportionately); others have a race/nationality basis. The emerging public policy model of limited, externally controlled development benefits or coopts few people while it maintains deep structures of race/nationality-based inequality in the distribution of resources (Chapter 10) rather than extending opportunities to all. This model forces minorities into a competition against each other for the privilege of development. The old consensus of inclusion, entitlement, and protection of opportunities for all residents is disintegrating. The new consensus poses serious challenges to most African Americans and Latinos.

THE COMMUNITY CONTEXT

Analyses in this book emphasize community as a critical referendum of Latino and Black struggles and relations in urban centers. Such an emphasis stems from objective and historical developments in U.S. society. First, power relations of oppression and exclusion have configured Blacks and Latinos as unique, unevenly developed, unevenly incorporated communities of condition. Racism has limited their options, segregating them socially and spatially. The convergence of interest, condition and place resulting from this, has given rise to movements of resistance and initiatives based on race/nationality and spacial concentration. Their convergent interests have reached extreme levels in cities, leading to locally based, intense movements of resistance against marginalization and comprehensive initiatives for incorporation. These concentrations are today the main arena and basis of their struggle.

Second, the concentration of Black and Latino communities in cities—usually in common or neighboring areas—along with their condition as "ascriptive class segments" (Barrera 1979) provides a strong foundation for joint organization centered on their shared conditions, issues and challenges.[7] Third, given the racial or nationality basis of oppression, the problem of their incorporation is a collective problem, which calls for a collective solution. Individualized solutions have been crafted by those in power selectively to promote a few who often become the outside-anointed elites, designated as leaders of their groups to further the (class) interests of the outsiders. Lastly, Blacks and Latinos have organized their struggles as discrete communities. While in the past more flagrant forms of segregation and exclusion brought each community together around a combined class/race struggle, more subtle forms of racism and the emergence of an elite sharing outside privilege have increasingly separated and confused the issues of race and class. Continued racism maintains the political communities. Class separates them.

CONTRIBUTING ARTICLES

This book examines contention and collaboration between Latinos and Blacks especially at the local level in the new context of globalization and neoconservatism. It examines common experiences, shared conditions, possibilities of joint action and lessons learned from uniquely Latino and Black community perspectives. It looks also at systemic and policy opportunities for advancement and joint action or, at least, strategic alignments.

A unifying thread, coursing through the articles in this volume, is that the urban setting is a unique context for dynamic interactions of race, class, nationality and other forces operative within communities of *place, condition*, and *interest*. This convergence of dynamic forces tends to facilitate popular and democratic mobilizations for deep changes in social relations. However, the realization of this potential requires significant foundational work, uncommon leadership, sustained dialogue and interaction between members of these communities.

In Chapter 2, John Betancur and Douglas Gills examine the global and urban contexts in which the dialogue about the nature of Latino and Black relations is placed. This chapter identifies some of the critical impacts globalization has on the struggles of these groups. It views Black and Latino relations as deeply affected or defined by a mix of past legacies and the new realities of global, political, economic restructuring. The authors illustrate their analysis with the concrete experience of Chicago to tie the global with the local while pointing to the ways in which their struggles for local power have been manipulated, preempted or suppressed.

The next three chapters examine experiences of collaboration/contention between African Americans and Latinos at local or regional levels. Examining the recurring cycles and circles of discrimination towards Puerto Ricans and Blacks in New York City, Frank Bonilla and Walter Stafford argue that political manipulation by institutional elites has seriously undermined their ability to work together. The local political machinery has manipulated both groups by fostering dependency, selectively providing services and using patronage to reward and to punish each one, alternatively. As a result, initiatives have been coopted and struggles defused. Restructuring of the economy has increased tensions and competition.

In Chapter 4, Betancur and Gills argue that the dynamic, at once convergent and divergent, character of national minority relations is the most reasonable alternative framework to examine cases of Black and Latino contention and collaboration. Examining the Black–Latino coalitional effort under the mayoralty of Harold Washington in Chicago, they claim that Blacks and Latinos were able to put together a successful electoral coalition but failed to stretch it into a successful governance coalition. While internal factors were critical in explaining this result, external forces also played a major role in bringing down the administration and coalition. These chapters suggest that the interests and aspirations of the elites, within the Black and Brown political communities alike, tend to thwart or undermine those of the masses. Implicit in the observation of the New York and Chicago cases is the apparent presence of a network of political and economic elites across racial and nationality lines formed to dominate poor and working class people.

In their analysis of historic coalitions in the southern United States (Chapter Five), Jerome Scott and Walda Katz-Fishman demonstrate that coalitions among members of the same class are most successful because their conditions and their class interests are similar. *Single-class coalitions*, organized from the bottom are more democratic and tend to be more effective in improving conditions for the poor and the marginalized than multiclass coalitions controlled by the middle or upper classes. The authors predict that this type of coalition is more likely in the future as the increasing polarization of economic restructuring brings different groups together along class lines in the struggle for more equitable redistribution and for social change.

The next two chapters discuss some of the objective realities facilitating or standing in the way of Black–Latino collaboration. In Chapter 6, Carmen Whalen suggests that African Americans and Puerto Ricans in Philadelphia confront shared obstacles as a result of migration histories, structural conditions and racial ideologies. Recruited as a source of cheap, temporary labor, they have become concentrated in low-end, dead-end occupations and neighborhoods. Economic change and residential segregation have created conditions of concentrated poverty and exclusion, while racial ideologies (e.g., "culture of poverty" and "underclass") blame them for their poverty. Whalen shows the need to revisit common experiences and conditions and to build strategies that address structural and ideological constraints as a basis for future coalitions.

Using survey and census data, Cedric Herring, Michael Bennett, and Douglas Gills (Chapter 7) conclude that prevailing economic and social conditions make it difficult for Latinos and Blacks to form meaningful coalitions. High concentrations of Latinos benefit Blacks in terms of employment and earnings. The opposite, however, is not true. Similarly, while Latinos show less resistance to Blacks than others do, they are more willing to live among others than among Blacks. The authors conclude that there are no foundations for blaming Latinos for the plight of Blacks and that Blacks and Latinos have to develop strategies to confront their objective and subjective differences head-on.

The last four chapters of the book examine collaboration and contention between Latinos and Blacks around specific areas and issues and the impact of concrete policies and programs on them. While recognizing that economic restructuring increases the sources of tension between Blacks and Latinos, Rebecca Morales and Manuel Pastor (Chapter 8) see the possibility of building Black–Latino unity around economic development initiatives that address common hardships. Based on four organizing projects in three cities of California, they compare the potential of *coalitional* and organizational strategies for building common ground between Blacks and Latinos around economic development initiatives. The authors conclude that organizational strategies may be more successful than coalitional ones in producing concrete gains that fare well in the realm of community building. The key to building unity, they claim, is the development of social capital across races from the bottom up through community organizing.

Teresa Cordova, Jose T. Bravo, Jeanne Gauna, Richard Moore, and Ruben Solis (Chapter 9) introduce the coalition building approach of the environmental and economic justice movement to tackle the local impacts of globalization on the basis of regional, democratic networks. They present the network in the Southwest as an innovative and effective response to the failures of earlier approaches, such as those used by the Chicano movement. While bringing together organizations representing all groups of color in the Southwest, this approach, the authors argue, operated as a dynamic and flexible block to confront the shared problems faced by the constituent communities.

In Chapter 10, Steve Alexander carries the analysis to a different front: the distribution of local revenues and expenditures. Using Chicago as his case study, he suggests that budget revenues and expenditures have a racial and class character. He argues that a socially aggressive budget policy is more compatible with an African American and Latino coalition than a social and fiscally conservative policy. Such a coalition holds the most potential for collective improvements in the conditions of these groups.

Edwin Melendez and Michael A. Stoll (Chapter 11) look at community development and its potential for addressing the conditions of Latinos and Blacks and conclude that the experiences demonstrate the inadequacy of single-minded strategies and the need for a combined space and people-based approach.

Finally, in Chapter 12, James Stewart examines the claims of futurists who view Blacks and Latinos as marginal in global economic reordering. According to him, their future role in the global society depends on their ability to gain control of their destiny. Juxtaposing the perspectives of futurists with the realities of Blacks and Latinos in the areas of employment, access to public goods and linkages to the international economic order, the author identifies specific strategies to facilitate Black–Latino collaboration that might alter the current trajectory. He emphasizes the need for organizations that focus on the interplay of domestic and international forces. For him, the color line remains a powerful tool for forging a sense of unity among oppressed peoples of color. While Blacks and Latinos are disproportionately at risk, he concludes, collaborative action that includes other populations of color can offer great hope in altering the current trends.

The volume concludes with a brief summary of action and research needs identified by the chapters and a discussion of the priorities emerging from the analysis.

NOTES

[1] The term "minority" is used very reluctantly here. Not only can it be demeaning of the groups characterized as such, but it has come to include a majority of the U.S. population as it has been extended to increasing categories of people (e.g., women, gays and lesbians, the handicapped, the elderly). In this book, it refers usually to racial and nationality minorities.

[2] The term dialogue refers here to interactions that, while addressing issues openly and candidly, are geared to reaching a new level of understanding and action among participants. It is not a simple matter of exchanges and give-and-take negotiations, but a transformative process of advancement— the development of a new consciousness.

[3] Since the early 1990s, the general media has been paying particular attention to conflicts among racial and nationality minorities. The most relevant for our case is the "Black versus Brown" debate. This is illustrated very well by an article in *The Atlantic* (Miles 1992) which blames the problems of Blacks on Latinos by suggesting that the latter are taking the jobs of the former. Papers such as *The New York Times*, *The Los Angeles Times*, *The Miami Herald*, *The Washington Post*, *The Chicago Tribune* and *The Chicago Sun Times* among many others have been consistently featuring articles on conflicts within and between the Black, Latino and Asian communities. In light of repeated claims of reverse racism, such coverage detracts attention from the fundamental problem of racism in this society while suggesting that the racial problem in America is between racial and national minorities rather than between Whites and minorities.

[4] The academy is predominantly interested in producing objective knowledge along the lines of hypothesis testing. In contrast, activists are more interested in communicating the inner learnings associated with their practice. The academic-activist dialogue helps activists in their reflection while instructing the academy about the possibilities of the struggle as informed by practice.

[5] The authors first gathered between September 7 and 9, 1995, in a Working Conference of Urban Challenges for Blacks and Latinos in the 1990s: Strategies of Contention and Collaboration at the University of Illinois at Chicago. Supported by the MacArthur Foundation, this conference brought the various research teams together with a large audience of researchers, scholars, activists, community practitioners and progressive politicians. At the center of the conference were presentations by the contributors to this volume as well as other academic and applied researchers. This work laid the foundation for the articles that appear herein.

[6] To what extent their class loyalties and aspirations prevail over those of their communities is an open question.

⁷ Using a model of internal colonialism to explain the conditions of Latinos—and Blacks—in the United States, Barrera argues that this system assigns class position on the basis of ethnicity and race. Blacks and Latinos have been assigned the role of subordinate class segments which includes labor repression, occupational stratification, lower wages and social and political marginalization. They have been ascribed the role of reserve labor and shock absorbers. Along with this, the system creates a privileged ethnic or racial segment whose class position is largely guaranteed by its monopoly of power—in all of its forms, also along ethnic, nationality or racial lines.

CHAPTER 2

The Restructuring of Urban Relations
Recent Challenges and Dilemmas for African Americans and Latinos in U.S. Cities

JOHN J. BETANCUR
DOUGLAS C. GILLS

African Americans and Latinos have come a long way, considering their respective histories of slavery and colonial domination and their ensuing marginalization in the United States. Still, as groups, they are at the bottom of the socioeconomic scale. After limited gains in the post war period, the gap between them and Whites is, again, increasing (Bean and Tienda 1987; Farley and Allen 1989; Jaynes and Williams 1989; Goldsmith and Blakely 1992; Cotton 1992; Morales and Bonilla 1993; Dawson 1994). Changes in the political economy (also referred to as globalization or restructuring), mediated by racism, chiefly are responsible for this retrogression. The ongoing challenge is to recast the movement against racism and to engage in new efforts for advancement.

Although, historically, Blacks and Latinos have waged separate struggles, recent processes associated with globalization have brought them together in U.S. cities and metropolitan areas. In these concentrations, they face common issues arising from similar objective conditions and collective experiences. They must turn their shared conditions and the possibilities for interactions that come from this geographic concentration into an opportunity for joint work around policies and strategies of group development.

This chapter examines critical changes brought about by globalization[1] and their particular impacts on Blacks and Latinos—especially policies and strategies of advancement. The discussion emphasizes key areas of intervention and strategizing and suggests a framework for collaborative action between the two communities. To illustrate concretely some of the implications of globalization on Blacks and Latinos, the

17

chapter briefly reviews the case of Chicago. The "successful" transition of this city from manufacturing to services contrasts with the dramatic losses of both groups. A concerted movement and coalition between Blacks and Latinos during the 1980s (see Chapter 4) showed the possibilities and the difficulties that can come from progressive undertakings between them. The succeeding regime under Richard M. Daley, meanwhile, illustrates the power of economic and political forces allied to control development and keep racial minorities and progressive forces at bay. The case of Chicago documents some of the dynamics and changes examined here and the challenges ahead.[2]

We argue that political economic reorganization is changing the foundations upon which Black and Latino struggles of resistance and advancement were previously organized and the bases upon which development policy initiatives were undertaken since the 1960s. Hence, there is a need to mobilize and construct new foundations, hopefully based on collaboration between communities of color as well as other progressive forces and classes around the new concentrations and conditions of national minorities.

REDEFINING THE PLAYING FIELD: GLOBALIZATION AND BLACKS AND LATINOS

Chronically handicapped by centuries of exclusion and limited opportunity, Blacks and Latinos are suffering disproportionately from the changes brought about by globalization. Four critical aspects illustrate this disparity: the new dynamics of labor, the redefinition of the political arena, the accompanying discourse of individual responsibility, and the concerted attacks on the organizational bases of Blacks and Latinos. Operating under a restructured form of accumulation based on the drive of capital for unlimited mobility, these factors combine to oppose collective or public responsibility for the condition of these groups and, hence, the need for specific race/nationality-based interventions to bring them to par.

The New Dynamics of Labor

The socioeconomic dislocations resulting from the global reorganization of production have been most damaging for Blacks and Latinos. Changes in manufacturing (differently defined in the literature in terms of deindustrialization, flexible production, sweatshop manufacturing, or automation) and, particularly, the end of mass mobility for unskilled or semiskilled workers—often immigrants—are cases in point. They took place at exactly the time when these groups started to make significant inroads into manufacturing. Not only did they deprive them of the opportunity to establish a solid economic floor, but they eliminated this traditional channel of mobility that was their main hope. Whites, in contrast, were able to use their economic power and position to transition successfully as a group into the new political economy. A polarized service economy lacking the entry-level jobs with career ladders and wages comparable to those in manufacturing mainly offers poverty jobs to the masses of displaced and dislocated workers, of which Blacks and Latinos are a disproportionate part.

Moreover, a highly racist labor market and city have segregated Latinos and Blacks from the jobs and opportunities of the emerging economy, while denying them the education and access that are the basis of mobility and success in this economy. This has been happening at a time when economic dislocations elsewhere resulted in the largest migration of Latinos and Blacks to U.S. cities. The result has been a city and metropolitan area and economy of extremes, the dual city that Smith (1996) and Mollenkopf and Castells (1992) have so vividly described. At one end, are the gentrified city core and self-segregated middle-class suburbs of wealth and prosperity. At the other, the expanding, predominantly minority inner-city and old suburbs showcasing the extremes of poverty and alienation of the new capitalist city.

Finally, relocation of economic activity has opened the traditional working class in U.S. cities to competition with Third World labor (Brecher and Costello 1990). Latinos and Blacks have been especially affected by this due to their clustering in competitive occupations and industries (Barrera 1979; De Freitas 1991; Jennings 1992; Morales and Bonilla 1993). Their wages and working conditions are deteriorating further with the addition of new immigrants (Torres 1991 and 1995). Employers are taking the opportunity to engage in sweatshop production and to replace resident Black and Latino with immigrant workers. This has led to new internal tensions within and between Blacks and Latinos.

Transformation of the Political Arena

The state has been the main vehicle for addressing the inequalities produced by the market system and, in our case, the inequities produced by racism and colonial oppression of Blacks and Latinos (Monkkonen 1995). The welfare state was critical in bringing about actions oriented toward leveling the playing field (Jennings 1992). Today, in its quest for unlimited mobility, capital is successfully pursuing the transformation of the state around the priorities of promotion of business interests, into the corporate state (Korten 1995). Under claims of competitiveness, this state is directing resources away from redistribution and redress toward facilitating globalization and accumulation of corporate capital. Many functions of the state itself have been privatized subjecting them—and affirmative action—to the logic and priorities of the private sector[3]. The bottom line is the construction of a society in which social and other consumption is ruled by this sector under the profit motive.

This transformation has handicapped very seriously the ability of Blacks and Latinos to resort to the political arena for the removal of the inequities of racism—a political factor—and the carving of opportunities for advancement. It has left them at the mercy of a highly unregulated private labor market in which they cannot compete in equal terms, given their accumulated, race-related deficits—e.g., education, access, networks, resources, and opportunities. In contrast, the state has been reshaped to serve growth coalitions and corporations primarily benefitting Whites-in-power. Such changes are redefining the political arena away from racial group claims.

The New Discourse of Individual Responsibility and Competition

The discourse legitimizing these changes has been especially damaging for Blacks and Latinos as groups. Central to it has been the claim of absolute individual responsibility. Arguing that success is the exclusive outcome of individual effort on a level playing field, it dismisses any need for public intervention to address race-related disadvantages. Under the assumption that race is no longer a factor in economic success and opportunity, it attributes the conditions of Latinos and Blacks to presumed or apparent cultural deficits and individual behaviors (Banfield 1970; Gecas 1979, 1980; Sowell 1981; Baca Zinn 1989; Steinberg 1989; Roth 1994). In this view, any redress is unwarranted. It is up to them to assume the right values and lift themselves up by their bootstraps—regardless of whether or not they have the resources and avenues to do it.

Furthermore, the new discourse works to scapegoat Latinos and Blacks for all urban ills. While many of them are dismissed under characterizations such as the underclass, others are blamed for taking the jobs of working-class U.S.A. or for threatening the unity of the country with their calls for diversity and plurality. Meanwhile, the discourse asks for strong intervention to punish/contain the poor and the outcomes of poverty—homelessness, alternative economic activities, dependency—and to eliminate all forms of assistance to them. Paired with the systemic underdevelopment of minorities, this denial of public assistance comes close to a call for their extermination (Smith 1996). Such a rationale certainly acts to perpetuate the position of the majority in these groups as permanent members of the low-class in U.S. cities (see Miles 1992; Quadagno 1994; Rothenberg 1995; Sklar 1995).

The Attack on Grassroots Struggles

A crucial aspect with a unique impact on Blacks and Latinos is the systematic, though mostly silent attack on the institutions and structures that have been the basis of their struggle.[4] Such an attack seems particularly aimed at depoliticizing and demobilizing the urban infrastructure of organization and political self-help built in the last three decades. It has ranged from the removal of funding for self-organizing, through stereotyping of grassroots struggles as anti-development, to the limitation of funding to categories determined by donors.

This attack is strategic for various reasons. The community-based, not for profit sector is capable of facilitating a front of resistance and advocacy against reactionary policies. It can fuel and sustain popular mobilizations and provide a medium for popular movements. It keeps a watch on the actions of the public and private sector and can mobilize against abuses and for promotion of progressive policies. In particular, it has had a strong race/nationality character. It has been well articulated with the social bases that drove the civil rights, social justice and race/nationality movements for self-determination and self-development. Hence, the attack on this community-based movement is a necessary condition in the consolidation of the emerging system and, in our case, for silencing or coopting the struggles of Blacks and Latinos against racial oppression and marginalization. It affects the ability of Blacks and Latinos to mobilize around the collective conditions and needs of their communities and to demand change.

Impact on Black–Latino Relations

Operating under the aegis of globalization and racism, urban restructuring has produced extreme—and segregated—concentrations of Blacks and Latinos in U.S. cities and low-income suburbs. It has dumped them in inner-city areas with the most deteriorated conditions, quite often dependent upon shared facilities, services and spaces. This concentration and common condition has intensified interaction and provided a new basis for solidarity between them. This is perhaps the single main opportunity and challenge: Bringing Latinos and Blacks together physically and socially can provide the opportunity for building a new consciousness and front of struggle.

At the same time, however, the conditions accompanying this physical concentration have pit them against each other in a competition for fewer opportunities. As the public budget is diverted into business assistance and social control, Latinos and Blacks, in fact, have been made to "compete" for declining resources in the context of increasing need. They have engaged also in competition for political position in local government.[5] Such dynamics have made them especially vulnerable to the manipulations of Whites-in-power who often use the elites of one community against the other. Additionally a small group of Latino and Black elites promoted by affirmative action, rather than exercising leadership in the collective affairs of their groups, has often identified with the class positions of elites in power. They have, in fact, engaged in unnecessary forms of nationalism to claim favor for themselves against their own race/nationality communities.

Multiple other dynamics have increased the possibilities of rifts between and within groups. Of particular relevance here are the dynamics of immigration and segregation. Public policies that pit recent and earlier immigrants against each other and that assign different immigrant status and rights to different groups and individual members induce tension. In turn, each community has used concentration in segregated areas as a foundation for its own struggles. Traditionally separated in their struggles and spaces, Blacks and Latinos can then see each other as a threat and compete for control of institutions, facilities, turf and services.

Lastly, the discourse of individuality is acting to eliminate any sense of collectivity between and within Black and Latino communities. This discourse puts forward the belief that success or failure are explained only by individual merit, disconnected from group drives or the effects of racism. Differences are manipulated to gain an edge against each other. Comparisons between groups are a case in point: the success of individual Asians, for instance, is used to disclaim racism; the work ethics of recent immigrants is appropriated to blame the conditions of other peoples of color on their values and behavior. Such discussions have opened the door for evaluating claims between peoples of color based on criteria such as *the most deserving minority* or for policies based on immigrant status.

In short, the opportunities for collective action have increased. Yet, to become effective, Blacks and Latinos need to find ways to deal with the new sources of tension.

BLACK–LATINO COLLABORATION AND THE NEW DYNAMICS OF RACE

The previous overview points to a changing playing field and reality for Blacks and Latinos in U.S. cities. It calls attention to some of the factors affecting collaboration or contention between them. Underlying this discussion is the transformation of U.S. cities and, specifically, the new Black and Latino urban reality described elsewhere (Morales and Bonilla 1993; Davis 1992; Galster and Hill 1992; Mollenkopf and Castells 1992; Massey and Denton 1993; Kleinberg 1995; Smith 1996; Wilson 1987). These communities are faced today with a more complex next stage in their urban struggle that calls for a serious assessment of the confluence of race and class, particularly as the political economy no longer provides the opportunities associated with manufacturing jobs and the welfare state. This section examines in more detail new dynamics of race with a critical bearing on current and future struggles in the Black and Latino communities.

To start, we argue that race is no longer the universal force bringing people of the same segregated group together as it had been before and during the Civil Rights Movement.[6] While the Movement obtained significant gains for peoples of color, it did not deliver the equality and resources demanded by them. It produced formal equality without power. It promoted a few while maintaining the general condition of underdevelopment of the majority. Thus, racial oppression continued, though in a reconstructed fashion. In the absence of the "coherent conflict" (Winant 1994:30) generated by the blatant racial oppression of the past and in a context of denial of racism, the ideological concept of race lost much of its universal, unifying power.

Today, we face a more disjointed racial front in competition with multiple other forces vying for public attention and redress. While racism is still a crucial factor in the distribution of resources and opportunities, its rhetorical and organizing power has been undermined by numerous factors.

First, since the 1980s, a political redefinition of discrimination as largely an *individual matter* has emerged. The resurgence of the New Right and recent rulings by the Supreme Court requiring plaintiffs to show intent of discrimination beyond reasonable doubt have weakened public sector proscriptions of racism at the *social, institutional, and interpersonal* levels. It has become the responsibility of individuals of color to show a conspiracy or intent to discriminate, to monitor compliance with the legislation and to bring cases to the courts. Recently, the Supreme Court has taken the position that group claims of racial discrimination will not be viewed favorably unless stringent legal tests are met. Individualization of claims of discrimination, coupled with the steering of collective action into mainstream processes of the political system, diverted the struggle away from its collective community basis and direct-action initiatives (Tate 1993) and turned it into a legalistic exercise.

Second, racial discrimination has assumed more subtle and coded forms.[7] These symbols are being used to deny the significance of racism and to protect the interests of the privileged majority by exempting them from any liability or accountability for social and institutional racism and the conditions facing racial or nationality groups. The form of these arguments and the self-serving policies of elites disguise the racial problem.

Third, as mentioned earlier, an increasing differentiation of interests and prerogatives among members of racially identifiable groups has driven a wedge between communities of color and has led to the partitioning of their struggles. The formation of a significant Black and Latino middle class is a case in point. This class has often directed the anti-racist struggle in its self-interest. Many of its members choose not to identify with the broader striving of their communities, claiming that they owe them little or nothing (Jennings 1992).[8]

Thus, racial/nationality unity, even within each of the groups, is by no means, a given. It needs to be built around specific projects addressing differences. While upwardly mobile Latinos and Blacks may be more interested in using their recently acquired political numbers and the power potential of their groups for their individual careers, the groups as wholes are not likely to realize their goals. In this sense, contention for position within a racially framed hierarchy may be the dominant driving force of upwardly mobile elements within these communities. In contrast, common struggle around issues of education, safety, housing, health, and other basic services may be the unifying priority of their less advantaged group members.[9]

Fourth, and closely related, the struggle for empowerment in the institutional political process has been pervaded by "plantation politics" and tokenism. Not only does this process coopt the community and confuse its interests, but it corrupts the leadership and increases dependency. It certainly prevents an up-front all-out struggle against racism.

Fifth, other groups (e.g. gays and lesbians, the handicapped, the elderly) have organized, particularly after the Civil Rights Movement, into racial/nationality equivalents of Blacks, Latinos and Native Americans. These *new minorities* have used political consolidation as a mechanism to achieve representation and political influence and to claim resources, benefits and opportunities for themselves above what they could claim, for instance, as Whites. While using the notion of *political mobilization of bias* themselves, they frown at efforts of Latinos and Blacks to mobilize politically around preference.

Even if all these claimants are pressing legitimate demands on the public policy agenda, government has not responded by expanding its commitment to the eradication of all forms of oppression, exclusion and discrimination. Instead, communities of color have had to *take a number* and put their dreams on hold. This development is making diversification of interests more evident and pervasive in the political process, while relegating diversity as a value to the scrap heap as a societal relic. It threatens to turn race/nationality-based efforts, at their best, into *merely one among many relevant and equal subdivisions* and to force them to compete with newly designated *minorities* for the same resources made available originally for the alleviation of their conditions of disadvantage.[10]

Within a restructuring economy and society—one that also threatens the economic security of a destabilized middle class (Rifkin 1995; Newman 1995), there is apparently little legitimate interest in the elimination of racism. Racism, in fact, helps consolidate a threatened sector of White Americans: better to blame Blacks and Latinos and to keep them off-balance than to allow the system to be blamed or its class disparities challenged.

Denial of racism has very damaging impacts on the struggle of Blacks and Latinos. First, it removes the onus of social responsibility and commitment from the larger society. Second, it deflects and throws systemic problems onto those who lack the resources to lift themselves by their efforts, alone. Third, it sends a message of low-value and worth to them, contributing to resignation to fate, self-blame and internal brutalization. Fourth, it works to dismiss the racial issue and replace it with a truncated, pseudo class framework that delimits social mobilization to the discrete acts of individuals and to their personal attributes, motivation and moral character rather than authentic class, nationality and consciousness. In the worst case, racism is not even being recognized as a significant factor in public policy. The notion is that Blacks and Latinos cause racism. From a bold point of view, this is a form of the *racialization of dispossession* (Webster 1992; Jones 1992).

These developments call for an aggressive stance on racism, White supremacy and White- skin privilege and for a careful revisiting of the racial issue. How could the struggle against racism possibly be maintained in such a context? How can divisive metaphors such as that of a *model minority*—applied almost universally to Asians—be counteracted?[11] While nationality groups are fragmented internally by class, individual interests, beliefs and loyalties, the association between racial status and underdevelopment is underscored as dominant in the U.S. As Winant states, "class position is in many respects racially assigned in the United States" (1994:34).

Finally, a discussion of the problems of Blacks and Latinos as a matter of class or race can be misleading and distracting. This tends to ignore the close association between race and class dynamics in the real world and the impossibility of examining them as two separate and discrete variables. As Mier (1993:191) argues, "Poverty seems an overwhelming issue; race is probably more intractable. Because poverty and race are so intertwined in this society, the inability to deal with race seems a major cause of the inability to deal with poverty."

This analysis calls for a careful discussion of racism in relationship to globalization and its associated urban transformation—its reproduction of race-based and racist initiatives among these groups, its impact on the Black and Latino communities and the relationship between city neglect and the neglect of communities of color, in particular.[12]

CHICAGO, A CASE IN POINT: BRIEF OVERVIEW

Transformation of the City and Its Impact on Latinos and Blacks— Some Indicators

The dramatic transformation of Chicago since the 1970s and the conditions of Blacks and Latinos in the city illustrate these points. An overview of indicators followed by a discussion of the political dynamics associated with the process expands on trends discussed earlier while shedding light on the conditions and challenges for Black and Latino struggles and relations.

Once considered *the* archetypal manufacturing city of the U.S.,

Chicago saw its manufacturing jobs shrink from 546,500[13] (nearly 41% of all local jobs) in 1967 to 216,190 (or 18% of total jobs) in 1990. In the metropolitan area, the corresponding figures were 1,064,500 (48%) and 653,411 (21%). In contrast, non-manufacturing jobs went from 797,867 (59%) in 1967 to 983,580 (82%) in 1990 in the city and from 1,136,366 (52%) to 2,402,100 (79%) in the metropolitan area.

This change in employment composition is clearly reflected in the city's physical landscape. While many manufacturing structures sit idle waiting for redevelopment or are being transformed into lofts, growth in Chicago's Central Business District (CBD) has been rapid (Ludgin 1989; Chicago Sun Times 1987; Chicago Tribune 1988). Office space went from 59.6 million square feet in 1970 to 81.3 in 1980 and to 116.6 million in 1989 (Ludgin 1989:21). Between 1979 and 1989, over $6.8 billion were invested in new and upgraded real estate (Ludgin 1989:4). This investment produced 45.2 million square feet of completed new or upgraded office space, with an additional 12.5 million square feet under construction or renovation; a total of 14,660 new residential units, with 3,114 new ones under construction; and 11,723 new or upgraded hotel rooms, with 2,944 under construction or renovation (Ludgin 1989:6). Also, between 1979-1984, 2.2 million square feet of new or upgraded space for government and nonprofit agencies were developed (Ludgin and Masotti 1985:6). Similarly, employment in the CBD and its outer ring went from 37% of total jobs in the city in 1967 to 44% in 1990 (IDES 1970 and 1990).[14]

In the last decades, Chicago has become home to strong financial, trade, insurance, legal, communications, accounting, exposition/convention and many other service industries. The metropolitan area hosts 18 headquarters of the top 500 transnational firms. It, in fact, was ranked 5th *in the world* in this category in 1986 (Smith and Feagin, 1987). Reed (1984) defined Chicago as a *first order international financial center*— after supranational centers. The city has been enlarging its cultural, sports and entertainment facilities at an impressive rate through expansion or construction of exposition centers, stadiums, marinas, and many others. Thrift (1989) classified Chicago among the main *regional centers* of the World—after global and zonal centers.[15]

The transformation of the region and the city has been accompanied by a dramatic population relocation. Growth and expansion in the suburbs have been paralleled by population loss and deterioration in the city, particularly in areas occupied by Blacks and Latinos. Most recently, construction of middle income housing has been promoted by a consortium of developers and City Hall in an effort to attract the middle class back to the city. In contrast, low-income housing has been allowed to deteriorate at a high rate (Chicago Rehab Network 1993).

The composition of the city by major racial/nationality group has changed from 43.6% White, 39.5 Black, 14.1% Latino and 2.8% other in 1980 to 38% White, 38.6 Black, 19.6 Latino, and 3.8% other in 1990. In 1970, Whites comprised nearly 60% of the population compared to 33% Black and 7% Latino. As a result, Chicago went from majority White in 1970 to minority-majority since 1980. In the suburbs, the Latino population increased by 83.6% and the Black by 45.3% between 1970–1990. With the exception of middle and upper class members of these groups, Latinos and African Americans are forming new low-income concentrations, especially in old suburbs of disinvestment in the inner ring of the city and in older satellite cities.

In the Chicago area, Blacks and Latinos are highly segregated in selected neighborhoods, suburbs and subsections of suburbs. These are the areas with the most depressed socioeconomic conditions. They have the lowest incomes and educational levels (Wiewel 1986:26–29; Betancur et al. 1993; Leadership Council 1991; The Chicago Reporter 1992; Orfield and Gaebler 1991; Tobias and Roy 1993). Latinos and Blacks, in this order, make the lowest average individual wages: the average for Blacks as a percentage of Whites for all industries was 66% for both 1970 and 1990 and for all occupations 66% for 1970 and 56% for 1990; for Latinos, the figures by industry were 64% and 59% and by occupation 64% and 50% (1970 and 1990 PUMS). As these numbers indicate, wages for both groups as a percent of those of Whites declined in the period. In other words, not only is income polarization very large, but the gap is increasing.

The percent employed in manufacturing declined very significantly for all groups in the metropolitan area but most dramatically for Blacks and Latinos. The figures for Whites were 31% in 1970 and 18% in 1990; for Blacks 31% and 15% respectively; and for Latinos 62% and 34%. In services, the percent increased from nine to 32% for Whites, from 14 to 35% for Blacks, and from seven to 22% for Latinos. Concentration of Blacks and Latinos in occupations such as operatives and crafts declined but increased in others such as clerical and service. Both groups made lower average wages than Whites in all of these industries and occupations.

In metropolitan Chicago in 1990, 13% of adult Blacks and 19% of Latinos were working poor, compared to 3% of White adults (Chicago

Urban League et al. 1993). The figures in the City of Chicago were higher, 14%, 21% and 6% respectively. The proportion of wage earners below the poverty level in metropolitan Chicago was 10% for Blacks and 9% for Latinos, compared to 2.4% for Whites. In the city, the percentage of Black persons below the poverty level was 31.7% in 1970 and 33.2 in 1990; the corresponding figures for Latinos were 24.1 and 24.2, and for Whites 10.6 and 11% (Chicago Department of Planning 1983 and 1992).

Thus, as a group, Latinos are moving from the bottom of manufacturing to the cellar of the service economy. This is where benefits are nonexistent, job turnover is high and underemployment is the norm. Similarly, Blacks, as a whole, did not improve their economic condition in the 1970–1990 period. A study by Ranney (1992) links closing or downsizing of a group of large manufacturing plants in the Chicago area to corporate transnational strategies. He (1992:11) estimates that 62% of job loss in these plants during 1979-1989 involved the parallel closure of Chicago plants and expansion of operations in other countries. He also points to the loss of 67,022 jobs between 1980-1990 in Illinois to firms with maquiladora operations (1992: 23).

In a separate study, Ranney and Cecil (1993:3) conclude that of the jobs lost in Chicago to transnational parents, 27% were held by Blacks and 23% by Latinos for a total of 39,873 jobs between the two. Meanwhile, downsizing or closure of plants in steel and other industries resulted in the devastation of minority communities such as South Chicago (Putterman, 1985), South Deering and Woodlawn, among others. Similarly, the closure of plants such as Sunbeam and Zenith had a devastating impact on Black communities in the West side of Chicago.

This is happening at a time when immigration is again dramatically accelerating. The Latino population in the city increased from 247,343 in 1970 to 545,852 in 1990. Fifty-one percent of this population (foreign born) immigrated to Metropolitan Chicago after 1969, compared to 2% of Blacks and 3% of Whites. Documented or undocumented, many of these immigrants are providing the low-wage, highly unprotected labor that allows sweatshops and other low-wage service industries to stay in business and thrive. Many employers, in fact, prefer them to other low-income Latinos allegedly because of their high work ethics—their lower expectations, lack of knowledge about labor struggles and alternatives and, hence, willingness to work for lower wages, we would argue.

The growing Latino presence in the area has met hostility in the media, multiple raids of firms with high levels of Latino workers and efforts by many suburbs to remove them, for example by code enforcement and redevelopment schemes. It is often argued that Latinos—especially undocumented workers—are *taking* the jobs of Blacks and other legal immigrants. They have, in fact, become the scapegoats for a society that is increasingly reneging on its social responsibility for all of its residents.

Development Approach of the Governing Regime

A crucial factor in the transformation of Chicago and, particularly, in its direction, has been the Chicago *growth machine* or *coalition* (Squires et al. 1987; Ferman 1996). Consolidated during the mayoralty of Richard J. Daley (1956–1977) and revamped by his son, Richard M. Daley (1989–present), this is a coalition of the city's Democratic machine (White) elites and the top central business district establishment (corporate and bank executives, developers, directors of civic, legal and architectural firms, trade and real estate business concerns) that has controlled development in Chicago. Predominantly focused on the CBD, large organizations, and their connections to the outside—highways, airports and other transportation infrastructure (Greer and Joseph 1989), the growth coalition has been also expanding its activities to the areas surrounding the CBD and to other development—cultural, entertainment, recreational, middle income housing.

These priorities are clearly spelled out in public documents and policy and development plans. In fact, development of downtown and its surrounding area has been steadily subsidized and promoted by City Hall, as has been the administration's commitment to the middle class. This has been done at the expense of low-income, Black and Latino areas in particular, which have been severely neglected or disrupted by gentrification. When the administrations of Washington (1983–1987) and Sawyer (1987–1989) tried to change this pattern, the coalition and, in general, the White political establishment fought to obstruct their work and managed to regain power.[16] Most recently, Richard M. Daley (1980–present) recaptured the mayoralty for these forces and brought the growth coalition in Chicago to its present, renewed prominence.

The coalition is carrying out a dual development strategy. On the one hand, it is promoting a model based on highly visible projects and aimed at increasing the attractiveness of the city for new residents, firms and visitors. It is focusing on expansion of the tourist, exhibition, and sports industries, coupled with the arts and culture, to attract and retain international corporations, finance capital and other global business activity. At the same time, the coalition is directing the main benefits—services, construction, contracts, etc.—to its members and supporters.

On the other hand, the coalition is seeking to weaken advocacy networks and community development and to keep them off the policy making and public leadership field. These networks had achieved great strength in the 1970s and 1980s through an alternative model fusing social and development goals and proposing a resident-based model of development. They contested generous public support of unregulated real estate development at the expense of low-income areas. They allocated federal and other public development funds to facilitate community-directed development in the neighborhoods (Clavel and Wiewel 1992; Mier 1993).

Rather than promoting appropriate neighborhood development led by local community corporations, the Daley administration has favored the redevelopment (gentrification) of low-income neighborhoods by outside real estate interests in order to create *middle income enclaves* without any regard for the impact on low income communities. Gentrification, hence, has advanced at the expense of low-income Latino and Black communities in the city—in this order, forcing residents to move toward the fringes into highly inconvenient locations.

The public budget gets compromised in such efforts. The city blames poor services and infrastructures in low-income and minority areas on budget constraints and federal cuts. As the bulk of steady revenues—from taxes, fees, licenses—goes to corporate and private activities, City Hall relies heavily on inadequate federal programs for the deteriorating services available to low-income Latinos and Blacks (Gills and Alexander 1997; Alexander 1995). The regime reserves the most solid municipal revenues for the priorities of the growth coalition. A look at the list and affiliations of the political contributors to the present regime—real estate and corporate-related, legal and accounting, construction firms—confirms this focus and its beneficiaries.

The growth coalition certainly has kept Chicago in the running for global status. But, how much have Latinos and Blacks benefited from this work? The actions of local government as part of the growth machine in Chicago have opened very marginal opportunities for Black and Latino developers. In fact, local officials have pursued a development route that has put their previous gains in these fronts at risk. A few points illustrate this.

Most of the public investment in infrastructure and brick and mortar projects has been contracted out to White firms with largely suburban,

White workers. The administration has never led efforts, for instance, to assure that residents of poor Black and Latino areas are trained and hired to do the work or that local Black and Latino contractors get the needed assistance to bid for these contracts. Hence, most of these contractors are left out of this market or are limited to small contracts or subcontracts. In spite of claiming support for affirmative action, the regime has resisted efforts to enforce affirmative action hiring or minority contractor set-asides that target workers and firms in areas of color.[17] Indeed, it pits Latinos against Blacks in the award of construction jobs and contracts. In this way, it forces Black and Latino elites to compete against each other for marginal opportunities rather than unite and demand a bigger portion of the pie.

The current regime has deflected the crisis of revenue generation by adding highly regressive consumption taxes and fees that place an inordinate burden on low income groups.[18] These taxes and fees subsidize services that low-income groups do not use while curtailing public or social services that they need (Alexander 1995). Other mechanisms of revenue generation include initiatives to increase the number of first-time home buyers;[19] redevelopment of large areas such as the South Loop for the middle class; facilitating the conversion of rental family housing units into condos; transformation of public housing located in prime real estate areas into so-called mixed-income housing; and heavy support of gentrification.[20] Such actions solidify the regime's ties to the development industry while building support within the middle class.

Another central strategy of the city administration has been privatization of services. This strategy also tends to benefit the urban growth coalition through development of a new private industry taking up many of the traditional functions of government—for profit. Not only does this industry supplant public employees but it undermines affirmative action in hiring and in contracts for services. Since a significant proportion of service employees in privatizing industries has consisted of Blacks, they have been most affected by the loss of meaningful employment in government organizations.[21] As privatization removes social accountability, it helps avoid the gains and demands of the Black and Latino communities.

Meanwhile, the federal government's withdrawal from education, health care, low-income housing and social and family welfare services has provided state and local government units with additional functions. The State of Illinois and the City of Chicago have engaged in privatization of such opportunities, hence passing up the opportunity of partnerships with communities and their organizations around systems of delivery that promote local development. Not only is this shift depriving cities of funds traditionally used for redistribution and minority opportunity, but it is leaving this role to a local government uninterested in national minorities and the poor.

All this work has been carried out without much community input or public debate.[22] Public agencies do not monitor the new firms and expanded businesses to see that they engage in fair employment practices. The policy priorities set, and partners selected by government in this endeavor have demonstrated that neighborhood and community development functions are tertiary priorities of the local government regime. While discouraging initiative and self-determination, City Hall uses funding to keep communities and their organizations in line. In this way, Black and Latino communities and their grassroots institutions and organization are excluded from the benefits of development. Their elites have been coopted into the role of government pawns depriving the masses of an effective institutional voice in governance.

Neutralization of the community movement and its organizational infrastructure has been part of the strategy of demobilization. Unable to operate without heavy public support, CDCs cannot continue developing and maintaining low-income housing or job generation and consumer markets for an under/unemployed population. Similarly, community organizations have been handicapped in their work for fair policy and against racism. The result has been the dislocation of minorities from their *communities*. Those CDCs which remain are being pushed to develop housing for higher income groups and to contribute to gentrification.

As a result of this policy, Blacks and Latinos with the fewest resources have become institutionally detached. This includes losses of churches whose congregations do not correspond to the composition of neighborhood residents,[23] and of public and community institutions and CBOs built around the needs of residents. CBOs, today, have a declining capacity to produce change in poor, minority communities. Disconnection from viable institutions further contributes to social destabilization, fractured and fragmented social networks and the emergence of truncated social infrastructures (i.e., undisciplined street gangs, drug dealers, etc.).[24]

In short, like other international cities, Chicago is building into an entertainment, tourist and cultural center—*core of prestige*—attractive to international travelers and investors. It is becoming a dual city, spatially and socially. While directing all development to upper and middle income groups and their physical enclaves, it acts to exclude and isolate racial minorities and the poor away from such spaces.[25] Proximity and ease of access to the centers of prestige are being assured through new street designs and rerouting that isolates these areas from less desirable neighborhoods. Control of public transit fares and routings is restricting access of non-working people to the CBD. Heavily biased in favor of the real estate industry, the regime has concentrated on public incentives and policies favoring middle income housing. In this way, it is helping recapture inner city areas—along the lake front and around the CBD particularly—for highly profitable real estate uses. The bottom line is to assure the city a competitive position in the global race (see Harvey 1995 & Castells 1989). Rather than acting to confront racism and to secure equal opportunity, the regime has operated as a vehicle for the growth coalition.

The Chicago Black and Latino Experience Today

While many Black and Latino areas in Chicago are being primed for gentrification, other, less conveniently located, former White areas undergoing disinvestment are being resettled by them. In this way, Latinos and Blacks are being increasingly pushed to the social and physical edge of the city. Residents control few of the remaining local businesses or the associated employment. Local accountability of business owners to residents also declines.

Meanwhile, a cadre of visible Black and Latino individuals has dedicated itself to delivering the Black and Latino vote to the current regime, in return for local political autonomy, party sponsorship and preferential treatment. Latino appointees have been used by Mayor Daley as a front to attack and undermine independent Black and Latino and other progressive leaders. This cadre has been helpful in displacing Blacks and Latinos from positions of power and influence within public agencies. Daley has visibly replaced "disloyal" Blacks with Latinos who are loyal to his regime. Many Blacks think that Latinos are being incorporated into government at their expense. Many Latinos suspect that Blacks will not support their needs and aspirations. Tensions are particularly high among Latino and Black elites competing for attention and benefits from local government. The reality is that both groups are being manipulated by the regime.

Significantly, White elites have fought to break apart efforts at Latino and Black cooperation by driving wedges between the two communities. In turn, mismanagement and fiscal crises have been the claims used to take away public agency control from Black leaders and place them in the hands of compliant White members of the growth coalition—Chicago Park District, Chicago Transit Authority and the Board of Education, among others.

While Black and Latino state legislators have maintained a working caucus, this has not been the case on the City Council. Although, together, Blacks and Latinos comprise a majority, they have been fractionalized by Daley's supporters on the Council and in the Democratic Party. In return for privilege within the affairs of particular Wards, these individuals have pledged fidelity to Mayor Daley. Many council members have negotiated away power and autonomy that were not mayor Daley's to grant in a formally weak-mayor/strong-council structure. The beneficiaries from this state of affairs are the Daley regime and individual Black and Latino politicians, while the vast majority of Latino and Black voters and their interests are marginalized.

To sum up, in Chicago a large majority of Blacks and Latinos is being destabilized and politically and economically displaced as a result of restructuring. Thus, transformation as well as the new contradictions it brings are undermining the bases of Latino and African American communities and their common, though frequently separate, struggles. The position of many minorities—Blacks in particular—tied to jobs in the public sector has become highly precarious in the wake of downsizing, privatization and the attack on the welfare state, affirmative action and civil rights protections. Politics of division and contention by the current regime are working to preempt Black and Latino coalitional efforts. The Black and Latino coalition and the Black-led regime of the 1980s has been dismantled and replaced by a new version of "plantation" politics.

A large proportion of Black and Latino elites and career politicians have disengaged from, and are no longer accountable to, the popular movement that paved the way for their ascendancy to political power and policy influence. While on the defensive, Black and Latino communities are rebuilding from the bottom and learning from past failures, integrating the new realities into their strategies. They are struggling to produce a new beginning against the new forms of racial and class domination.

Contention has been promoted by a forced competition for declining poverty budgets, jobs and opportunities; control of local institutions; elite rifts over position and opportunity in the public sector; and limited or negative experiences of collaboration, among others. The main source of this contention seems to lie with outside manipulation of differences and needs, and elite opportunism.

NOTES

¹ The concept of *globalization* is controversial. It refers to the new phase of capitalism that, many authors argue, became dominant after 1970. The controversy spans from the explanation of this change to the claim that capitalism has entered a new phase. For a summary of contending explanations see Amin 1995. While accepting the basic premise of change, some authors focus on the debate between the local and the global (Lipietz 1993; Keil, Wekerle and Bell 1996; Cox 1997). The related urban change is widely discussed in the literature (Friedman and Wolff 1982; Harvey 1989; Castells 1989; Sassen 1992; Mollenkopf and Castells 1992; Smith 1992; Barnett and Cavanagh 1994). Some prefer to talk about restructuring (Soja 1992). While inspired by this debate, our analysis proposes some applications of globalization to Latinos, Blacks and other national minorities in U.S. cities. In the text, we make reference to works that support our conclusions directly or indirectly. We also have the benefit of multiple presentations and discussions of these issues in academic and non-academic circles and the feedback from a large diversity of participants. Similarly, we have been following the case of Chicago (illustrated at the end of the chapter) both qualitatively and quantitatively and have identified these matters in the city. Comparable or relevant conclusions for other cities and populations include Mollenkopf and Castells 1992, Morales and Bonilla 1993, Carnoy et al. 1993, Sassen 1992, and Smith 1996.

² The transformation of Chicago from a manufacturing to a service economy has not been discussed much in the literature. This analysis provides a general overview of the most visible changes, particularly as they suggest how urban revitalization is eroding conditions of under represented groups in the city and Metropolitan area.

³ To the best of our knowledge, the impact of privatization on Blacks and Latinos has not been carefully assessed and analysis is largely limited to the insights of participants and observers. A central policy of Mayor Washington in Chicago (as well as of progressive administrations throughout the USA) has been the use of public sector opportunities for the advancement of members of such communities. This policy has been dropped by Mayor Daley. His administration has privatized public functions on an ad-hoc basis (Mahtesian 1995; Mason and Siegel 1997). Although private concerns often kept many of the employees and were asked to maintain minority hiring goals, monitoring has been loose and nobody has watched for compliance. Many cities have dropped this issue from their policy priorities. Since minorities hold a disproportionate share of the unskilled and semi-skilled service jobs—the most amenable to privatization—they tend to suffer disproportionately from privatization. A study of the Chicago Institute on

Urban Poverty (Mason and Siegel 1997) points to the deteriorating quality of jobs, particularly in these categories, through privatization. Perhaps the best kept secret of privatization is that cost reductions result from lower private wages and short-term public costs. Moreover, privatization raises serious issues of account-ability as service and working standards are privately dictated. Our discussion reflects these analyses along with insights shared with the authors by people in-side and outside the Daley administration. See also Ascher 1987, Finley 1989, Uhlfelder 1996, and The Civic Federation 1996.

[4] We have been active in the community movement in multiple capacities (researchers, volunteers, staff, activists). As such, we have studied, taught, and followed it very closely. This analysis is informed by this experience.

[5] By no means do we disclaim the potential merits of competition. In this context, however, competition is a zero sum game as the gains of one occur at the expense of those of the other. For obvious reasons, Latinos and Blacks are sensi-tive to the social budget. Declining allocations in the face of increases in popula-tion and the concentration of poverty pits them against each other in a war of mutual exclusion (called competition).

[6] *Racism* and *the idea of race itself* is socially constructed and historically conditioned (Winant 1994). It is, to an extent, a moving target. The dynamic fea-tures discussed here are particularly important for assessing the possibilities of Latino-Black collaboration and contention.

[7] Quotas, human capital, reverse discrimination, charges of cultural deficits and lack of individual responsibility, immigration and welfare reform are sam-ples of the rhetoric of retrenchment and infringement on the status of people of color in the public discourse.

[8] Note that since the tailspin of the mass movement and direct assaults on oppression in the mid-1970s (when Blacks turned from protest to electoral poli-tics), there has been an increasing assault on civil rights, affirmative action and equal opportunity and a mounting social and institutional racism at the national and urban levels.

[9] The elitist position should be distinguished from the community empow-erment movement that it parallels. The former accepts the orientations of the New Right as opposed to community-directed decision-making, accountability of leaders to constituents, participatory democracy, self-determination, collective discipline and cooperation around a common agenda (Jennings 1992 & 1994; Betancur and Gills 1997; Fletcher and Newport 1992; Craig and Mayo 1995; Mier 1993; Klein 1994; Cogan 1994). For elites, social promotion and position are explained in terms of "meritocracy." They claim that they got their relative positions of privilege and authority on the basis of individual industry, high moral conduct and personal efforts to overcome adversity—not as a result of the

collective struggle of their communities. Moreover, as the argument goes, they, too, do not have any responsibility to those left behind (Fletcher and Newport 1992). Under these circumstances, race-based initiatives need to have a clear sense of class interest. A false identity allows for manipulation of mass movements and facilitates efforts by elites promoting their own agendas.

[10] This is a case in which a law is enacted without new funding to implement it. In the ensuing competition for a fixed budget now stretched to serve multiple groups, those with a higher standing (White males, White females, etc.) are at a competitive advantage over the next in a new hierarchy among "minorities." It is also in this sense that collective status claims of race/nationality groups are viewed by the majority as coming at the expense of other recognized minorities. This appears to be the new game: if the majority cannot overcome them, then it joins them.

[11] The example of the *Avis dilemma* speaks very powerfully to this question. Asked about his membership in the *model minority, an* Indian professor pointed out with righteous indignation: "Should we be proud of the fact that European ethnographers and racists regard us as a 'number two'? Are we to be complacent and reconciled? Or, are we to be like Avis—the rental car company, second in sales in the USA? We are to be applauded by Whites and hated by Black and Brown peoples because 'we try harder?' Would we be trying harder to be as racist as some Europeans or Americans? Sorry, we reject the distinction. Being the 'model American minority' or the 'model global servant' of White racism is not our aspiration. To accept this appellation is to be victimized or to be a willing peon of the same game of division and dominance of all peoples of color on a national or global scale. Only Whites would win this game; anyone else would be still relegated to the status of subhuman."

[12] Nationality/race-based survival efforts and collaborations need to be tied to the class interests of the masses of Blacks and Latinos—and to sectors whose conditions did not improve significantly with the Civil Rights Movement and may be actually worsening in the last two decades. It requires the development of common consciousness about their interests. This point of view does not reject all-class collaborations, especially around collective racial attacks. However, a more appealing strategic response for promoting social change appears to rest with efforts that link progressive forces to single class, democratic and popular coalition across cultural or race/nationality lines.

[13] These figures include only unemployment insurance-covered jobs as reported by the Illinois Department of Employment Security (IDES) for 1970 and 1990.

[14] Construction stopped in the city in the mid-1980s to resume in the late 1990s. Most development activity today focuses on residential, commercial and

entertainment. The figures in this analysis illustrate the main period of transformation of the City of Chicago from a predominantly manufacturing to a service economy.

[15] Surprisingly, Chicago has been largely absent from discussions of globalization. Thus, it may be underrated.

[16] The growth coalition continued its activities throughout the progressive regime of Washington/Sawyer (1983-1989). Rather than opposing the development agenda of the coalition, this regime tried to work around it and to promote development linkages between the CBD and the neighborhoods. The coalition survived outside of City Hall and worked to undermine and obstruct the work of the regime. Since it regained power in 1989, the Daley regime has kept a tight grip on the City and has worked closely with the coalition around an agenda of globalization, gentrification and economic and political consolidation.

[17] A different model was pursued under the Washington-Sawyer regime (1983-1989). It sought ways to direct a share of public development expenditures to low-income communities and residents, to allocate jobs created by public funds to city workers and low income residents, to train residents of these communities for the construction jobs generated by publicly subsidized development and to award contracts to Black, Latino and female contractors.

[18] For example, Cook County has instituted a "pop" tax that is excessively paid by young people as the main consumers of beverages.

[19] While heavily promoting middle income housing of all types and home ownership, the Daley regime is severely restricting subsidies for rental multifamily housing production. Along the way, the administration has satisfied other industries—e.g., banking through sponsorship of first time buyer subsidy loans administered by the banks—and has discouraged development or rehabilitation of low income housing.

[20] Notice that these initiatives are aimed at the middle class and, in fact, facilitate the displacement of Latinos and Blacks from many of their neighborhoods—particularly those in prime locations.

[21] An alternative model is for policy makers to explore alternative avenues of privatization around *community-based organizations* (CBOs). CBOs could use these contracts to hire residents and promote local development.

[22] The coalition and regime have worked to take total control away from communities and the interests of low-income groups. This is reflected in a top-down policy and decision-making bent on repressing alternative forces while heavily rewarding supporters within a reshaped system of patronage and mutual loyalties. The mayor has gained control of a Black–Latino majority City Council through the running of its handpicked candidates. The large campaign war chest provided by the regime's wealthy supporters guarantees their election. He can,

then, give control to alder persons of their home Ward's affairs in exchange for unconditional support of the coalition's priorities. This is clearly reflected in the passing of the 3.9 billion dollar 1988 Municipal budget by a 49 to 0 majority in record time with only token debate. Local government is run like a quasi-corporation largely limiting the democratic process to Machine electoral politics and excluding it from governance.

[23] These churches are referred to as *drive-in* churches in the Chicago community lexicon.

[24] Similar patterns are being observed in the implementation of the Empowerment Zone (EZ) in Chicago. It appears that this national policy initiative will fail to prevent existing poor residents, the majority being Latino and African American, from displacement related to the absence of opportunities to accumulate personal, family and community-controlled assets and access to capital. In fact, the EZ may be used as a mechanism to dislodge the same people it was intended to assist. The EZ initiative has already failed as a thrust to empower local residents and to reinvent government through greater citizen and community participation in all aspects of the program and policy development—plan design, implementation, monitoring and oversight, and evaluation. The suspicion has been raised, in fact, that the administration is using EZ allocations to replace other sources such as CDBG funds.

[25] Furthermore, Chicago is a prime example of local government- assisted gentrification and redevelopment of property for new residential, commercial and institutional uses. Policy makers are presiding over the displacement of large sectors of poor, less advantaged Latinos and Blacks. The growth coalition is encouraged by this policy. The upward revaluation of property close to central city amenities and deliberate tax reclamation policies are associated with de-densification of housing affordable to low-income families and the re-attraction of affluent households.

CHAPTER 3

African Americans and Puerto Ricans in New York
Cycles and Circles of Discrimination

FRANK BONILLA
WALTER STAFFORD

Cities serving as global and regional economic centers in the United States are becoming important sites for concentrations of people of the Black and Latino Diaspora. While there have been major settlements of Blacks and Latinos in some of these same cities since the 1800s, the number of these locales and the density of their populations have increased dramatically since the 1960s. By 1990, Blacks and Latinos made up 54% of the nation's five largest cities (U.S. Bureau of the Census 1994).

To understand the effects of this clustering and the opportunities and problems it offers for interethnic collaboration, we have chosen to focus on Puerto Ricans and African-Americans in New York City. Their coexistence stretches over more than a century, providing a fertile setting to explore persistent features of inequality and the reproduction of modes of marginalization over time. Distinctive, yet parallel, configurations of Black and Latino group interactions mark other major cities such as Los Angeles, Miami, Chicago, and Washington. These similarities have led to recurrent efforts by Blacks and Latinos to reach out to one another to confront and contest exclusion and subordination. Our work seeks to redress the exclusion of these actions from most studies of U.S. urban history. Although Blacks and Latinos manifestly share their positioning in structures of oppression, directly or indirectly linked to U.S. colonial involvements, this commonality is often overshadowed by the particular combination of economic, political and cultural features of each instance and historical period.

The entry into the work force of sizeable contingents of new immigrants has added to intergroup tensions over jobs, wage scales, and urban spaces. The composition of Latino and African-origin groups in these cities has also diversified substantially over the last decades. Competition for place-linked economic development and empowerment resources between inner city entrepreneurs and community organizations newly fuels intergroup economic and political rivalries. The immigrant groups' differential success in penetrating particular economic sectors or building substantial ethnic enclaves[1] has also brought a growing number of Black organizations to view their communities as anchors for a new wave of Black self-employment.

Political conflicts increasingly are linked directly to economic interests within and across ethnic and nationality groups. The high levels of poverty among both Latinos and Blacks mean, as well, that organizations in both communities are commonly dependent on governmental assistance. Since in most cities, neither group controls the local political machinery, these organizations are often susceptible to manipulation by contending factions within the power elite. They are also in competition with older, White ethnic, nonprofit and charitable groups, which claim that they are best equipped to provide services to Black and Latino clients.

Beyond the economic and political realms lay a broad range of cultural conflicts. Although there are strong commonalities in the cultures of Blacks and Latinos, both with African antecedents, language often becomes a significant barrier. Intercultural communication is further constricted by the limited availability of institutional spaces that respect and nurture common elements and seek to mediate differences, including churches and schools.[2] Similarly, stereotypes of individual character and of cultural practices are generated and reinforced by tensions about the ranking of particular values, claims and the appropriation of public goods and services.

EXAMINING CIRCLES OF DISCRIMINATION

This essay examines commonalities and conflicts in New York City between Blacks and Puerto Ricans, the two minority groups widely acknowledged to have the oldest settlement patterns in the city and who still face the most intense discrimination. These patterns of sustained inequality and disadvantage have been characterized as "a circle of discrimination." According to Herman Bloch (1969), a circle has four components: (1) political subordination, (2) social subordination, (3) restrictive social mobility, and (4) noncompetitive employment status. While Bloch formulated this framework to describe the social and economic barriers facing African Americans, we contend that the scheme is more broadly applicable. We also argue that:

1. Once a circle is institutionalized the structure of subjugation is transferable to other groups.
2. The circle opens the way for extensive cooptation and manipulation of groups.
3. The longer a group has been subordinated within one dimension of the circle, the poorer its chances are to improve its condition on other fronts.
4. Because of the complexity of the internal dynamics of the circle, affected groups often have difficulty clearly identifying the principal individuals and organizations managing this apparatus of domination.

In our view, a key dimension of this notion of circles is to grasp the systemic qualities and adaptability that make for the reproduction of these relationships over time and their manifestation in distinctive configurations in a broad range of social formations. We will return to these considerations in our closing section.

CYCLES AND CIRCLES OF DISCRIMINATION IN NEW YORK CITY

Circles of discrimination in New York City originate with the enslavement of Blacks in the early 17th century. Although southern slavery has long overshadowed the bondage of Blacks in the North, in the 1600s and 1700s, slaves were about 16% of New York City's population and 11% of Whites were slave holders (Mabee 1979; Bloch 1969; Phillips 1918). New York's Blacks were formally emancipated in 1827 and joined the small population of free Blacks in creating small businesses and offering themselves as labor for hire. These economic gains were short-lived. By the 1840s, Blacks were displaced in many of the lower wage jobs by European immigrants, notably by the Irish. Bloch argues that, by the 1850s, New York had institutionalized job ceilings for Blacks in trades, industries and unions in ways that would shape political struggles for the next 150 years.

As Bloch documents extensively, the social and cultural subordination of Blacks in the city was essentially defined in the period between the 1600s and 1800s. Black values and culture were degraded and ignored in the building of public institutions. Most of the city's public infrastructures, including the New York City Board of Education, were set in place during the 1800s with little consideration of the Black community. The political dominion of Whites over Blacks was effectively maintained statutorily and through violence. Following emancipation, Black suffrage was restricted by a variety of property requirements. The state legislature did not remove these barriers until 1870. By then, the party political machine had begun to build a formidable base among European immigrants (Buenker 1973).

By the early 1900s, the circle of institutionalized discrimination had become well nigh intractable. Blacks had not gained significant access to jobs outside of early established sectors and ceilings. They were vastly outnumbered in the political arena. There were, however, a growing number of civic organizations in the Black community and a new radicalism represented by the creation of the National Association for the Advancement of Colored People (NAACP). Black churches had also, by then, become a leading voice of Black advocacy.

When Puerto Ricans and fresh contingents of Blacks from the South and the Caribbean arrived in large numbers in the 1920s, the interlocking apparatus of discrimination in the city was firmly anchored in official policy and practices. The depiction of Puerto Ricans as a culturally inferior and racially suspect group had been extensively elaborated from the beginning of the colonial relationship. The first U.S. occupying authorities in Puerto Rico declared the population to be submissive, unproductive, inferior and, essentially, a "surplus" human aggregate. These stereotypes continued to flourish even after Puerto Ricans were legally declared free to travel within U.S. territories, cultivated as a useful stock of cheap mobile labor, awarded formal U.S. citizenship, and conscripted into military service during World War I (Bonilla and Campos 1981).

Puerto Ricans arriving in New York, as elsewhere in the continental U.S.A. were readily incorporated into racially defined institutional arrangements that they only dimly understood. A major difference from African Americans in the way they were included in the circle of discrimination was the nature of their work. Because of new restrictions on European immigration in the 1920s, some Puerto Ricans gained access to low wage manufacturing jobs which, until then, had been reserved for native Whites and European newcomers. This undoubtedly cushioned some of the potential job competition with Blacks, who were more highly concentrated in services and transportation.

Still, the continued economic subjugation of both groups sparked new efforts at political and cultural self-determination in the 1920s. Marcus Garvey's United Negro Improvement Association and the Harlem Renaissance reflected the cultural and political spirit among Blacks. Faced with discrimination and violence from Whites, who perceived them as threats, Puerto Rican's also organized to promote unity and combat prejudice. Though Island political concerns continued to dominate community interests, the raw conditions of housing, social services and political exclusion soon drew Puerto Rican's into local action. A Porto Rican Brotherhood of America (Hermandad Puertorriquena) with an explicit class and nationalist agenda surfaced in 1923. Some efforts demonstrate early recognition of shared interests between the two groups. For example, a prominent figure in the powerful revival of interest in Black culture and history in that decade was Arturo Schomburg, a Puerto Rican scholar-activist, whose extensive art, literary and document collection was to become the core of the Division of Negro Art and Literature of the New York Public Library (Ortiz 1988). Archives (held at CUNY'S Centro de Estudios Puertorriquenos and the library of the University of California at Los Angeles) also record efforts at collaboration between Garveyites and the Liga Puertorriquena in New York later in the decade.

The 1930s depression hampered such coalition efforts as the weak economic base of both groups gravely eroded. Blacks were displaced from jobs at twice the rate of Whites and were widely discriminated against by relief agencies. Return migration to Puerto Rico soared for the first time (History Task Force 1979: 112). The Harlem riots in 1935 dramatized the problems of both groups. Frustrated by police brutality, White gang violence, lack of jobs within their neighborhoods, job discrimination, and chronic health problems, the Black community exploded. Mayor LaGuardia appointed a distinguished group of citizens to review conditions and hired E. Franklin Frazier, a Black sociologist, to write its report. Frazier's report detailed the interlocking networks of structured discrimination. However, LaGuardia refused to publish the report, exposing again the limited civic and political power of Blacks in the city (Commission on the Harlem Riots 1969).

It is worth noting that, though both Blacks and Puerto Ricans embraced nationalist causes in the 1930s, cross national unity came notably under the mantle of the Communist Party and the banner of socialism. The broad, non-racial agenda advanced from these sectors of the left held a strong appeal for groups consciously bent on structural reforms. In Puerto Rico itself, strikes and other disturbances accompanied a rising tide of nationalist resistance and threats of insurgency, eliciting ominous rumblings from Washington ("Put aside radical nations . . . or be cut adrift to certain economic doom") and legislative initiatives in the U.S. Congress for Puerto Rican independence (History Task Force 1979:117).

BEYOND WORLD WAR II

With the advent of World War II, there was an increased demand for Black labor in northern industries. As a result, several Presidential Executive Orders attempted to reduce discrimination in industries and unions. Black politicians became more vocal. A new period of civic and political activity was emerging. Adam C. Powell, Jr., became the first Black elected to the City Council (1941) and the first to represent New York in the House of Representatives (1947). Puerto Rican migration to the city slackened with the imposition of the military draft on the Island and the active recruitment of Island labor for military and war industry projects, especially in the U.S. Midwest.

After the war, the assertive political voices of Blacks and the rising numbers of Puerto Ricans posed new threats for local politicians. Congressman Powell consistently challenged barriers to racial equity in the city. The greater accessibility of air travel dramatically accelerated migration flows from Puerto Rico. Anticipating future turmoil and chagrined by continuing manifestations of racism after a major war fought partially against this heritage, Mayor Wagner during the course of the 1950s urged public agencies to increase the numbers of Black and Puerto Rican employees.

Despite modest inroads in the public sector, postwar economic realities for both groups remained grim. Most employers refused to heed Black and Puerto Rican political protest and returned to prewar exclusionary practices. These practices, combined with a decline in manufacturing jobs, created an ominous vision for the future. In 1950, nonWhite males earned 61% of the income of Whites. In each succeeding year, that income gap widened. Large increases in population further weakened the economic base of both groups. The 1950s brought a dramatic renewal of migration flows from Puerto Rico that trailed off only as the decade ended. Continued migration from the American South simultaneously increased the size of the Black population.

By the 1960s, there were 1,087,931 Blacks and more than 600,000 Puerto Ricans in the city. Together they represented nearly 22% of the city's population (U.S. Bureau of the Census 1960). Still, despite the passage of a host of federal and state anti-discrimination statutes and a vigorous civil rights movement, the jobs ceilings and segmentation instituted in the last century remained essentially intact. Public sector advances by Blacks were still not matched by Puerto Ricans. The exodus of manufacturing continued. The racial gap in incomes among males continued to widen.

Confronted with the stark reality that the city's leadership was unlikely to bend to the moral suasion deployed by the civil rights movement, local Blacks and Puerto Ricans created a host of new organizations that mounted joint campaigns for equity in education, housing and employment. Puerto Rican youth in the Young Lords adopted many of the principles and strategies of Black revolutionaries, creating a new generation of activists seeking cross-cultural communication. At the same time, appeals from the Rev. Martin Luther King for a break from a sterile cultural pluralism in which people came together episodically but remained locked in worlds apart produced only limited effects in the main body of the civil rights movement and the more established Latino organizations (Bonilla 1988).

The power structure of the city, while somewhat daunted by the rising militancy of Blacks and Puerto Ricans, once again manipulated the operations of public agencies to create political dependencies and patronage. Great Society Programs initially enhanced opportunities for both Black and Puerto Rican politicians to increase their power. But soon the White establishment used turf conflicts between the two groups to divide and disparage both. White politicians and researchers, building on evidence of a growing neo-conservative movement in the city and beyond, shifted the blame for the shortfalls in these reforms from the failures of public institutions to the "weaknesses" of Black and Puerto Rican family structures (Glazer and Moynihan 1963).

By the 1970s, the inability of Blacks and Puerto Ricans to develop a common political agenda was costing them dearly. In the 1973–74 fiscal crisis, both groups lost considerable ground. Blacks suffered major setbacks in their newly found jobs in government. Persistent Puerto Rican protests on this front had produced no significant breaches, and their base in manufacturing steadily continued to erode. Poverty among both groups began to increase, predictably accompanied by a decline in family stability. One report signaled that the highest proportion of children in

poverty were Latinos. Together with Blacks, these youngsters constituted nearly three-fourths of the city's children living in poverty (*New
York Times* 1979:4:2).

Politically, both Blacks and Puerto Ricans lost ground vis-a-vis their
counterparts in other major cities. While Chicago, New Orleans and others prepared for a "new era" of Black Power, New York's political establishment held a tight rein on its public institutions. The city refused to
pass a strong public sector affirmative action plan despite the clear record
of disproportionate layoffs of Blacks and Puerto Ricans under financial
pressures. It balked as well at developing set aside procedures to increase
contracts with minority businesses. In addition, at the close of the decade,
Mayor Koch reconfigured antipoverty programs to curb Black and Puerto
Rican influences.

New York City's Blacks and Puerto Ricans won their single major
advance during the 1970s through legally mandated scrutiny of discriminatory practices in education and employment. In 1974, the courts or-
dered the New York City school system to develop a bilingual education
program. Three years later, the Department of Health, Education and
Welfare charged that the schools were not providing adequate services to
Latino children and that New York City violated civil rights law by discriminating against minority students in its spending patterns. Five years
later, the federal government threatened to withhold 300 million dollars
in revenue sharing because the city was discriminating against six hundred Black and Latino police officers.

Despite, or perhaps as a consequence of this closer federal monitoring of racial inequities in the city, the New York Urban League contended
in 1978 that race relations were at their most troubling level in twenty
years. A League report argued that, without major improvements in jobs
and a reduction of tensions in economic and social policy, the nonWhite
community was poised for an imminent explosion (*New York Times*
1978:3:1).

Rather than concede that the historical circle of institutionalized
discrimination was bringing the city into a new crisis, White neoconser-
vatives and their political allies set out to reinforce the view that weaknesses in the social fabric of disadvantaged communities best explained
their social disarray. For some prominent analysts such as Roger Starr,
the best solution to these problems would be "planned shrinkage" of
these unassimilated groups in places such as the South Bronx, Harlem
and Brownsville. Felix Rohatyn, the head of the Municipal Assistance
Corporation, suggested similar measures.

Thus, by the 1980s, Blacks and Puerto Ricans found themselves once again at a crossroads. The federal government had become less vigilant in monitoring racial equality issues in the city and Mayor Koch had emerged as a vocal opponent of "racially based" measures to increase Black and Puerto Rican access to desirable jobs. In confirmation of Urban League auguries of coming racial violence, the city teetered on the edge as White mobs assaulted and killed ten Blacks and Latinos and racial disturbances broke out in high schools. Demonstrations led by Blacks and Puerto Ricans against Mayor Koch grew in number. He promised to hold town meetings to address some of the issues, but noted that he could only conduct discussions with "decent people."

In the face of continued slippage of their already limited political openings, Blacks and Puerto Ricans again saw a need to work together. A 1982 Federal Appeals ruling, which found the city's at-large council system unconstitutional, paved the way for another attempt at coalition building. The power of the Black and Puerto Rican vote showed immediate, in spite of limited results. Blacks used their political muscle to shape the outcome of local and gubernatorial races. They also demanded greater control in the selection of candidates for major offices, notably the Board of Education. The first Puerto Rican Chancellor of Education was selected in 1983 as a compromise to a Black candidate. The access of Blacks and Puerto Ricans to higher paying, more visible private and public jobs increased and several Blacks became heads of leading voluntary agencies.

The limited bonds between Blacks and Puerto Ricans were weakened, however, in an intense political battle in 1985 over who would challenge Mayor Koch. Herman Badillo, a Puerto Rican, announced that he would run for Mayor and sought the endorsement of Blacks. However, the more established Blacks in Manhattan felt that Badillo's entrance into the Mayoral race in 1977 had shattered the chances of their candidate, Percy Sutton. Rather than nominate Badillo, the Blacks selected Herman "Denny" Farrell, a state assemblyman. Farrell's selection exacerbated tensions between Blacks and Latinos. With a split in the Democratic Party coalition, Koch overwhelmingly won the race (Falcon 1985; Green and Wilson 1989).

The modest political gains of the two groups during the 1980s were not paralleled in the world of work or reflected in household conditions. Although, by 1980, Blacks and Latinos made up nearly half of the city's population, they remained rigidly segregated in the labor market— Puerto Ricans still mainly locked in manufacturing and a limited number of health-related occupations; Blacks most visible in banks, insurance and social service agencies in the private sector. In the public sector both groups were largely confined to human resource and juvenile justice agencies. Poverty rose as the wages of both groups lagged behind those of Whites (Stafford 1986; Torres 1995).

Hence, as the 1990s approached, New York was commonly referred to as a "Dual City," alluding to the vast discrepancies in living standards and wealth of abutting communities (Mollenkopf and Castells 1992). The relative status of Whites compared with Blacks, Puerto Ricans and other Latinos remained roughly the same. Survey findings by the Roper Organization for the American Jewish Committee revealed that Blacks and Latinos were viewed by New Yorkers of all races as the primary targets of discrimination. According to respondents, 55% of Blacks and 41% of Latinos were discriminated against a lot compared to 23% of Asians, 13% of Jews, 6% of Italians and 3% of Irish (Roper Organization 1992). Still, there was, in fact, a new dimension to this duality. The overall process of social polarization had begun to set off a more clearly defined class differentiation within each group, generating new forms of fragmentation that may bring further complications into coalition building in the near future. Blacks and Puerto Ricans came together around redistricting for seats in local and state legislatures. However, they were unable to coalesce on congressional boundaries.

Thus, the modest gains in restricted sectors of each community may hold as much negative potential as political promise. While the 1989 election of David Dinkins as the first Black mayor of the city appeared to open new possibilities, his "gorgeous mosaic" was seen by some more like a tectonic plate than a harmonious construction. Faced with shrinking revenues and a hostile federal government, Dinkins could not appease his various constituencies. While privately supporting him, Puerto Ricans often publicly challenged his policies and his slow appointment of Puerto Ricans who had strong community ties. Dinkins also avoided appointments of Blacks who had a strong base in their community. Many of the Blacks appointed to head agencies in his administration were recruited outside New York City.

The Dinkins regime (1990–1993) is important because it presented one of the few opportunities for Blacks and Puerto Ricans to create a common agenda. The heads of the two leading unions in the city were Black and Puerto Rican, the School Chancellors were Black or Latino, and the heads of many of the social service agencies were now Black.

Yet, the possibilities for coalition were strained by internal and external forces that the administration could not control.

Mayor Dinkins was confronted with demographic realities unlike any of his predecessors. By the late 1980s and 1990s, the full impact of the 1965 immigration law, which abolished national origin as the basis for U.S. immigration policy, was being felt as Asian, African, Latin American, European and Caribbean immigrants surged into the city. "Post modern" identity politics had also blossomed, as gays, lesbians and others demanded government recognition. Dinkins initially claimed that he could resolve the residue of hatred inherited from the Koch administration and calm the incendiary conflicts plaguing the city. He soon realized the limitations of "managing diversity."

Turf conflicts between groups, including two events that drew national attention, shattered the mosaic. The first occurred when a Korean merchant mistreated a Black Haitian customer. Blacks boycotted the store, leading many groups to charge that they were infringing on Koreans' rights to own businesses. The tension between the groups was further strained when a report issued by one of Dinkins' allies minimized the conflict. Another racial controversy emerged in Brooklyn when a young Jewish male killed a Black child with an automobile. Blacks rioted and, in the process, a Jewish male was slain. The Black community blamed Dinkins for allowing the Jew who drove the car to flee the country, while Jews blamed him for failing to intervene more quickly and forcibly to quell the disturbances that followed the accident. Crown Heights, the area of Brooklyn where this incident occurred, at the time had also become the center of Latino and Jewish conflicts around housing (redistricting fusions/splits).

Economic conditions showed little improvement during this period. As Table 3-1 shows, nearly one-third of New York's non-Latino Blacks were in poverty in 1993, and the poverty rate for Puerto Ricans had reached 50%, nearly eight points higher than the previous year (Community Service Society 1995). Unemployment rates for both groups in 1994, with the exception of Black females, also remained in double digits as they had for most of the decade (Table 3-2). Both groups faced increasing competition from new immigrants for skilled and low wage jobs (see Table 3-3). White foreign-born workers continued to dominate construction jobs, which Blacks and Puerto Ricans had unsuccessfully pursued for decades. Foreign-born Latinos had also increasingly moved into lower wage manufacturing jobs. The only employment sector in which Blacks and native-born Latinos held a decided edge was the public sector.

Table 3–1. Poverty Rates by Race/Ethnicity: New York City, 1985, 1986, 1987, 1990, 1991, 1992, and 1993

Race/ Ethnicity	1985	1986	1987	1990	1991	1992	1993
Total	23.9	20.6	23.2	25.2	24.2	23.9	27.3
Non-Hispanic White	9.7	8.9	8.4	11.6	12.4	12.3	13.4
Non-Hispanic black	31.6	26.5	33.8	33.0	28.8	32.7	31.3
Hispanic	44.4	36.2	41.6	43.1	43.6	39.9	46.5

Source: Data for each year from 1984 through 1993 from the March Current Population Survey tape file of the following year (July 1995). Updated Poverty tables for New York City with March 1994 Current Population Survey Estimates. Population Studies Unit, Community Service Society. 1995. New York, New York.

Poverty Rates for Puerto Ricans and for Other Hispanics

Ethnicity	1985	1986	1987	1990	1991	1992	1993
Puerto Rican	52.4	47.7	47.7	54.5	52.2	42.8	50.0
Other Hispanics	34.5	24.7	35.5	32.2	34.6	37.3	43.5

Source: July 1995. Updated Poverty tables for New York City with March 1994 Current Population Survey Estimates. Population Studies Unit Community Service Society. New York, New York. Data for each year from 1984 through 1993 from the March Current Population Survey tape file of the following year.

With the 1993 election of Rudolph Giuliani, the fortunes of Blacks and Puerto Ricans took yet another turn. Giuliani's victory can be attributed, in part, to the low turnout in both communities. This low turnout has been repaid with a new disdain from City Hall. Although during his campaign Giuliani had courted a few Blacks and Puerto Ricans, he also promised to slash municipal budgets and to reduce welfare spending. He has kept these promises and reduced the public workforce, eating again into the small gains of Blacks and Puerto Ricans in the last decade. When asked how his policies would affect the poor, Giuliani echoed the ideas of "planned shrinkage" voiced by Roger Starr nearly twenty years before. To facilitate this "shrinkage," Giuliani reduced or eliminated contracts to many of the Black and Puerto Rican nonprofit agencies serving and advocating for the poor.

Table 3–2 Labor Force Participation Rates and Unemployment Rates by Race/Ethnicity and Sex, New York City, 1980, 1985, 1986, 1987, 1988, 1991, 1992, 1993, and 1994.

Race/Ethnicity and Sex	Civilian Labor Force Participation Rate*								
	1980	1985	1986	1987	1988	1991	1992	1993	1994
Total									
Male	69.2	66.6	69.5	69.4	67.8	66.3	66.4	64.9	63.3
Female	47.1	46.4	44.9	45.1	44.9	46.6	44.8	46.1	47.6
White									
Male	70.7	68.1	69.7	70.7	69.7	66.5	66.0	64.2	61.4
Female	46.1	45.6	42.8	42.8	43.6	45.5	43.9	45.3	43.5
Black									
Male	64.5	60.9	67.6	61.9	59.8	61.2	65.1	64.5	63.2
Female	51.5	48.7	50.5	48.7	48.0	46.6	44.4	46.3	53.3
Hispanic									
Male	70.1	64.1	69.0	71.8	68.2	65.0	65.6	59.6	62.0
Female	41.0	33.8	38.0	37.8	38.9	37.9	35.6	39.6	38.4

Unemployment

Race/Ethnicity and Sex	1980	1985	1986	1987	1988	1991	1992	1993	1994
Total									
Male	7.7	10.0	8.7	5.2	5.2	5.8	12.1	10.8	12.1
Female	7.7	8.3	6.6	5.0	4.4	3.2	7.2	8.1	8.8
White									
Male	5.9	8.3	7.2	4.7	3.8	5.0	11.6	10.0	10.6
Female	6.3	7.7	5.1	4.6	3.9	3.3	7.3	7.1	8.1
Black									
Male	12.8	16.2	13.7	7.5	9.7	8.1	15.8	12.2	17.1
Female	9.8	10.3	11.0	6.9	5.0	3.0	8.3	12.0	8.7
Hispanic									
Male	10.2	17.4	16.5	9.3	5.9	6.5	15.2	16.2	15.1
Female	11.8	13.3	9.0	8.6	7.3	3.5	8.3	14.1	12.4

*Employment figures are for persons 16 and over.

**The unemployment rate is for persons in the civilian labor force.

Source: Data for 1980 are from 1980 *Census of Population, General Social and Economic Characteristics, New York,* Tables 120, 128, 134, and 152. Data for each year from 1985 through 1994 are from the March Current Population Survey tape file of the same year. (July 1995). Updated Poverty tables for New York City with March 1994 Current Population survey Estimates. Population Studies Unit, Community Service Society. 1995. New York, New York.

Table 3-3. Representation of Employed Foreign Born and Native Born Workers by Race/ Ethnicity by Industry

	White Non-Hispanic		Black Non-Hispanic		Asian, Pacific Islander		Other Non-Hispanic		Hispanic		Total
	Foreign Born	Native Born	Foreign Born	Native Born	Foreign Born	Native Born	Foreign Born	Native Born	Foreign Born	Native Born	Total
Construction	16.50	35.00	9.46	11.25	5.19	0.35	0.13	0.05	12.24	10.05	100
Manufacture nondurable	8.87	36.50	5.32	8.60	13.80	0.70	0.13	0.02	16.00	10.10	100
Manufacture durable	10.62	26.88	6.90	10.90	7.08	0.40	0.06	0.11	23.11	14.00	100
Transportation, Communication	7.20	37.00	8.24	23.31	5.60	0.5	0.08	0.04	8.00	10.00	100
Wholesale durable	10.75	45.83	6.89	10.15	5.97	0.55	0.08	0.06	10.36	9.24	100
Wholesale nondurable	10.15	41.32	4.04	9.44	11.12	1.21	0.20	0.04	11.57	10.77	100
Retail Trade	11.11	32.32	5.75	10.44	13.48	0.77	0.18	0.07	15.30	10.35	100
Finance, Insurance, Real Estate	7.87	48.14	7.72	13.88	5.67	1.02	0.08	0.07	6.07	9.36	100
Business Repair	8.88	40.69	8.36	14.60	4.69	0.78	0.17	0.13	12.38	9.10	100
Personal Service	10.47	21.38	13.89	13.21	10.89	0.61	0.22	0.06	19.53	9.57	100
Entertainment, Recreation	6.88	63.24	2.42	11.42	2.18	0.40	0.04	0.10	5.35	7.76	100
Professional, Related Services	6.91	43.86	10.08	18.22	5.26	0.59	0.07	0.07	5.49	9.27	100
Public Administration	4.64	40.06	7.11	28.80	2.91	0.42	0.04	0.02	4.15	11.54	100

Source: 1990 Census Public Use Microdata. New York City Department of Planning.

The new regime has forced Blacks and Puerto Ricans to reexamine their political and economic strategies. Politically, both communities are in serious disarray. Where brutal internecine conflicts do not prevail, there is a resigned effort to survive with marginal, fragile budgets. Although both communities join in protest against budget cuts, there is no clear strategy for dealing with economic disorder. Union leaders from both groups choose to protect minimal benefits for their members rather than engage in a confrontation with the administration. Social infrastructures crumble in lower income areas; police brutality and corruption become more visible; and poverty and homelessness become accepted realities of the current order.

TIGHTENING CIRCLES

This essay suggests that an institutionalized circle of discrimination is difficult, although not impossible, to overcome. The complex, interrelated components of the circle help explain why effective Black–Latino coalitions have not yet emerged in New York City.

Among the best passages in Bloch's study of circles of discrimination are his accounts of how "mores", that is, cultural practices and institutional standards prescribing the status, duties, permissible movements and other attributes of subordinate groups, are periodically sanctioned in law. This is often accompanied by penalties beyond those arbitrarily applied by slave masters, overseers, and others in power. Benjamin Ringer (1983) has charted these same processes as they bear on Puerto Ricans, Africans and Native Americans during the constitutional period in his *We the People, and Others.* These interventions in the legal order generally follow when perceived challenges from or behavior at the bottom of the social order appear threatening or involve "high" costs, especially economic ones.

Today, the much touted *Contract with America* and subsequent initiatives reproduce this particular cycle in the periodic reconstitution of the circles of discrimination. Reviving the death penalty, mandatory sentencing, deportations, denials and restrictions on social services and asylum, militarization of borders—all are familiar elements in this historical merry-go-round. Numerous observers point to this feature of the current political and social conjuncture. While touted as a "watershed" era, there is ample awareness that the nation simply is reliving ups and downs from its past (Mansfield 1995; Taylor 1995).

As we have argued elsewhere (Bonilla and Campos 1982), the social polarization that has come into being over the last two decades and the measures contemplated as remedies are intimately tied to the process of economic globalization and its enduring colonialist dimensions:

> The present fluidity of movement of factors in production may mean that the colonial experience is running in *advance* of social processes in the metropolis rather than recapitulating earlier phases in capitalist development. ... [B]y interjecting the colonized through immigration, the metropolis not only imports and reproduces in new ways colonial relations formerly screened from direct social experience at home, but eventually embraces colonial "solutions" for its own internal social dislocation.

This chapter has only hinted at the intricacies of questions of theory, method, research practice and policy implications implicit in this account of a small part of what is happening to Blacks and Puerto Ricans in urban America. We are at a moment of crisis that reaches into the academy. All our disciplines openly acknowledge the insufficiencies of existing competing paradigms. The precariousness and shortfalls of available data are a constant object of lamentation. Those concerned with shaping policy or guiding movements for radical change can muster only feeble ideological grounding for responsible counsel on these fronts. Hopefully, we may together begin to draw on the legacy of pertinent critical scholarship and institutional construction to press forward in mutually supportive ways that transcend past divisions and self-defeating contention.

As suggested in later chapters, opportunities to break through the cycles and circles can emerge, or may be produced, through social practice. The dynamics of globalization, the endemic nature of the urban crisis, and the emergence of grassroots movements can certainly produce such openings. Since Blacks and Latinos are at the center of populations adversely affected by globalization and the attendant urban crisis, they can be in a unique position to respond. The nature and work of the leadership in both communities may be decisive in determining whether relations of collaboration or contention are built and whether or not social movements are developed in the cities of Latino and African American concentration.

NOTES

[1] New European and Asian immigrants often enter the country with established job and business ties. Historically, Jewish communities have maintained highly effective advocacy and social service organizations, which Latinos and African Americans have, in fact, often sought to emulate. The Puerto Rican Diaspora has been historically coordinated by a combination of corporate and government entities that scattered Islanders around the Caribbean, as far as Hawaii, and to a variety of mainland locales aside from New York (e.g., Arizona, Pennsylvania, Connecticut, Illinois). Black internal migrations within the U.S. have been driven by yet another configuration of forces that still make African Americans one of the most spatially mobile contingents in the nation (Long 1988).

[2] The Black church, a main anchor of Black culture, has not manifested a great deal of interest in cross-cultural communication. Research on the role of religious institutions, Catholic and Protestant, in shaping Puerto Rican social activism in the city has surged recently. As elsewhere around the country, church-based Black/Latino unification efforts are only now gaining prominence (Stevens-Arrogo and Diaz Stevenz 1995). Schools, which should provide an appropriate site for principled and informed linkages, are often a center of conflict around the question of bilingual education. Blacks often resent the use of scarce public resources for bilingual education when similar cultural enrichment programs for native Blacks are declared suspect. Even when well disposed to have their children immersed in bilingual settings, Black parents may encounter practical difficulties in adapting to the needs of children gaining facility in a second language.

CHAPTER 4

The African American and Latino Coalition Experience in Chicago Under Mayor Harold Washington

JOHN J. BETANCUR
DOUGLAS C. GILLS

This chapter analyzes the African American–Latino coalition experience under the mayoralty of Harold Washington in Chicago.[1] This work is critically important in light of the continuing deterioration of socioeconomic conditions for Blacks and Latinos in U.S. cities and the need for renewed efforts to reverse this trend. Intensification of interracial conflict likely will lead to further subordination and marginalization of these two groups. Cooperation, on the contrary, can provide new avenues for empowerment and improvement.

As the first major undertaking of Latinos and Blacks in Chicago, the Washington mayoral experience sheds light on the possibilities for joint action between them in the City. It provides rare lessons for interracial or multinational social practice within the urban policy environment. We argue that the movement and coalition supporting the election and regime of Washington were, at once, successful in getting a Black mayor elected for the first time in Chicago and, yet, unsuccessful in consolidating a sustained governance coalition led by Blacks and Latinos.[2]

This analysis pays special attention to the common ground upon which the coalition experience was fashioned and might be reconstructed in the future and describes the basis of contention and collaboration between Blacks and Latinos in the political process in Chicago. It identifies the specific set of historical elements that broke the hold of the reigning regime while opening the doors for new options. Finally, it examines crucial elements in the process of building and maintaining a progressive, reformist and inclusive government.

We start with a methodological note followed by a background summary of the conditions that led to the electoral coalition and the Washington mayoralty. Next, we describe the coalition's developmental phases and their aftermath. We conclude by discussing findings and implications.

METHODOLOGY

This work is based on documents and literature, interviews of central players and outside informants, and the experiences of the researchers. The literature on urban political coalitions (Clavel and Wiewel 1991), on sociopolitical movements for minority empowerment (McAdams 1982; Hanks 1987; Villareal and Hernandez 1991; Hero 1992; Jennings 1992a and 1994a) and on local political regime displacement (Cole 1976; Eisenger 1980a and 1983a; O'Laughlin 1983) helped identify the analytical framework and the major issues and indicators for research. Writings specifically documenting the Washington administration were used to determine the forms of the coalition and the role of Black and Latino coalitional politics in the election and in the Washington-Sawyer regime (Alkalimat and Gills 1984, 1989; Green 1990; Holli 1991; Green 1990; Clavel and Wiewel 1991; Nyden and Wiewel 1991; Gills 1991, 1993; Grimshaw 1992; Betancur and Gills 1993). Few works have addressed this aspect of coalition politics in the Washington mayoralty; none has discussed it in detail.

Between May 1994 and August 1996, the authors conducted intensive interviews and focus groups with more than 30 persons who have been central to the Chicago political scene during the past 10 to 15 years. Interviewees included activists, politicians, regime officers, observers, and scholars.

The researchers, themselves, participated in the community politics that gave rise to the electoral movement and played roles in the campaign.[3] They bring a combination of academic practice and social action to this work. The techniques employed are consistent with accepted practices; their community change perspective follows the approach of social action research (Stanfield and Dennis 1993:53–74; Stanfield II and Dennis 1993). While focused on the Washington-Sawyer regime and the support coalition underpinning it, of necessity, the chapter provides a historical context and makes certain comparisons and references to the current Richard M. Daley administration. The presentation summarizes the history and insights extracted from documents, interviews and discussions with participants and the experience and insights of the authors.

BACKGROUND

The Black–Latino coalition around the election and government of Harold Washington (its significance and difficulties, in particular) cannot be properly understood outside of its historical context. The Black and Latino experience of displacement and domination, the dynamic between these two communities, their struggles for empowerment, changes in the political economy, the crisis of the early Daley regime and increases in the Black and Latino populations in Chicago are of foremost importance. While we could not possibly discuss each of these factors in detail here, we briefly point to those aspects that propelled both of these political communities toward alliance-building and that can help understand the limitations of this experience. We wish to communicate the need to see this experience in its historical connections.[4]

Domination

The Latino and Black experiences in Chicago have been harsh and oppressive. They are characterized by high levels of residential segregation, job segmentation and social separation (Ano Nuevo Kerr 1976; Padilla 1987; Galster and Hill 1992). In spite of this segregation and concentration, machine and "plantation politics"[5] did not allow Blacks and Latinos to select and elect candidates of their choice in local elections until the late 1970s. Such experiences have translated into histories of disadvantage and limited opportunity. As a result, the two groups face similar problems and challenges in the city.

Community Dynamics

The separate histories and insulated experiences of African Americans and Latinos have reinforced their distinct and often contending political identities, often leading to mutual suspicion, competition and mass ignorance of each other's circumstances and legacies of struggle. This separate development hindered their chances to build an effective, enduring coalition in Chicago in the 1980s. Latinos and Blacks had not developed the bonding necessary to confront the dominant outside forces, while addressing their own internal tensions.

Added to this is the significance of race/nationality and class dynamics as a basis of political struggle in Chicago. Although the antiracist struggle presents opportunities to unite them, nationalism tends to break them apart. Yet, both are salient components of their respective political and social experiences. Moreover, Blacks and Latinos are highly hetero-geneous in their composition—especially in terms of class. Ideology, origin, culture, political practice, linkages, loyalties and immigrant sta-tus give rise to a diversity of priorities, responses and initiatives in the broader as well as in the local political process. While Blacks have a longer tradition of struggle together, Latinos have organized into a social aggregate only recently.[6] Moreover, the literature does not begin to ad-dress the Latino presence in Chicago as significant until the mid 1970s when this group increased dramatically (Travis 1987; Gove and Masotti 1982; Pinderhughes 1987). These factors make joint Black–Latino un-dertakings as complex and difficult as they are important.

The Struggle for Black–Latino empowerment

Three anti-institutional political movements defined the dynamics of the insurgency underpinning the Washington election: the nationalist, the re-formist and the community-based movements. The main motion was the reformist minority empowerment movement with roots in the civil rights and Black and Latino power movements of the 1950s, 1960s, and early 1970s (Alkalimat and Gills 1984, 1989).

In spite of its community control and self-determination content, the nationalist movement was led by the Black and Latino middle class seek-ing inclusion into the local economy and into political and public institu-tions (Gills 1991; Rivlin 1992). The reformist, efficiency-in-government, antipatronage movement, targeting corruption in public expenditures (Starks and Preston 1990; Simpson 1993; Grimshaw 1992; Holli and Green 1987) cut across social segments—race included—but was partic-ularly strong among middle-class liberals. While opposing waste and corruption in local government, this movement sought the inclusion of groups traditionally excluded from government, particularly through the (White elite) Democratic machine. The community development move-ment, also comprising multiple forces, was led at the time by a progres-sive, democratic and inclusive wing calling for balanced development, equitable resource allocation, community reinvestment and community-based planning and development (Squires et al. 1987; Gills 1991; Betan-cur and Gills 1993; Ferman 1996). This movement was particularly, though not exclusively, active in Black and Latino communities.

Under Washington, for a fleeting political moment, these three mo-tions converged in the form of racial/nationality community empower-ment, greater citizen and community participation in urban governance and more equitable (race and class) allocation of public resources.

Historically, the local Democratic machine had selected or coopted Black candidates for office. Latinos, meanwhile, had not received this attention partly because of their small electoral numbers before 1980. Lacking or having a puppet representation, Blacks and Latinos waged many of their struggles at the community level through efforts of advocacy and self-help. This essentially not for profit, place-based, organizing infrastructure became central in the late 1970s. It brought the two communities together around issues of common concern and collective need, preparing them for larger undertakings. It provided the foundations for independent bids for office and for the election of Washington.

Restructuring and the Urban Crisis

As Chapter 2 explained, with industrial decline, the opportunity for mass, entry level jobs paying livable wages and for upward mobility dwindled at a time when Blacks and Latinos were increasing their share of the city's population. Unfortunately, their experiences under the local Democratic machine were similar to those in manufacturing. Since they were the last to be absorbed, they were relegated to the margins and participated in the party as a reserve army of voters. Access to the machine's patronage system was restricted by a dwindling local tax base and by racist practices of the political elite leadership (Pinderhughes 1987; Grimshaw 1992).

Black and Latino political insurgency and urban restructuring since the 1970s further polarized middle- and working-class Whites. Within an environment of growing job insecurity, the latter feared losing the secure, well paying public sector jobs and contracts to Blacks and Latinos (Squires et al. 1987). Here, class reaction had racist effects. Faced with these challenges, Latinos and Blacks had to develop collective strategies to access the political arena and to create new opportunities for themselves, while directing public resources to their communities. Along with this, they had to compete with new urban growth coalitions of the private sector looking to the local government to supply their margins of profit (Squires et al. 1987; Ferman 1996). Together, Blacks and Latinos could become a formidable force in local politics. Apart, they could cancel each other or fall prey to the manipulations of reigning White elites in power.

Deepening Crisis of the Democratic Machine

With the death of legendary mayor Richard J. Daley in 1976, the struggle for control over a fractured Democratic machine broke loose in Chicago. Blacks and Latinos saw this as the best opportunity to get "one of their own" elected mayor (Alkalimat and Gills 1984, 1989) under an agenda that brought their largely neglected priorities to center stage.

The Black community had been preparing for this opportunity (Travis 1987; Rivlin 1992; Grimshaw 1992; Alkalimat and Gills 1984, 1989). Latinos were exploring options about supporting a candidate willing to promote an agenda of community development, jobs, contracts, economic venture opportunities, protection of immigrant rights, access to public health, human services assistance, schools and bilingualism. Washington attracted progressive Latino sectors who saw him as a reform-minded candidate deeply committed to fairness, equality and diversity.

Dynamics of Demographic Growth

The Black population reached nearly 33% of the city's total in 1970 and 40% in 1980. Similarly, Latinos grew from 7% in 1970 to 14% in 1980. Despite this, the White elite-dominated Democratic machine kept tight control of power through mechanisms such as handpicking candidates and the gerrymandering of Latino and Black areas to reelect its candidates and to preempt an independent takeover by these groups (Grimshaw 1992). The concentration and growth of the Black and Latino population increased their possibilities of electoral gains. For the first time, their electoral numbers provided the foundations for challenging the entrenched elite Democratic machine. Moreover, Latinos and Blacks expected that redistricting would substantially increase their representation in public office (Pinderhughes 1987:3–17). The opportunity was ripe to organize around a coalitional government.

LAYING THE GROUNDWORK: EARLY COALITIONAL EXPERIENCES

The movement underpinning Washington's election originated outside the political mainstream, from within Black and Latino communities and limited groups of Whites interested in government reform (Starks and Preston 1990; Grimshaw 1992; Gills 1991). It was inspired by the experience of exclusion and the feeling of alienation and anger caused by years of monopoly of power and racism by the local Democratic machine. It was a moment of hope: the hope that the election of a reform-minded Black mayor would open up City Hall to them and direct public resources to their communities. Washington was a viable and attractive candidate. Although a product of the machine, he had distanced himself from it and, later, ran against it. He was particularly troubled by its corruption and racism. His progressive legislative record and his advocacy of justice, equal opportunity and reform[7] fully qualified him as a reform candidate.

Starting in the late 1960s and 1970s, the community development, nationalist and reformist movements had been setting the groundwork and building support that proved crucial when the opportunity arrived. In the early 1980s, the motion to run a unity candidate against the machine took on a sweltering intensity. The overt abuses of the Byrne administration (1979-1983) and the national advance of a conservative agenda left Latino and Black activists smoldering with anger while the candidacy of Washington ignited the fire. The pieces fell together in the early 1980s.

In 1981, following the election of President Reagan, the Illinois Coalition Against Reagan Economics, I-CARE, was formed as an urban policy advocacy and protest force linking welfare rights groups, community organizations, social workers and labor unions. In 1982, on the eve of the Illinois gubernatorial election, People Organized for Welfare Economic Reform (POWER) was established as a direct action coalition of grassroots activists, welfare recipients and disabled and unemployed workers. Sponsored by community-based groups from within Black, Latino and poor White communities, POWER and I-CARE expressed the progressive, populist spirit of the broad social change movement underpinning Washington's run. POWER was particularly successful in expanding the popular electoral base. It ran a registration campaign that added 160,000 voters for the gubernatorial elections of 1982 and the local elections of 1983. These mobilizations first tested the Latino and Black alliance, prior to the Washington campaign. Black and Latino activists supported reform candidates with varying levels of success.

Other experiences of multinational, multiracial progressive coalitions organized around grassroots issues and platforms since the mid-1970s include CWED, the Community Workshop on Economic Development, a coalition of community development corporations and support intermediaries; the Housing Agenda, a network of housing and tenant advocacy groups; the Chicago Rehab Network, the first multiracial coalition of community-based housing rehabilitation and development groups; and the Community Renewal Society, which brought groups together from within the communities of color to expose racism and poverty through public forums and direct assistance to community groups.

Coalescing around common causes and collective issues important to their respective communities, organizations learned the power that could come with joint action. Without this groundwork, participants who were interviewed explained that coalition could not possibly have happened in the way in which it did. Thus, the man, movement and moment of opportunity came together. The convergence was electric, innovative and promised great possibilities for change.

THE BLACK–LATINO COALITION PROMOTING HAROLD WASHINGTON

The Electoral Coalition

While the mutual bonding between the Washington candidacy and predecessor networks and groups brought them together, formation of the Black–Latino electoral coalition did not take place without difficulties. Latino support was initially limited. It came from leaders of citizen and community groups previously involved in joint actions with Black activists around community organization action and progressive agendas. It started with meetings in the early 1980s in the Puerto Rican and Mexican communities to consider the possibility of electing Latinos to office and promoting a Latino agenda in the public political economy (Latino interviewees).

Progressive forces tied to solidarity causes, Puerto Rico's independence and churches led the way in the near northwest Puerto Rican community. CASA, Center for Autonomous Social Action, a group advocating for the rights of Mexican workers, headed the effort in the near southwest Mexican community. Other Latino nationals, brought in by the struggles of the 1970s, were also involved. This core leadership held joint meetings to discuss overall strategy, including conversations about the benefits of forming a Black–Latino coalition and electing a Black mayor. Participants decided to support Washington and joined in actions to get him elected.

Of special importance in forging a Black–Latino electoral coalition was the independent political organization (IPO) in the west and near southwest sides of the City. IPO was formed in the early 1980s around independent political activists. Not only did these ties develop trust and the ability to work together, but they became the nucleus of the Black–Latino coalition.

In the Black community, Washington's candidacy benefitted from a massive upsurge of community-based political and civic activism from every segment of the political spectrum in the late 1970s and early 1980s. But the most important umbrella coalition was the Task Force for Black Political Empowerment, which united all segments of political activism in the community. As an all-class, all-sector unity body, the Task Force was the principal force of mobilization and coordination. Initially started by a reform, community-oriented leadership, it became the main source of nationalist influence on the Washington-Sawyer regime (Alkalimat and Gills 1984, 1989; Starks and Preston 1990). But the main forces of Black–Latino coalition work in the Black community were political progressives on the left, community-based organization activists and the Black labor and workers' movement under the banner of the Coalition of Black Trade Unionists.[8]

The motion to elect a Black mayor brought new actors into the political arena. They came out of neighborhood struggles, the fight to save the welfare state, and from antiracist battles. They were young, electoral neophytes. When the prospects for success had increased significantly after Washington's victory in the primary elections, the traditional Black and Latino middle classes came on board, as did elites in business, institutional and civic settings and some political elites tied to the machine.

Thus, there was a fusion of the mass base with the traditional elite players. The latter brought to the process considerable resources but also the conventional political expectations that have fettered Black and Latino popular efforts historically. Their narrow, self-interested activities, coupled with the rise of petty nationalism, would later serve to derail the political coalition and topple the new regime after Washington's demise. Such a divergence of interests became a continuous source of tension throughout the campaign and administration, particularly among class forces in positions of leadership or power. While successful at the grassroots, the coalition ran into difficulties at the electoral level. They had to contend also with politicians demanding special considerations because of their status in political and public offices. These factors proved to be a liability at a subsequent phase of the alliance-building process.

Finally, Washington's candidacy attracted progressive, liberal, good government reformers and the radical left. Excluded from the political process, or deeply opposed to the corrupt and monopolistic ways of the Democratic machine, these reformers saw Washington as a once in a lifetime opportunity for development of new power relations between the people and City Hall, between citizens and the local bureaucracy (Coleman and Atkins 1989; Simpson 1993; Grimshaw 1992).[9]

Two facts stand out in the history of Black–Latino political relations in Chicago (there was near universal agreement among our informants about them). First, in spite of a tradition of community-based coalitions prior to the 1982-83 campaign, there was barely any tradition of electoral coalition building between them. Second, the coalition building efforts came from outside the extant political system.

Although the Washington campaign perceived the need to attract non-Black voters, it had a hard time integrating even those Latinos who volunteered their support. It was difficult, for instance, for the Washington camp to accept that Latinos run the campaign in their own barrios. This reluctance to decentralize the election process and pursue non traditional political tactics was experienced within Black wards as well. According to one respondent, Washington had learned to trust few political leaders within and outside the Party.[10] This practice became a continuous source of tension while keeping potential supporters away and alienating some allies.

Initially, support for Washington came from Blacks (most sectors) and from progressive Whites and Latinos. Once he won the Democratic primary election in late February, sectors supportive of defeated candidates joined. While only 15% of all Latino voters supported him in the primary elections, 75% cast their ballots for him in the general election. Interviewees credited this change to different factors including: strong commitment of and campaigning by progressive Latino leaders; an agenda supporting Latinos for office, jobs and contracts; Latino loyalty to the Democratic Party; opportunism; the expectation that he would win; and vote by default (with the defeat of Richard M. Daley and Jane Byrne who had captured the Latino vote in the primary elections, they had no where to go but to Washington).

Two strong White Democratic candidates had split the White vote in the primary election, facilitating the victory of Washington. With reunification of White voters under a White Republican candidate, the support of Latinos and White progressives made the difference for Washington in one of the most vicious and racist campaigns in the country's history. This split also suggested that his mayoralty would have serious difficulties with governance. To confront this, his transition organization adopted a combined strategy of inclusiveness and fiscal conservatism. The former attempted to include all groups in governance; the latter was a conscious effort to send a message to the business elite that there was nothing to fear from a Black-led reform government. This gesture, however, did not appease the entrenched political opposition, more concerned about losing power than about the efficacy of a government that was more representative of local sociodemographics and that was committed to a pluralist agenda.

In short, the electoral coalition, particularly between Blacks and Latinos, was based on limited relationships and networks. It paid little attention to its consolidation through a mechanism of agreement and accountability. It operated on the implicit assumption of a coincidence of interests and commitment to the sharing of power and resources. Early tensions over control of the campaign, inclusion of non-Black groups and the electoral agenda pointed to the limitations of these assumptions. Such matters, though, were never frontally addressed. There were few efforts to build a mass-based organization. Commitment to the cause and Washington's mediation efforts kept tensions swept under the rug. In spite of this, the coalition was able to defeat the machine and to elect Washington to office in 1983 and, again, in 1987.

The Governance Coalition

Washington's government was submitted to the persistent and vicious attack of the defeated Democratic machine. With a majority in the City Council, the machine engaged in every possible effort to stand in the way of the new regime, aided by a bureaucracy dominated by employees inherited from earlier administrations. It also received the assistance of the media and a business elite determined to obstruct the work of the administration at every step of the way. The strategy of the defeated Democratic machine and its allies was clear: to obstruct, frustrate and embarrass the emerging (predominantly Black and Latino) coalition to the point of making the city ungovernable and consolidation of the new regime impossible.

This environment did not help the young electoral coalition, unprepared for coalitional governance. Given the uncertainty of the election, the difficulties in integrating other groups, the largely ad-hoc nature of the coalition and the uphill battle of Washington's candidacy, little attention had been paid during the campaign to the day after: the role and maintenance of an electoral coalition; distribution of power and opportunity; and the process for governing together.

Once in power, members of the electoral coalition were anxious, and now divided, about the opportunities and resources and the purposes of the new regime. They were no longer outsiders ignited by the common forces of abuse and exclusion, but insiders confronted with the task of distributing power, opportunities and resources. Largely unprepared for this task, the coalition was pulled in multiple directions.[11]

Meanwhile, having reached its delimited goal of electing a progressive Black mayor, the community-based movement dissolved, with the expectation that City Hall would fully represent the interests of its constituents. Similarly, coalition members operated on the assumption that the new government would be coalitional and would represent their interests without their vigilance. After all, people believed that this was their government and that they should not embarrass it, and themselves, by keeping the inside-outside divide.[12] These proved to be mistaken assumptions. Supporters paid little attention to the capability of government to carry out policy and agenda changes without outside pressure and the legitimacy of mass demands.

Deprived of the dynamics of the movement and lacking a clear-cut coalitional agenda and accountability mechanism, the administration became highly vulnerable to the agendas of elite politicians, government bureaucrats, and other influential individuals. An attempt to put together a balanced government of movement leaders and established bureaucrats proved counterproductive. Not only were the progressive elements far outnumbered by bureaucrats, but they became isolated from their social bases as the movement took a back seat to City Hall.

Hence, the coalition inside City Hall got reduced to its City Council members and the small circle of activists that Washington had integrated into the administration. Outside, it became practically inactive. Hence, efforts to further the advance of a coalitional agenda were thwarted. There was no coordinating organization or forum facilitating broad unity of action. Every spectrum of the movement was busy promoting its own agenda, while the opposition-out-of-power was plotting to topple the new regime before it could consolidate.

The only remaining independent coalitional action linked to the community consisted of the growing number of CDCs that came together around specific policies and projects—housing, economic development, health and human services. While Black and Latino activists were most visible in these networks, they generally were middle class professional practitioners, speaking for poor and disadvantaged lower class communities. Few voices of the poor were projected, especially voices from among poor Blacks and Latinos. Moreover, there was no outside-inside center of the coalition. There was no joint work to bring about a coherent, comprehensive public policy action agenda, one going beyond discrete urban development policy reforms. It was as if most activists felt that the problems of racism and nationality exclusion, which had characterized race relations in Chicago for a century, had all been resolved by the ascension of a Black mayor.

Shortly after Washington took power, the outside electoral infrastructure started falling apart. POWER folded. The Task Force for Black Political Empowerment embraced a restricted Black nationalist power program. The left organizations moved into the Jesse Jackson Presidential bid. The labor movement was engaged in sectarian economic struggles, disjointed from the initiatives of communities of place and condition. In short, the left wing of the movement failed to consolidate its gains and to coordinate reform initiatives. Meanwhile, in City Hall, Washington had his own problems of coordination and regime consolidation.

On the defensive for the first three years, Washington tried to recruit blue chippers, blue ribbon commission members, the cream of the crop at the expense of other, less educated, but more committed and sensitive political activists and planners. The practical qualifications of the latter were overlooked, perhaps weakening the new government, but most certainly injuring the coalition. Some ranking appointees and close advisors lacked an affinity or an orientation for addressing the concerns of and exchanging experiences with ordinary folks and grassroots activists (interview with former alderman Jesus Garcia and community activist Pablo Medina, 1996). Many had not been part of the campaign nor the movement and had no appreciation for the sensitive nature of binationality coalition-building and the brittleness of its relations.

The absence of a strong independent coalition or mass movement watching over City Hall, in fact, made room for opportunists who were able to pursue their own, often anticoalition or antipopular priorities (Rivlin 1987). Although citizens from all affiliations and orientations had access to government officials and gave input into the policies driving decision making, some individuals surrounding Washington isolated him from his constituency, pushed him in the direction of reelection politics and countered the influence of more progressive elements. The agenda of the regime and the coalition suffered from the resulting tensions (Interview with MACLA's former director, Maria Torres 1995).

Latino interviewees claimed that while many Blacks were empowered in the process, the dynamics of governance pushed Latinos back to the role of outsiders in City Hall. Blacks, surrounded by Whites, held the upper hand. Latinos were largely limited to the role of a support cast. This situation precipitated the need for a Mayor's Advisory Latino Commission (MACLA) in City Hall that could articulate and advocate for their community's priorities. Although partners in government, they felt that their agenda had to be pushed from the outside (Torres 1991).

Latinos were particularly frustrated by their representation. In spite of their highest ever participation in public sector jobs and contracts, they felt underrepresented particularly at the executive and decision-making levels. Washington's failure to fulfill his promise of proportional representation in jobs, contracts and other opportunities for members of the coalition limited the incentive for Latinos to stay within the coalition (Torres 1991).[13]

In contrast, Black elites increased their share of the public sector very significantly and played a dominant role in the administration. According to interviewees, some of them operated under the "it's our turn" perspective and made sure to accommodate their own first, giving a message of exclusiveness to the outside. From our research, this view was promoted by some narrow, middle-class strata and did not reflect the sentiment of the majority, who did not expect to benefit as individuals from public jobs and contracts and were, therefore, more concerned about collective benefits, respect and fairness. Certainly, such agenda clashed with those of grassroots activists, distracting the movement from its original intent and aims.[14]

Such class-motivated actions produced mutual distrust between Blacks and Latinos. They diluted the ability of the regime to advance progressive and plural, social and human development policies.[15] Too many Black and Latino political elites subordinated the agendas of their people, the movement and the coalition to their own and to those of political entrepreneurs and businesses seeking public contracts, privilege and special favor. Under such conditions, the nationality/race question could not be adequately subsumed under Washington's agenda—its progressive character notwithstanding (City of Chicago 1984; Gills 1991; Clavel and Wiewel 1991).

Some interviewees pointed to Washington's administrative style which combined progressivism and pragmatism in governance and management of public affairs. While willing to carry a progressive agenda as far as possible, he was also willing to change directions and make adjustments as needed. A discussion took place at the end of the first term between him and his close circle of advisors over the nature and character of the regime's power base. While some believed in creating a structure based on a grassroots movement, others were convinced that it was more expedient to take over the machine and to reform it. Washington's policy advisors opted for the latter (interview with former Commissioner Timothy Wright 1995). Our research suggests that, at the end, Washington believed that he could achieve the same progressive goals through a reformed machine as he might through a grassroots movement (Interview with activist Robert Lucas 1997). This proved to be a misadventure.

Washington's election ticket at the time of his death reflected this move toward conservatism as he bowed to the "realities" of reelection. It extended an olive branch to the machine by including its less reactionary, more conciliatory members. This was viewed by some interviewees as a way to work with the center of the Democratic Party. It was a move toward securing reelection through more traditional and stable means. The rationale behind this was that by securing the electoral machine, the administration would be in a better position to affect change. It was at this point that the progressive, reformist character of the regime was lost.

In short, the governance coalition became more virtual than real. It was vulnerable, fragile and precarious, as it depended so much on the leadership of Washington and a few leaders and their ability to keep it together. According to some interviewees, the coalition held together because Washington's strength of integrity and charisma "willed" the collaboration of progressive Blacks, Latinos and Whites. While the electoral coalition was able to elect Washington to a second term, it never gained control of government and, in fact, was supplanted by other groups and individuals not necessarily committed to the priorities of the movement and coalition (Mier and Moe 1991; Hollander 1991; Clavel and Wiewel 1991).

The broad-based coalition, at least its Latino-Black aspect, faded into the background after his election. Its fragility was most clear in the inability to reorganize around a single successor candidate at Washington's death. Black and Latino political forces broke into pro-reform and pro-machine members. Aware of the contradictions of the administration, the deposed machine leaders went after unsatisfied constituencies and were able to regain control by intensifying their internal divisions and determining Washington's successor. Meanwhile, people changing their loyalties argued that their political survival and that of their communities rested with the best deal they could get (Rivlin 1987).

THE AFTERMATH OF THE COALITION

Mayor Washington died in November 1987, less than a year into his second term. Following his death, the old guard in City Council embraced

Eugene Sawyer, the mayor pro term, opposing both Tim Evans, the late Mayor's floor leader in the Council, and alderman Danny Davis, who offered himself as a compromise candidate. Black aldermen split on the candidates while Latinos supported Evans, who appeared to have the backing of popular and progressive forces outside of government. Latino aldermen were distrustful of Sawyer and his supporters—narrow Black nationalists—on the one hand, and reactionary machine hacks, on the other hand.

The strategy of the "old guard" was to allow Sawyer, viewed as a weak Washington supporter, to complete Washington's term and, then, to defeat him in the regular election of 1991 by running a machine candidate. The strategy worked: the mass electorate was demobilized; Black politicians were divided and Latinos were further alienated within Sawyer's government.

Fretful and anxious that reformers had been driven from power and unwilling to compromise, the more radical reformers organized a new municipal party, the Harold Washington Party. They pressed a suit calling for a special election to force Sawyer from power. This proved to be a huge strategic mistake. Failure to unite Blacks and Latinos behind a single candidate opened the door for Richard M. Daley to oppose Sawyer in the primary election in 1989. Daley easily defeated Sawyer behind united White support and a divided Black and Latino vote. In a last ditch effort to retain City Hall under Black leadership, Timothy Evans, Washington's floor leader in the City Council, ran under the banner of the Washington Party. Without united Black support but with consensus Latino backing, Evans fared better. He too, however, was defeated in the general election (Holli 1991; Grimshaw 1992).

Over the ensuing two years, Daley was able to garner sufficient Latino voters for the "old guard" and to obtain substantial Black support. He did this by focusing on unsatisfied sectors of the Washington coalition, while successfully pitting Latinos against Blacks. He also obtained the support of lakefront neo-liberals with his antimachine rhetoric and his opposition to big, wasteful, inefficient bureaucracies. Since 1991, Mayor Daley has engineered a restructuring of the administrative cadre which has now systematically dislodged Blacks from high positions of city governance and other public institutions under the mayor's control.

The Chicago growth coalition reconsolidated itself beginning in 1987 with the resurrected remnants of the old machine and some newly-activated forces (Squires et al. 1987). This is reflected in hefty elite contributions to Daley's election campaigns of 1989, 1991 and 1995 (Ferman

1996). It also resulted in a significant increase of expenditures on construction to the benefit of this industry and its workers—both disproportionately White and suburban. Composed of real estate, banking, and development finance interests, construction along with big-time lawyers and architectural firms, this consortium embraced Daley as the new political chief executive officer. Its support and resources, coupled with the debilitation of the grassroots' political movement in Chicago, have enabled the current regime to consolidate control without any effectual resistance (Ferman 1996).

Although highly pragmatic in its approach, Daley's regime can be characterized by:

- dominance of the interests of the new growth coalition led by large businesses;
- focus on development of a business climate conducive to making Chicago an elite, world-class city;
- dramatic cuts in social expenditures;
- a conservative electorate of the old guard Democratic machine voters, homeowners, and the middle class in particular;
- a top down, centrally controlled, closed-door administration;
- the systematic attack of independent forces with the potential to challenge the regime;[16]
- renewed efforts to keep workers' demands at bay; and
- recruitment and cooptation of individuals from minority communities as fronts against forces of opposition or disagreement in these communities.

Daley's regime has favored mainstream sectors over community efforts of self-determination and self-representation. Some examples of this follow.

He has satisfied the mortgage banking and real estate industries by sponsoring programs such as first time home buyer subsidy loans administered by the banks instead of the city (as under Washington), while severely restricting subsidies for rental multifamily housing for low-income households. He has engaged in privatization of public services and has used the power of local government to buttress commercial and industrial park property through tax increment financing (TIFs) programs supporting the subsidy of market development, even in areas of the city where development would have occurred, otherwise.

Unlike Mayors Washington and Sawyer who used the powers of the executive to reach out to independent community-based, non profit development groups, Mayor Daley has limited the city's promotion of such groups which tend to be populist, democratic, and a potential source of opposition. By turning away from these community-based development groups concentrated in Black and Latino neighborhoods, he has directly undermined the capacity of these communities to oppose injurious urban development policies and to promote pluralist and collective consumption agendas. He has favored instead church-based community development agencies, citywide service agencies, and partnerships between selected community and private developer interests. The leadership of these institutions is more autocratic and less capable of independent political mobilization as well as less inclined to undertake it.

Daley has promoted housing and economic development programs targeting the middle class as part of his policy to attract the support of this group. This strategy allows him to control property tax rates, offering a timely rebate to homeowners around election time while broadening the overall tax base of the City with highly regressive sales taxes and fees paid disproportionately by the poor and lower income groups. His regime has assisted large institutions with their real estate expansion, while applying each available public instrument to the development of the central business district and the gentrification of its surrounding neighborhoods.

COALITIONAL EXPERIENCE: SUMMARY, FINDINGS AND IMPLICATIONS

The story of the systematic demobilization of the political base energizing Washington's coalition is very significant. Not only has the coalition dissipated, but community-based forces and disadvantaged sectors have been rendered politically ineffective in developing and promoting an agenda capable of winning broad support within or outside the electorate. Resources from the city and from foundations that support community empowerment and organizational capacity have been drying up under Daley's regime. Thus, there are fewer resources to support advocacy and constituent-driven mobilizations. Although significant networks and coalitions have been organized or maintained around empowerment and community development, they have failed to launch a counteroffensive to the new growth consortium.

Unable to coalesce around an agenda, a movement or a leader, the progressive mass movement has receded and the reform coalition dissipated. Apparently dominated by the ascendency of Black nationalists and would-be machine aspirants, the Sawyer administration precluded an inside-out progressive Black–Latino coalition. The remnants of the progressive movement outside of City Hall were demoralized and exhausted. Once Washington—the element that held things together was gone—many individuals and forces who had gained power, privilege and access panicked and opportunistically looked for a place for themselves in the midst of an unsettled scramble for power. Daley provided that opportunity.

This discussion has identified two overall aspects in the Black–Latino coalition associated with Washington's mayoralty, an electoral and a governing one. A shared consciousness of exclusion, the struggle and opportunity to bring down the Democratic machine and the drive to build an alternative government brought the coalition together. Excessive dependency on the mayor and a few others, unevenness in the distribution of opportunities and roles, limited Black–Latino coalitional experience, absence of agreements on distribution and accountability, inability to work out differences and expectations, class differentiated agendas and competing nationalisms (Rivlin 1992; Torres 1991), lack of a conscientious effort to develop a truly coalitional government, dissolution of the community movement after the election, mismanagement of pivotal sociocultural dynamics within the new regime, the unresolved trauma of moving from opposition to institutional leadership, and efforts to attract the White vote by broadening the support base (Grimshaw 1992) were among the internal factors undermining the coalition.[17]

Equally important were external factors such as the bitter attacks of the defeated machine determined to regain power by any means, the less visible efforts of an emerging urban growth consortium to erode the gains or control the new regime (Squires et al. 1987) and the accelerated urban crisis brought about by globalization and neoconservative politics.[18] Driving these factors were the ever present dynamics of class interest and divergence.

The inability to build a more solid Black–Latino coalition had to do with the historical dynamics of the progressive movement itself. Dominated by multiple other immediate tasks, the coalition movement did not pay much attention to its goals beyond the election. A coalition builder, Washington's commitment to an all-inclusive governance composition,[19] to equitable minority participation and multinational collaboration (Miller 1989; Travis 1989; Clavel and Wiewel 1991; Green and Holli

1990, 1991; Kleppner 1985; Wiesberg 1983)[20] held the forces together. This, however, proved catastrophic after his death.

Formed to gain power, the coalition did not materialize into an alliance to share power. It was undermined by contradictory, divergent class and political interests and the individualistic or myopic agendas of many members.[21] Meanwhile, those with a legitimate commitment to a progressive agenda were outnumbered and pushed to the side, having waning influence on public policy. Polarization prevented formation of a more inclusive, expanded effort.

An obvious weakness of the Washington administration was that a large proportion of the staff consisted of career politicians, upwardly mobile technocrats and nationalists who did not share the vision of the regime. Progressive as Washington might have been, he did not have a majority in his own group committed to the coalition. Thus, the coalition lacked the mystique, discipline and loyalty that were necessary to withstand the attacks of the old guard.

Like most Black and Latino urban mayoral regimes, this regime was adequate, if not superlative, in terms of crisis management in all but one respect: it allowed the tensions from the crises to be internalized within its own support coalition. This served to undermine its support base. Also, as in other cities with Latino and Black mayors (Eisenger 1980b, 1983b; Karnig and Welch 1980; Browning, Marshall and Tabb 1982; Clavel 1986; Tate 1993; Stone 1989), the power of White elites remained intact outside City Hall and was able to undermine the regime.

Urban mayoral studies across the country point to the tendency for Black and Latino administrations based on insurgency politics and popular support to shift to the right in subsequent reelection efforts (Eisenger 1980a, 1983a; Browning, Marshall, and Tabb 1982; Jennings 1992a). Our analysis suggests that the regime, especially in its second term, was, in fact, making special efforts to appeal to a White constituency through adjustments in its message, through integration of other sectors and responsiveness to their demands. Similarly, it was working to bring the expectations of its own constituents to more manageable levels.[22]

The perceived electoral vulnerability of Washington convinced him to work to attract the liberal and moderate wings of the old Democratic Party, in an effort to expand its White base and to gain control of Cook County politics. This shift was resented by grassroots groups deeply involved in the election who had advocated for a new form of politics based on a network of community organizations and progressive groups. In spite of its shortcomings, the coalition and movement produced significant increases in the electoral representation and in the number of

Blacks and Latinos in positions of authority and influence.[23] It created new, inclusive and open processes of policy making and service delivery.

The Washington administration affected politics in the long run, as it forced the next regime to continue some of its policies and to include members from underrepresented groups, even if for electoral purposes or within a context of tokenism.[24] Similarly, some neighborhood and other agendas and programs of central importance to Blacks and Latinos stayed in place, though at a smaller scale and often redirected to the new priorities. New networks and ties formed between Blacks and Latinos. The experience taught crucial lessons about the possibilities of future coalitions between them. It showed the feasibility of other approaches to government and policy making. The limitations of the coalition experience are rooted in the middle-class political elite which led the movement to consolidate the regime. This stratum played a progressive role in getting Washington elected but failed to remain accountable to the grassroots base.

The contrast between Harold Washington's and Richard M. Daley's regimes demonstrates that White-elite led governments can be very unresponsive and insensitive to minority communities, which must organize and coalesce to attract attention to their particular needs.

There are three central implications of Latino and Black coalition efforts in the political processes of cities like Chicago. First, these grassroots coalitions advance as a result of the fusion of place-based, condition-based, and interest-based community politics. Such politics activate and mobilize the grassroots to raise democratic, antiracist, and egalitarian demands promoting cultural and multinational diversity as a value. All of them tend to be progressive. They present serious, but popularly legitimate challenges to mainstream political elites and privileged strata in politics.

Second, this research points to the need to develop clear agreements on distribution of opportunities and sharing of power and on mechanisms of accountability and processes for working out conflicts between coalition members as well as between elites and grassroots. They speak to the necessity of inclusiveness; commitment to the coalition at all levels but, especially, in the key locations controlling policy making and implementation; sensitivity to and respect for difference; insertion of coalitions' priorities in each initiative; and open partnership between members—as opposed to coalitions in which the minority partner is excluded from major decisions and benefits.

The third implication for students of politics is the need to struggle earnestly and to have continuous dialogue in order to build and maintain coalitional unity around an agenda that is acceptable to the mass electorate. A vitally important corollary for crossnationality coalitions is that without such unity building and maintenance, consistent support from other communities cannot and perhaps should not be expected. Similarly, members need to work to make sure that their constituencies are clear about and strongly committed to their goals as part of the coalition, as well as to the goals of the coalition as a whole.

An obvious but overlooked dictum is that unity is a prerequisite for collective action.[25] Coalition members must constantly maintain unity above all other priorities. Since minority coalitions are, by definition, engaged in an uphill battle, their members need to be disciplined, alert and obsessive about these matters. Within progressive, grassroots politics, the interests of upwardly mobile middle class members need to be kept in check or they will tear the coalition apart. The selection of people with a firm commitment to the coalition's priorities is crucial.

Other lessons can be learned from the Chicago experience. First, any new coalitional effort that seeks to realize substantial benefits for the vast majority of Blacks and Latinos requires building on a broader social basis than narrow electoral politics. Electoral activity is too subject to crass opportunism to be a source of lasting, principled relationships.

Second, the coalition must work to overcome nationalisms. It would appear that the success of political struggles to come lies in the realization that the main sources of oppression of urban Blacks and Latinos are within the prevailing political-economic relations that bind members of both groups to oppression, domination, and exclusion.

Third, effective political coalitions are built on the basis of traditions of interaction and joint activity where people learn trust through testing of each other in practical struggles, under conditions of risk and sacrifice. This experience has made clear the critical importance of ground work to develop networks, which are the pillars of coalitions. Fourth, it is crucial for the leadership to remain accountable to the mass-based organization if it is to retain its legitimacy and progressive character.

In short, the frame for building effective coalitions between under represented groups must be broadened beyond election mobilizations to embrace more substantial reforms that could weaken the extant system that reproduces racism, national oppression and political polarization in order to sustain the status quo. The greatest shortcoming of the Washington period was the failure of progressive leaders to assist in building sustainable mass organization with the capacity to fight for power and to hold reform government accountable.

CONCLUDING REMARKS

This study has identified several sources of optimism. In our interviews with Black and Latino activists and others closely associated with Washington's mayoralty in Chicago, we were encouraged by their honest and frank dialogue and perceptive review of the political history. Many felt that the main period of Latino-Black coalition building was yet to be experienced.

Various factors led to this optimism. The shared economic conditions among the vast majority of Black and Latino people and the persistence of racial and nationality-based exclusion in political and social life provides a structural context for unity building. Moreover, continuing networks facilitate dialogue and enable Latinos and Blacks to work together on common issues ranging from struggles against displacement and residential gentrification, through initiatives of education improvement, to efforts to resist the dismantling of the social system of health care, human capacity enhancement and social service support.

The overall rise of the New Right to political dominance has led to extremely reactionary policy agendas locally, regionally and nationally. On the perceptual level, the brunt of these attacks is aimed at the masses among, and the most vulnerable sectors within, Black and Latino communities. Such attacks provide a new basis for the formation of a united front of Latinos, Blacks and others who feel their impacts most directly. Aggression towards one group effects all others because it gives legitimacy to further, more blatant actions.

This environment calls for extreme efforts and discipline in coalition formation and maintenance. Initiatives for Latino and Black unity are often perceived as a threat by the larger society. As the Chicago experience demonstrates, elites expertly manipulate the fears and inner prejudices of U.S. society to undermine attempts at unity and grassroots mobilization. They have certainly used the expectations and fears of upwardly mobile elements in the Black and Latino community to cause intragroup and intergroup contention.

Collaboration in Chicago was facilitated by common actions and networking around the conditions and needs of the two communities. The trust and experience of earlier joint efforts between members of both groups made united action feasible. While these two factors are mutually dependent, the experience demonstrated that the strength of collaborations had a lot to do with the strength and commitment of those involved.

Black and Latino activists with previous experience of collaboration provided the bridges between the two communities and kept the coalition alive in spite of difficulties. The slow, patient work that went into forming these relationships provided the foundation for coalescing at levels of increasing complexity. Hence, there is a critical need to promote close interactions particularly among progressive individuals and sectors in these communities. Since the potential for contention exists at every step of the way among all sectors, leadership interactions are crucial in facilitating or obstructing collaboration and trust between the two groups.

Blacks and Latinos are at an early stage in their process of collaboration. That their electoral coalition under Mayor Washington disintegrated is not surprising. That it did so abruptly is a cause for inquiry and assessment that can teach social action researchers and political activists invaluable lessons.

Before closing, one note of caution is in place. While diverse class interests can topple regimes, it has yet to be demonstrated that more than one class can share governance. Heretofore, the managing element in Chicago has come traditionally from one class, centered in a coalition of European American ethnics led by the Irish minority, with unity forged around the hypothesis of "White power." Although multinational coalitions have come to power in Chicago and elsewhere, the leading ruling and managerial element of the regimes has been the middle class of professional politicians and professional bureaucrats. Chicago's political progressives and community activists, romantically perhaps, attempted but failed to build a multiclass, ruling power coalition during the Washington-Sawyer regime. This chapter and the previous two pointed to the limitations of electoral alliances as they reflect multiclass, multiracial collaborations. While we should be open to challenges and new approaches, expectations should be realistic. Coalition builders should insist upon types of coalitions that hold most potential. In the light of current research, the single class coalition should be considered seriously as the basis for new multinational or biracial politics of collaboration of the type discussed in the Scott and Katz-Fishman chapter.

NOTES

[1] This work is part of a larger project by the co-authors addressing collaboration and contention in the social relations of Latinos and Blacks in major U.S. cities and the possibilities of building a joint agenda of urban research, public policy advocacy and social action. An earlier version of this paper, "Understanding Black–Latino Conflicts and Concerns," was published in Jennings 1997.

² The Black–Latino coalition examined here was the central expression of bi-nationality coalition building in the campaign to elect Harold Washington. Thus, we cannot discuss it in isolation from the overall mayoralty experience. Notice that we treat the Washington-Sawyer administration as a clearly distinct order of government or *regime-in- formation*: it had its own supporters and approaches to government and public policies that differentiated it from previous and succeeding regimes (Gove and Masotti 1982; Grimshaw 1992; Green and Holli 1991).

³ Both researchers have been activists in community organization in Chicago. Dr. Betancur served as executive director of a leading Latino community organization in the city. He is also one of the founders of a well-known city-wide Latino housing advocacy group. Dr. Gills was executive director of CRN—mentioned here—during the campaign. He was the executive director of a prominent Black community group. He co-founded CWED—also mentioned here—and was instrumental in the neighborhood orientation of the early Washington regime. Both researchers have retained strong ties to the community and have continued their development practice and research work. As applied researchers and planners with the University of Illinois at Chicago Center for Urban Economic Development and as members of the boards of several coalitions and organizations shaping public policy, they are well positioned to assess the policy impacts of local governments on the affairs of their communities.

⁴ This is a rather sketchy attempt to cover an extremely complex history. However, we include it to suggest the need for a historical understanding of the coalition—its urgency, moment, fragility, uphill struggle, unrealistic expectations and, very particularly, the fact that it took place *against all odds*.

⁵ The term "plantation politics" is used to refer to the politics of integration of minorities along the lines of the plantation, that is, under the control of White elites who decide who to support and in what terms.

⁶ The primary identity of Latinos in the U.S. has been their nationality of origin. Their bond in the USA is a common root in a region of U.S. domination, Latin America (Hayes Bautista and Chapas 1987) and a condition of discrimination and exclusion related to this origin. This bond has slowly evolved into a Latino *identity,* indeed a *political construct* much like the term *Black community.* The primary identity of many Latinos, however, is still their nationality. This situation affects any efforts at Latino unity as nationalisms can be called upon to fragment it.

⁷ Latinos were most likely to recognize Washington's legislative record given his support of bilingual education, progressive immigration policies and other matters of vital interest to Mexican descent persons in particular.

⁸ These groups saw in Washington's mayoral campaign the potential to empower Black and Latino sectors and strata, to share power under a realignment of

political forces and to create new relations of power between members of these communities and the White minority power structure at the helm of the local political economy.

⁹ The core supporters of the new regime included: neo-liberals, community development and empowerment activists. Neoliberals were antipatronage and advocated "good government" reform (Grimshaw 1992). Many of them held closet neo-conservative positions and were among the first to abandon the coalition after Washington's death. The group of community development activists came from the emergent networks of community-based organizations, coalitions and associations of community-oriented service and technical assistance providers (Gills 1991; Brehm 1991; Betancur and Gills 1993). Their leadership strata consisted of middle-class, professionally, if not institutionally trained administrators, social workers, and program directors, along with a small, but growing number of university-credentialed community development planners. The group of empowerment activists came from within the Black and Latino empowerment movements. They tended to center their points of view around the nationalistic demands promoted by leaders of these communities. While in absolute numbers, the Black community provided the bulk of the votes that helped Washington win, he could not have been elected without the additional votes of the other constituencies mentioned here.

¹⁰ He was particularly unfamiliar with the Latino leadership and had difficulty deciding which representatives from this community he could trust.

¹¹ Alkalimat and Gills (1984, 1989) use the terms convergency and divergency to explain the political behavior of class forces within the Black community during Washington's election and governance. These authors assert that he had been elected on the bases of multi-class unity and critical linkages to Latino and White sectors. After the election, however, unity gave way to the politics of divergent class interests led by strata within the Black middle class. The ties Harold enjoyed with the popular masses of voters and his commitment to plurality allowed him to keep these disparate forces together. But, once he died, the strata could operationalize its agenda abandoning the masses to fend for themselves in the confusion of the period. This allowed them time to make private arrangements to secure their personal interests.

¹² This was a point of view expressed by most of the respondents. On the surface it appears politically naive. However, most of them had not been students of electoral politics nor had been involved in government.

¹³ Clearly, the administration rested on this partnership and depended on it for reelection and governance. The claim that power should correspond to the size of the vote contributed by each constituency undermined the coalition because it downplayed the importance of non-Black groups. The leaders and ac-

tivists of each of these support bases in the coalition contained class representatives who had an interest in Black and Latino coalition-building for political, social welfare, and development reasons. However, the mixed class character of this leadership stratum also hampered the coalition's advance into a governance coalition. Harold Washington, and perhaps most Blacks and Latinos could support a progressive agenda based on fairness, equity, and openness. These principles, however, if acted upon would fetter the aspirations of class elites for privilege and favoritism over time. Therefore, many would-be coalition activists, who saw that Washington was serious about reform, silently opposed him. Some opposed him openly after his death.

[14] This criticism is most prevalent among Latino respondents. Yet, it must be made clear that the Black leadership should not be absolved. In fact we make a distinction between the overall progressive character and content of the Washington-Sawyer regime and the practices of some of its leading policy makers. That Washington himself was aware of some of the criticisms of his regime was shared by at least two respondents who noted that the Mayor had scheduled a staff retreat to deal with some of the issues raised by Latinos and others about some of his ranking personnel and was prepared to discipline them. However, he died a month before it.

[15] This does not discount the great strides of the regime in affirmative action, expansion and capacity-building of community-based organizations (CBOs) and neighborhood improvement. CBOs increased from less than 100 under Mayor Byrne to well over 500 by the end of the Sawyer mayoralty. One of Washington's first acts was to allocate $13M in CDBG funds to support capacity building among CBOs. In the first four years, he spent over $100M annually in neighborhood improvements. More funds were spent to rehabilitate privately-owned rental housing for low income families than at any other time in the city's history. But perhaps his single greatest accomplishment was citizen participation in policy formation. He established a neighborhood-based approach to public policy, including community planning and program implementation through partnerships with CBOs and private concerns in local communities. He emphasized capacity-building for under-represented constituencies to participate in the mainstream of governance along with encouragement of creativity within high standards of performance and accountability.

[16] The Daley administration removed most appointed Black and Latino officials in high positions; it has run its handpicked candidates against grassroots Latino and Black candidates; and it has reinstated the top-down, elitist and less transparent policy making process of the previous era (Green and Holli 1991; Ferman 1996).

[17] Several works have explored the coalitional and social movement aspects of the Washington experience. However, while some have explored the internal

collaborations and points of divergence among Blacks and between them and the broader community, scanty efforts have been made to examine the sources of tension leading to the unraveling of the coalition. This work attempts to fill this vacuum.

[18] The *urban crisis* meant that Washington inherited a city with a declining manufacturing, employment and tax base and a restructuring economy demanding additional services from the local government. Numerous studies affirm the relationship between Black and Latino movements for empowerment and the increasing systemic problems of the economic and fiscal crisis (Jennings 1992a, 1992b; Hanks 1987; Clark 1994, 1996; Karnig and Welch 1980; Stone 1989; Tate 1993; Eisenger 1980, 1983; O'Laughlin 1983).

[19] The best testimony to his position on nationalism was the assertion by well-known Black activist Lou Palmer that Washington had nearly killed the (nationalist) movement. Palmer had assumed that, as the voice of Black political empowerment in Chicago, he would get Washington's endorsement to replace him in Congress. Instead, Washington endorsed a labor leader, Charles Hayes. The situation under Sawyer, however, was slightly different. After Sawyer's unpopular, controversial selection to succeed Washington he was desperate for some legitimacy and was prone to embrace a compromise with nationalists in the Black community.

[20] The authors have access to a full collection of his campaign speeches, briefing books, formal policy and staff development documents and leadership training materials that testify to his commitment to equity and equal access as well as to other progressive principles of coalition building—fairness, respect for diversity, sensitivity to difference, support for affirmative action and set-aside programs for women and minority businesses. His work and commitment to strengthen the coalition obviously were not sufficient. Discrepancies existed at the level of practice, particularly from the vantage point of Latinos. This demonstrates the extreme difficulties of bringing about systemic and bureaucratic change. Efforts of government units such as the Chicago Public Schools and the Chicago Public Housing Authority to reform themselves from within ran into similar difficulties. Current federal initiatives to reinvent government as aspects of the Empowerment Zone and Consolidated Planning Initiatives led by HUD represent other example in which bureaucracies have proven to be resistant to change. These cases suggest that bureaucracies are fetters on themselves with respect to reform from the inside-out and that the character and courage of executive and political leadership are crucial ingredients of change. Finally, these initiatives of policy and executive leadership must be coupled with a vigilant, enabled movement outside urban government if substantial and authentic procedural change is to occur and to be sustained.

[21] After all, many of them had opportunistically joined the coalition after the defeat of their mainstream candidates; many others were seduced by the bureaucratic or electoral opportunities opened to them by the regime; most did not identify at heart with the class interests of the grassroots movement; finally, many had joined the coalition in search of individual opportunities rather than because of conviction or commitment to it.

[22] Limitations related to the persistent *economic and fiscal* aspects of the urban crises and the need to expand its electoral basis (certain segments of the Black community—e.g. public housing residents and youth—were becoming disaffected and the internal dynamics discussed earlier compromised the commitment of many Latinos) justified this move. Besides, Washington's commitment to a government that included all social forces convinced him to engage in efforts to integrate other forces to his constituency and administration.

[23] Many Latino leaders in Chicago argue that the Washington administration was the main vehicle of Latino political empowerment in the City.

[24] Under Daley, the policy making process is circumscribed by an adherence to formalism and legalism. The overall planning and policy development process limits citizen and community participation to the design phase and excludes participation in implementation, oversight and assessment of process, program and impacts. This reliance upon formalism results in less concern about equality and equity in the outcome and more stress on the definition of the steps of the process. Thus, procedural democracy prevails over substantive democratic outcomes and ends.

[25] As one avid supporter of progressive politics and an advocate of Latino-Black political unity building asserted: "How can the Black community expect Latinos to follow when even the Blacks who want our support do not know where they are going?" Yet another respondent noted that: "We cannot simply pass a resolution and wave a proclamation of unity between our communities despite all the objective and subjective reasons that we should unite; unity has to be worked at just like a good marriage. It is built over time and is tested in practices over time."

CHAPTER 5

Race and Class Coalitions in the South

JEROME SCOTT
WALDA KATZ-FISHMAN

> *"Ain't no foreign country in the world foreign*
> *as Alabama to a New Yorker. They know all*
> *about England, maybe France, never met one*
> *who knew 'Bama.'"*
> — ANONYMOUS BLACK COMMUNIST, 1945 IN
> KELLEY (1990:XI)

In this chapter we examine the nexus of race and class in coalitions[1] in the South from the 1500s through the 1990s to understand when and under what circumstances these differences of color have been transcended and to identify current conditions and prospects for multiracial working class coalitions in the South. We trace the confluence of historical forces that has periodically brought Black and indigenous women and men, as well as Black, White, and Latino peoples together in multiracial coalitions. We further identify the conditions that can give rise to their success, failure and dissolution. We conclude with a tentative model of multiracial working class coalitions in the South and some projections for the near future based on our understanding of these historic and contemporary coalitions and the current stage of high-tech global capitalist development. We pay particular attention to Southern history because of its significance in shaping the institutions of our society.

The examples of coalitions we discuss are (1) the Maroon communities in the period of the conquest and initial penetration of capitalism from the early 1500s to the early 1800s; (2) the abolition movement in the antebellum period of chattel slavery and southern agricultural capitalism; (3) the Farmers Alliance and Populist movement of farmers and farm workers in the period of continuing southern agriculture, burgeoning northern industrialization and rapid westward expansion in the late

1800s and early 1900s; (4) the citizenship schools and farm workers' movement in the period of U.S. ascendancy to power within world capitalism in the early to mid-1900s; (5) the civil rights movement in the period of the expansion of industrialization and urbanization into the South in the post-World War II years; and (6) the economic justice and political democracy movements in the postindustrial hig-tech period of the 1980s and 1990s.[2]

A few key observations about race and class in America and especially in the deep South contextualize our analysis. Race and class relations have been central organizing features of American society from the European conquest to the present. However, while race and color differences have been at the cutting edge of economic exploitation and political and ideological hegemony,[3] class relations, in contrast, have remained deeply submerged within the institutions and ideology of the American experience.

It was not until the most recent post civil rights period, which produced significant class stratification within communities of color, that class relations diverged in a substantial way from race relations and color differences. This reality, coupled with the transition of American society from late industrial capitalism to post industrial high tech capitalism, has created the conditions for a new kind of coalition building between working class women and men—peoples of color, oppressed nationality groups, and dislocated White workers.

While many of the goals of contemporary coalitions are continuous with earlier struggles for economic well-being and political control, this new stage of capitalism, with its labor eliminating technology and hemispheric economic integration, is forging a new kind of working class coalition, often led by women of color.

Understanding the bases for past coalitions in the South, where race historically has been the fundamental organizing principle, is critical in identifying coalition strategies for Blacks and Latinos in today's U.S. cities[4]. This perspective (1) identifies structural and historical dynamics in U.S. society that have interfered with, prevented or perverted such multinational coalitions; (2) provides broad insights, precisely because this region has played such a special role in defining race relations in the U.S.; (3) increases in importance as the Latino presence expands throughout the South; and (4) focuses on a restricted regional level where coalitions can pursue broader issues. By addressing head-on the dilemmas of race and class, it not only sheds light on the complications of that intersection, but also claims that conditions are ripe for single class-based, multiracial coalitions to succeed in introducing fundamental changes for peoples of color.

This chapter is particularly important because it addresses head on the dilemmas of race and class examined earlier in this book. Not only does it shed further light into the complications related to their intersection, but it claims that the conditions are ripe for class-based multiracial coalitions and that these can succeed in introducing fundamental changes for people of color.

THE SOUTH IN THE AMERICAN EXPERIENCE

From the moment of European conquest, the genocide of the indigenous peoples of the hemisphere, and the enslavement of the African peoples, the political, economic, and cultural institutions of the Americas have been built upon White supremacy and capitalist class domination. The colonial government and, later the U.S. federal government embodied in their legal and political structures principles and practices of inequality and oppression.

The United States of America, at its inception, was a southern nation (Alkalimat 1984, 1989; Peery 1992, 1994). The earliest coalitions of African and indigenous peoples taught the colonists the powerful lesson that this unity must be destroyed if the colonists were to retain power and control. Race and class divisions were essential to the southern experience in U.S. history and remain so in the contemporary context. These divisions and the role of the South have been key to the ruling class strategy for political power in the U.S.A. from its beginning to this day.

Race divisions and the hegemony of White supremacy, embedded in political, economic, and cultural structures, particularly of slavery and of the post-Reconstruction, Jim Crow South, undermined possibilities for multiracial coalitions. Such coalitions have been largely absent within the agricultural and trade union movements. This lack of enduring organizational forms rooted in working-class experience that bring African Americans, Latinos, Native Americans, and Whites together around concrete issues of mutual concern is even more pronounced in the South today than in the rest of the country because of this history.

Maroon Communities One: A Challenge to the European Colonists

The European invasion of the "New World" marked the early stages of the formation of the world capitalist system and the accompanying era of colonial domination and world slave trade. Millions of indigenous peoples inhabited the *new* world in the pre-Columbian period. Van Sertima (1976) suggests an African presence in this period, as well.

Soon after the first African slaves arrived (probably in April 1502 aboard the ship carrying Nicolas de Ovando, the new governor of Hispaniola) some of them escaped, finding a welcomed home among the Native Americans (Katz 1986:28). Ovando requested of King Ferdinand that no more African slaves be sent—a request he later retracted. But the reason he gave, that "They fled amongst the Indians and taught them bad customs, and never could be captured," anticipated problems of the European colonizers in the Americas (Katz 1986:28).

On Christmas Day, 1522, the African and indigenous slaves on the plantation of Diego Columbus on Santo Domingo rebelled, killing their masters and overseers. Free Native Americans in the area joined the slave rebellion, which was quelled three days later. The European colonizers learned an important lesson: that "it was absolutely necessary to remain armed, and use one race to fight the other." A colonial dispatch later stated: "Between the races we cannot dig too deep a gulf" (Katz 1986:33–34).

The first colony in what is today the U.S.A. was founded in 1526 near the mouth of the Pee Dee River, in eastern South Carolina. The wealthy Spanish official Lucas Vasquez de Ayllon, along with five hundred Spanish men and women and one hundred African slaves from Santo Domingo, settled San Miguel de Gualdape. Within months Ayllon died; fighting broke out among the Spaniards. The Africans rebelled and fled among the Native Americans, who sided with the slaves. The remaining 150 Spaniards returned to Santo Domingo. Katz (1986:25–26) observes with irony:

> The Black Indians of Pee Dee River became the first colony on this continent to practice the belief that all people—newcomer and native—are created equal and are entitled to life, liberty, and the pursuit of happiness. . . .
>
> The story of this new community shows that our vaunted democracy did not march into the wilderness with buckled shoes and British accents. . . . This dark democracy lived in family groups before London companies sent out settlers with muskets, Bibles, and concepts of private property.

Despite their unity and their humanity, the coalition of Native and African Americans was not able to return the fire power and to protect themselves from the imperial ascendancy of Europe in the West. The Native American population plummeted from between 80 and 100 million native peoples throughout the hemisphere in 1492 (including 40 million in geographic areas encompassed in today's United States and 25 million in Mexico) to 10 million one century later (Katz 1986:29; Kirkpatrick 1991; Williams 1971:33; Yeoman 1992:17). More than one million Africans were enslaved in the Americas by the early 1600s (Dennis 1984:16–17; Zinn 1980:25). In the English colonies of North America, and later the U.S.A., the labor of African slaves played a key role in the vast accumulation of wealth—the basis of U.S. economic expansion and political domination.

Maroon Communities Two: The Seminole Nation

Southern slavery made American *democracy* a farce. The national ideology of White supremacy and institutional racism were solidified in the struggles around slavery and its abolition. The *founding fathers,* all White, male property owners, drafted the U.S. Constitution empowering and privileging those in their own image. Roughly 15% to 20% of the U.S. population was eligible for the franchise. Of those, about half exercised that right. Slaves were not recognized as people, only as property. They were, however, counted as three-fifths of a person in determining Congressional representation.

Scholars estimate that, by 1800, between 10 and 15 million Black Africans had been forcibly enslaved in the Americas, actually only about one-third of those who had been taken from Africa. In toto, the modern slave trade deprived Africa of the lives and contributions of roughly 50 million men, women, and children who either were sold into slavery or died during the harsh passage (Zinn 1980:29). African slavery in America was extremely cruel for two important reasons: the integration of the plantation economy into the world market with its drive for limitless commodities and profits; and the imposition of a sharp color line drawn to reduce slaves to less than human status, and continuously to generate new forms of racial hatred and White supremacy.

The market expanded rapidly with the development of the industrial revolution, first in Europe and later in the North. The expanding market and chronic labor shortages fueled the growth of the slave system. As the slave ranks swelled, so did the capital accumulated by the slave owners. In the immediate pre–Civil War period, more than 60% of all U.S. capital was invested in slaves (Keller 1983:58–59). By the time of the Civil War, the South was 15% richer than the North, including $4 billion in the form of slaves (Peery 1992:4, 15; Katz-Fishman and Scott 1994:570–71).

Resistance and revolt to the conditions of genocide and slavery began with the slave raids and the transatlantic slave voyages, and continued on American soil (Dennis 1984:65). The Maroon communities and the Underground Railroad were among the most highly organized expressions of slave resistance involving multiracial coalitions. Throughout the Americas fugitive African slaves and Native Americans established coalitions in the form of Maroon communities. The most renowned Maroon community in North America, formed in Florida by the runaway African slaves and runaway Native Americans, became the Seminole Nation. ("Seminole" in the Creek language means "run away.")

The Black Indians of the Seminole Nation were a threat to developing U.S. capitalism. The runaway Native and African slaves organized independent Maroon communities, defended themselves, and prospered. They also raided slave plantations, freeing thousands of slaves. This was more than the slaveholders could tolerate; and the Seminole Wars ensued (Katz 1986; Zinn 1980). Possessing great military ingenuity, the Seminole Nation was able to fight three major wars between 1816 and 1841 against the U.S. military machine and to win many major victories. With its agricultural skill, the Seminole Nation was able to sustain itself. In the 1830s and 1840s, after the third great Seminole War, many—though not all—of its members joined with members of the five southern Native Nations in the forced march out of the southeast to Oklahoma, recorded as the "Trail of Tears" (Katz 1986:53-69).

The increasingly powerful U.S. government was also successful in its imperialist expansion into Latin America—making the Louisiana Purchase in 1803, declaring the Monroe Doctrine in 1823 and annexing much of Mexico in 1848. U.S. efforts at economic and political domination of the hemisphere set the stage for conditions of political struggle and economic crisis that would create a surge in Latino migration to the U.S.A. more than a century later.

The Abolition Movement: A Brief Victory

Throughout the 1800s, slave rebellions in the South continued, with the one led by Nat Turner in August 1831 among the most renowned. State and federal troops quelled the rebellion, and Turner himself was executed. The increasing number of rebellions sent a signal to those in the

North as well as the South who were willing to fight to end slavery (Dennis 1984:65–69).

The abolition movement represents one of the best known coalitions of Blacks and Whites in U.S. history. The central guiding force was a commitment to end slavery. The runaway slaves and free Black women and men of all social classes who instigated the movement were joined by middle class and a few elite northern Whites and even a few Southern Whites, mostly middle class and a few working class. People entered the coalition for a variety of reasons. The self interest of Blacks in wanting to end slavery is the clearest. Whites were motivated by morality and religion, as well as by politics and economics. The abolition movement was, thus, a multiracial and multiclass movement, with the leadership controlled by the Black and White middle class.

Even within the abolition movement, however, the powerful presence of White supremacist attitudes and practices confined the possibilities for real coalitions. Meier and Rudwick (1993:134–136) note:

> In the early years, certain auxiliaries [of abolitionists] excluded Black people entirely. . . . Militant Blacks made numerous references to the insincerity of "professed abolitionists." They reported that many White abolitionists refused to admit Negro children to their schools or to employ Black men in their businesses other than in menial capacities. . . .
>
> The Blacks were right about the prejudice within the White anti-slavery groups. . . . [T]hey [Whites] were, in fact, ambivalent in their relationships with Blacks. One must therefore distinguish carefully between their egalitarian rhetoric and their paternalistic and prejudiced actions.

Meier and Rudwick (1993:173–74) also explain the exaggeration of the role of Whites in the freedmen's aid societies in the early 1860s: "The activities of the White societies are better known, both because of White tendencies to ignore what Negroes were doing and because the work of the White groups had greater financial resources and was therefore more extensive." These themes of ambivalence among Whites continued throughout the abolition struggle and resurfaced one hundred years later during the modern Civil Rights Movement.

Some abolitionists adopted more immediate, individual approaches to ending slavery. Through the Underground Railroad, more than 3,200 Blacks and Whites worked between 1830 and 1860 to transport about 2,500 slaves a year to freedom. Harriet Tubman, after freeing herself and her family, became the most famous conductor. On 19 trips between the South and North, she brought more than 300 slaves to freedom. Carrying a pistol, she told the runaways: "You'll be free or die" (Zinn 1980:171; Dennis 1984:71).

John Brown, a determined White abolitionist, raided the federal arsenal at Harpers Ferry, Virginia (now West Virginia) to secure the arms needed for a slave insurrection. Federal and state troops easily overwhelmed Brown's strike force of 22 men (5 Blacks and 17 Whites). Of the 5 Blacks, 2 were killed in the raid, 2 were executed by the authorities, and 1 escaped. John Brown was executed by the Virginia authorities, with federal government approval, on December 2, 1859 (Zinn 1980:181–82).

There also were scattered instances of poor Whites aiding slaves in their struggle and even of slaves helping poor Whites. While these cases were not numerous, they were frequent enough to cause severe police measures against those Whites fraternizing with Blacks, and vice versa (Zinn 1980:172). More widespread and somewhat less threatening to the established social order in the South was White, mostly middle-class and northern, participation in benevolent associations (nonsectarian and sectarian) and in the freedmen's aid societies in the Civil War and Reconstruction periods (Meier and Rudwick 1993:174–175).

The Civil War and the Union victory represented the first time that the interests of the African American masses struggling for freedom from chattel slavery coincided with the interests of a section of the ruling class. This coincidence of interests was critical for victory—however fleeting and fragile it was—in the long war against White supremacy and fascism in the South. The fledgling industrialists of the North, fighting the entrenched slavocracy of the South over political control of the country, found the cause of abolition to be a crucial tactic in winning the Civil War and preserving the Union in the interests of the ascending industrial North.

By 1861, with Lincoln's election, the secession of eleven southern states, and the formation of the Confederacy, the North had to move decisively to end the stranglehold of the slave power over the national government and to save the Union. Lincoln had originally proposed eliminating slavery gradually, with its final abolition *in 1940!* However, with the war going badly for the Union, the northern section of the ruling class concluded that slavery would have to be abolished if the war was to be won (Peery 1992; Zinn 1980). Meanwhile, the southern slave reserves freed capable White southerners to serve in the front lines. Although a few southern White yeoman farmers and other non slave owners sided with the North, most White Southerners supported the Confederacy. Finally, many northerners, won over to the cause of abolition for a variety of reasons, would not fight for a Union that did not end slavery.

The Emancipation Proclamation signed by Lincoln, January 1, 1863, freed only the slaves in rebel hands and allowed Black troops to serve in limited capacities. The proclamation was silent about slaves behind Union lines and in the Border States and did not even free slaves on some plantations of slave owners who had taken an oath of *loyalty* to the national government (Meier and Rudwick 1993:159). As the *London Spectator* observed: "The principle is not that one human being cannot justly own another, but that he cannot own him unless he is loyal to the United States" (Zinn 1980:187). The full legal emancipation of all slaves had to wait until ratification of the Thirteenth Amendment in December 1865.

Even as the Civil War was ending and the northern section of the ruling class was vacillating about what to do with the freedmen and women, the southern states of the former Confederacy were definitive. In 1865 and 1866, they passed the extremely repressive Black Codes, laws attempting to return Blacks to a virtual state of servitude and to insure an abundant supply of really cheap labor for the agricultural work that still needed to be done. The defeated planter class also promoted and funded extra legal reactionary and terrorist organizations. The most well known is the Ku Klux Klan, founded in 1866 in Pulaski, Tennessee by six ex-Confederate officers—all educated men and some holding positions of prestige in the community.

Congress passed the Civil Rights Act of 1866—over President Andrew Johnson's veto— granting citizenship, certain legal and property rights, and the full protection of the law to U.S.-born Blacks. The Reconstruction Act of 1867, enacted by Congress and enforced in the former Confederacy by occupying federal forces, was necessary to consolidate the transfer of power from the slave owners of the South to the industrialists of the North. The Act called for a military governor for all southern states until each could hold its own constitutional convention based on universal male suffrage and the requirements of Congress. Newly arrived northern immigrants, middle-class and a few elite Whites were the primary coalition allies of freed Blacks of all social classes in the Reconstruction period (Meier and Rudwick 1993:183–85).

Surmounting the powerful history and state policies of White supremacy was difficult. The Fourteenth Amendment, ratified in 1868, conferred only general and vague protection against discrimination by the states and guaranteed full constitutional rights to all U.S.-born and naturalized persons. The Supplementary Civil Rights Bill, specifically protecting Blacks from forced segregation in transportation, schools, and public accommodations did not pass until 1875, and only after deletion of the section calling for mixed schools. Blacks tested the law in cities in both the North and the South—only to find many evasions and outright violations. Then in 1883, in the era of Jim Crow, the term used to describe a broad range of segregation laws and customs, the Supreme Court found the law unconstitutional (Meier and Rudwick 1993:183–84).

However briefly, Blacks, with the support of their White middle- and upper-class allies and backed by federal legislation, had made discernible gains in the political arena. The Reconstruction Act of 1867 and the Fifteenth Amendment, ratified in 1870, extended the vote to all men, including ex-slaves. Black men participated in all southern state constitutional conventions. Both antebellum free Blacks and ex-slaves were elected to local, state, and federal offices in all southern states. Their ranks included two U.S. Senators, twenty U.S. Congressmen, five lieutenant governors, and several secretaries of state, state treasurers, and superintendents of education (Zinn 1980:195; Meier and Rudwick 1993:185-86).

Free and integrated public education was instituted by several state Reconstruction governments. The Freedmen's Bureau and the churches also established a network of schools from the primary level through professional education. Again, the primary coalition partners were working and middle-class Blacks and their carpetbagger allies—mostly middle-class and a few elite Whites.

Throughout the period of Reconstruction, southern Whites, led by the ex-planter class, resisted and rebelled against the Reconstruction governments and the federal occupation. They resented and feared the participation of Blacks and disliked their northern White coalition allies almost as much. Race riots beginning in 1866 and peaking in 1874-76, led by White Democrats to *redeem* the South from radical Republican control, anticipated the even greater violence of the post-Reconstruction era (Meier and Rudwick 1993:189).

The Farmers Alliance and Populist Movement: The Pull of Reaction is too Strong

By 1876, three factors converged and led to the end of the occupation and Reconstruction. Ex-slaves and poor White farmers increasingly demanded radical land redistribution. Federal power had been effectively transferred from southern planters to northern industrialists and bankers.

The low level of agricultural technology required large numbers of laborers to farm the land in the revamped "plantation" system of sharecropping (Katz-Fishman and Scott 1994:572).

The 1876 presidential election between Democrat Samuel Tilden and Republican Rutherford Hayes, deadlocked in the electoral college, provided the ruling class the opportunity to reunite the North and South. Republicans offered a compromise that the Democrats accepted. Democrats gave Hayes the 19 electoral votes needed to win the presidency, and in return, the new Republican administration withdrew federal troops from the South, promised to fund infrastructure (mainly railroads), and repealed the Southern Homestead Act that gave federal land to Southern farmers of all races (Katz-Fishman and Scott 1994:572).

The 1877 Hayes-Tilden Compromise spelled the death knell not only for Reconstruction, but for any sustained multiracial coalition building in the South that would be supported by any section of the ruling class. The unprincipled compromise between the northern and southern sections of the ruling class exposed the truth of why the Civil War had been fought—to defeat the slave power of the South, not to free the slaves. The northern section of the ruling class returned power in the South to the ex-Confederate Dixiecrats (Southern Democrats) and their extralegal White supremacist organizations. Can there be any question about its chilling effect on the masses? (Katz-Fishman and Scott 1994; Woodward 1951).

With the defeat of the unbridled power of the planter class in the federal system, the Union could return to the business of southern agricultural production. Chattel slavery, as such, was no longer an option for satisfying the labor needs of the low-tech agricultural system. The sharecropping system and the land lease system provided ways out. Virtually all the ex-slaves and many poor White farmers were bound to the land producing agricultural products and huge profits for the ex-planter class and, perhaps more importantly, for the northern banks. Under the rule of the Black Codes and the rapidly changing legal structure of state and federal governments, this new economic system represented slavery in a new and sanitized form.

During Reconstruction the ex-planter class, dethroned but armed, had terrorized Blacks and their southern White allies. The defeat of Reconstruction and the withdrawal of federal troops unleashed a horrific reign of terror. This fascist era of Jim Crow—of lynchings and burnings, of Dixiecrats, of sheriffs and goons with guns and hoses, of rapes and mayhem, of legal apartheid southern style—is still recent history and fresh in our memories.

From 1882 to 1900, 2,833 people were lynched: 1,726 Blacks and 1,107 of their White allies. Another 1,903 lynchings took place between 1901 and 1962: 1,716 Blacks and 187 Whites (Lindemeyer and Kaiser 1971 in Harris 1994:105,108-9). The vast majority of these occurred in the South. The states with the highest number of lynchings were Mississippi (578), Georgia (530), Texas (493), Louisiana (391), Alabama (347), Florida (282), Tennessee (251), Kentucky (205), South Carolina (160), Oklahoma (122), North Carolina (100), and Virginia (100) (Lindemeyer and Kaiser 1971 in Harris 1994:108–109). From 1882 to 1890 more Whites (680) than Blacks (594) were lynched. From 1891 to 1900 the number of Blacks lynched jumped to 1,132 compared to 427 Whites (Lindemeyer and Kaiser 1971 in Harris 1994:105). Lynchings, as well as other forms of terror and violence, taught Whites and Blacks an important lesson— not to fight the powerful fascist government of the post-Reconstruction era.

Jim Crow state constitutions rapidly replaced Reconstruction constitutions. By the early 1890s, a new legal structure replaced or supplemented the direct violence of lynching as a means of social control. White lynchings decreased dramatically as new legal institutions increasingly restrained the actions of Whites allied with the Black cause, while a renewed and invigorated ideology of White supremacy undermined arguments of human equality. The emerging fascist state governments and the extralegal terrorist organizations had effectively broken the nascent coalitions between poor Whites and ex-slaves. For Blacks, who had to rebel and resist to establish their very humanity, the law was their enemy.

One economic and political movement indigenous to the South that held promise as a Black-White coalition for economic justice and political participation was the Populist movement of the 1880s and 1890s. The powerful monopolies of railroad and industrial capital and the economic stranglehold of Wall Street financiers over the economy confronted small farmers, tenant farmers, and farm workers, both Black and White, with common enemies

The Populist movement and the Populist Party emerged from the actions of the Northern and Southern Farmers' Alliances and the allied Colored Farmers Alliance in Texas in 1886 (Meier and Rudwick 1993:196) and spread throughout the country. By 1892, its organizers had spoken in 43 states and reached two million farm families (Zinn 1980:280). In the South, the Alliance was concentrated in Georgia, Tennessee, Mississippi, North Carolina, Louisiana and Texas (Zinn 1980:280). Estimates of membership of the Colored Alliance vary from 800,000 to 1.3 million nationally and 689,000 to 825,000 in the eleven states of the Confederacy (Gaither 1977:12-13). Sources indicate it peaked at one million in early 1890, was concentrated "in the South Atlantic and Gulf states," and collapsed by the end of 1891(Gaither 1977:12-13).

From the beginning, the alliances were also fraught with contradictions. Whites were primarily small farmers and Blacks were, in the main, farm workers. In some states the Colored Alliance worked in concert with the Southern Farmers Alliance and in other states the Southern Farmers Alliance was thoroughly White supremacist. In addition, Blacks and Whites were never equal partners in the coalition. In the Farmers Alliance movement, even the Colored Alliance was led by a White man, R. M. Humphrey (Gaither 1977:6–16; Zinn 1995:276–286).

In the early 1890s the Colored Alliances, representing farm workers, called for a nationwide strike for higher wages for cotton pickers. The interests of the White farm owners in the Farmers Alliances were at odds with the strike call, which created a serious split between the Black and White farm alliance groups in the Populist movement. This marked the disappearance of the Colored Alliances and the dissolution of the multiracial coalition within the Populist movement. By the time the movement ended in the 1900s, it had embraced the reactionary and racist tendencies in the soil that nurtured it.

In the words of C. Vann Woodward: "Never before or since have the two races in the South come so close together as they did during the Populist struggles" (Zinn 1980:286). But the weight of Southern history, i.e., of White supremacy and of the repressive legal institutions of the late 1800s was too great to overcome. By 1905, Jim Crow constitutions were in place in all ex-Confederate states. Blacks and poor Whites were disenfranchised; the last Black southern elected official left Congress in 1901. Thousands had been lynched. The Ku Klux Klan and other extralegal White supremacist organizations were riding high. Dixiecrats held power throughout the South. The federal government had totally deserted the cause of freedom and democracy (Katz-Fishman and Scott 1994:573). But the struggle continued.

Citizenship Schools and Farm Organizing: A Prelude to The Modern Civil Rights Movement

African Americans in the South have never stopped trying to escape lynching, to eke out an existence as tenant farmers and sharecroppers, to attain political rights promised in the Constitution, to gain literacy and an education, to secure health care, and to build a better future for their children. But historic changes require more than determined actors ready to take on the seemingly impossible. Objective conditions in the national and global political economy also must be ripe if people are to live out their hopes and visions of equality, justice, dignity for all peoples, and respect for mother earth. It was the historic destiny of the courageous women, men and children (mostly Black, with a few White allies) of the South, the most economically underdeveloped and politically oppressed region of the USA, to step forward into this role.

During the first half of the 20th century, the South did not experience the same kind of industrial expansion as the rest of the U.S. because of its underdeveloped economic, political, and social infrastructure. But in the 1930, some truly southern and multiracial grassroots institutions, such as Citizenship Schools and farmers' unions, helped nurture the conditions for extension of industry and political rights into the South. One of the most significant, the Highlander Center for Research and Education (founded in 1932 as the Highlander Folk School) (Bell, Gaventa, and Peters 1990; Couto 1991), offered literacy and political training for the nascent civil rights movement through the Citizenship Schools. The Highlander staff was primarily White working- and middle-class southerners. Those who attended Highlander included Black and White working- and middle-class women and men. Highlander alumni who made their mark on the civil rights struggles include Septima Clark, Bernice Robinson, Rosa Parks, Martin Luther King, and Andy Young (Bell, Gaventa, and Peters 1990; Couto 1991).

In addition to political reform, economic change was critical, not just for the South's workers—Black and White—but for industrialization and modernization to occur. Struggles over land reform and the working conditions of tenant farmers, sharecroppers and farm workers continued. Two of the most important multiracial coalitions in the 1930s were the Southern Tenant Farmers Union (STFU) in Arkansas and the Alabama Sharecroppers Union (Couto 1991). In July 1934, 27 Black and White men gathered in Poinsett County, Arkansas, to found the STFU. They discussed whether or not to have separate Black and White unions, and were persuaded by the words of one attendee, an old Black man to have one multiracial union.

> He recounted his membership in the Progressive Farmers and Household Union and how that union had been wiped out and many of its members massacred in Elaine in 1919.... "For a long time now the

white folks and the colored folks have been fighting each other and both of us have been getting whipped all the time. We don't have nothing against one another but we got plenty against the landlord. The same chain that holds my people holds your people too. If we are chained together on the outside we ought to stay chained together in the union. It won't do no good for us to divide because there's where the trouble has been all the time. The landlord is always betwist us, beatin' us and starvin' us and makin' us fight each other. There ain't but one way for us to get him where he can't help himself and that's for us to get together and stay together" (Couto 1991:183).

The STFU organized a strike to demand land reform, better working conditions and higher wages. Despite unity across color lines, the strike brought reprisals. Strike leaders were arrested, jailed, and forced into convict farm labor, for 75 cents a day. The Earle town sheriff arrested 13 strikers and forced them into peonage; he was subsequently arrested and punished himself. In a 1936 strike over raising wages from 70 cents to $1 a day, union officer Reverend William Bennett was beaten to death and strike breakers were brought in. After additional violence and the death of two strikers, the Union called off the strike (Couto 1991:184).

The Alabama Sharecroppers Union, another effort at a Black and White coalition of poor farm workers, had a similarly brief life. Their strike for higher wages and better working conditions against the Bell Plantation in Lowndes County, in September 1935, also ended in failure, violence against the 25 strike leaders and their flight from the county to save their lives (Couto 1991:179). Couto's (1991:179) comments about the strike sum up the political climate of the South: "The strike surfaced the violence constantly at hand to enforce the system of scarcity and to suppress attempts to organize to improve conditions."

Trade union organizing in this period involved few, if any, multiracial coalitions because racial segregation ensured that factory workers were almost all White. Nevertheless, the violence ready at hand to suppress the organizing efforts of the multiracial farm workers' unions was as readily applied to the organizing efforts of southern White workers.

The Modern Civil Rights Movement: The Black-White Coalition Revisited

The modern civil rights movement like the Civil War and Union victory almost a century earlier, was possible because the yearnings and struggles of the African American people for freedom coincided with the interests of a section of the ruling class, this time finance capital, in the post-World War II period of economic expansion. The impetus to embrace aspects of the civil rights agenda on the part of this section of the ruling class was threefold: significant changes in southern agricultural production, the expansion of industry into the South, and global economic and political developments putting the U.S. on the side of anti-colonial movements.

The 1940 invention and refinement of the mechanical cotton picker and the 1952 development of weed-killing chemicals provided the technological and economic basis for forcing millions of agricultural workers off the plantations and thousands of small farmers off their land (Katz-Fishman and Scott 1994:574), creating a large pool of urban Black workers. Between 1940 and 1970, 4 million Black Americans migrated from the South to the North and from country to city. By 1965, 80% of African Americans lived in urban America—both South and North (Tidwell 1993:261; Zinn 1980:451; Katz-Fishman and Scott 1994:574). This historic demographic transition occurred precisely at the moment that industrial production to rebuild war-devastated Europe, to satisfy the needs of the commodity-starved American people, and to consolidate the U.S. military-industrial complex demanded an expanded workforce.

Again, there were contradictions between the modern civil rights movement and the interests of its ruling class allies. Blacks were fighting for freedom, equality, and democratic rights. Finance capital was seeking profits, i.e., the lowest possible cost of production and the cheapest available sources of labor. The South and its potential pool of cheap labor, Black and White, held great promise. The obstacle was Jim Crow segregation. Truman recognized this problem as early as 1947:

> One of the principal economic problems facing us and the rest of the world is achieving maximum production and continued prosperity. . . .
>
> Discrimination imposes a direct cost upon our economy through the wasteful duplication of many facilities and services required by the "separate but equal" policy. That the resources of the South are sorely strained by the burden of a double system of schools and other public services has already been indicated. Segregation is also economically wasteful for private business (Blaustein and Zangrando 1968:377-78).

Finally, the changing postwar international economic and political environment placed U.S. finance capital on the side of the anti-colonial movements in some developing countries. This was an opportunity to penetrate previously closed markets; but for the U.S.A. to be seen as a credible ally for third world peoples, it had to address its own apartheid in the South.

Within this context a Black-White coalition emerged and was consolidated in the struggle for the civil rights agenda of the twentieth century. It included Blacks of all social classes from throughout the country, and was led primarily by middle class Blacks from the South. The White members of the coalition included northern Whites, e.g., students, clergy, working-class people, and some economic and political elites, as well as some working-and middle-class southern Whites. The coalition initiated sit-ins, marches, freedom rides, boycotts, demonstrations, lobbying, voter registration drives and freedom schools in the renewed struggle for civil rights.

The Student Nonviolent Coordinating Committee (SNCC) was among the best known of the Black–White coalition organizations of this era. Zinn (1965) calls them the "new abolitionists." Their numbers swelled from 16 in 1961 to 150 in 1964 (Zinn 1965:3–4). SNCC workers, mostly Black with some White students, youth, and advisers, formed the backbone of the civil rights movement in the South. Unlike many activists who came out for specific, isolated events, SNCC workers were the *guerrilla fighters* who moved in with the people of rural communities throughout the deep South, tutored adults for voter registration, and educated youth through freedom schools (Zinn 1965:3).

SNCC workers and other movement activists met terror, violence, torture, and even death at the hands of the southern fascist and White supremacist legal system (police, sheriffs, courts, jails) and at the hands of extralegal vigilante organizations such as the Ku Klux Klan and White Citizens Councils. The federal government reluctantly intervened only after the burning of a freedom riders' bus, the death of four small Black girls in the Birmingham church bombing, the mounting death toll of freedom fighters in the deep South, and the local and state *law enforcement* officials refusal to stop participating in and covering-up the carnage and terror.

Finance capital knew that if higher profits and workplace integration were to be achieved, the heavy hand of southern history would have to be held at bay. But only after President John F. Kennedy's assassination was Lyndon Johnson able to strike a deal with the southern Dixiecrat wing of the Democratic party to push through the 1964 Civil Rights Act and the 1965 Voting Rights Act.

Although these victories addressed the need for greater political inclusion of Blacks and other peoples of color, the reforms fell short of the remedies that would address the economic inequality of Black workers and farmers—women and men, the poor and near poor—and the working class of all colors and nationalities. As the economic crises of late-20th-century capitalism deepened in the U.S.A. and globally, even these political reforms came under attack.

Economic Justice and Political Democracy Movements of the Late 20th Century: The New High Tech Poverty Crosses the Color Line

Recent history demonstrates that hard fought civil rights victories, much like the victories of abolition and Reconstruction in the 1860s, have not fundamentally and permanently provided economic well-being to Black or Brown or Red or White working-class women and men, especially those at the bottom of the class structure. The abolition movement and the Civil War did end chattel slavery, and the modern civil rights movement did end segregation in public accommodations, offer legal remedies for discrimination, and provide access to the ballot box. But, the quality of life of the ex-slave in the sharecropping system under Jim Crow laws was as close to chattel slavery as it could be without being such. Today, 35 years after the Civil Rights Act and 34 years after the Voting Rights Act, the quality of life of the Black, Brown, and Red masses, women and men and youth, suffers from disproportionate un/underemployment, poverty, incarceration, hunger and homelessness. These conditions are rapidly worsening, despite the so-called *economic recovery*. The quality of life of the white masses deteriorated more rapidly in the 1990s than at any other time in the post-World War II period.

What is new and what is at the root of the deteriorating quality of life of the masses is the revolution in today's economy. The global integration of the economy, the high technology revolution, and the reengineering (downsizing) of corporations, the government, and social institutions are transforming every aspect of society and our lives. Greater use of new technologies in the workplace—i.e., computers, robots, automation, permanently eliminates jobs in agriculture, manufacturing, and even in the service sector and the knowledge industry. The question is "What does this high tech revolution and global integration of the economy mean for multiracial working-class-based coalitions in the South?"

There was much discussion in the 1970s and early 1980s about the decline of the *rustbelt* and the *snowbelt* in the Northeast and Midwest and the rise of the *Sunbelt* in the South and West. The truth is that the sun never shone in the Black Belt South. By 1986, the Commission on the Future of the South issued a Report "Shadows in the Sunbelt" (1986) suggesting that the *economic boom* was much overstated (Gaventa, Smith, and Willingham 1990; Falk and Lyson 1988; Slaughter 1992).

As agriculture mechanized and industrialization of the South moved forward, small farmers were faced with extinction. The Federation of Southern Cooperatives has led the fight for survival of the small, primarily Black farmer from the late 1960s to the present. With its training center in the heart of the Alabama Black Belt in Epes, the Federation has been important as a training ground for many leaders in the region's political and economic rights' struggles.

The plight of the small farmers, continuing impoverishment of the South, the bankruptcy of the Democratic Party, the Jesse Jackson campaign in 1984, and the *rainbow* movements contributed to the rise of two multiracial coalitions in the South. The Alabama New South Coalition (ANSC) was formed in 1984 as a reaction to the Alabama Democratic Conference's endorsement of Walter Mondale over Jesse Jackson. The Southern Rainbow Education Project (SREP) formed in 1990 and organized throughout the South, including West Virginia, for political power and economic change in the region. Both coalitions were composed of middle-and working-class Blacks and Whites, with middle-class Blacks making up the majority and serving as leaders (Slaughter 1992).

These coalitions have attempted, through electoral politics and grassroots organizing, to expand the political power of African American working- and middle-class people and their White and Native American middle- and working-class allies. Their objective has been through political power, to gain control over the economic development of the region. Though they have had some success in getting elected to political office, they have not been the least bit successful in controlling the economy of the region (Bethell 1982; Katz Fishman and Scott 1986; Slaughter 1992; Alabama Blackbelt Defense Committee n.d.; Workers Press n.d.).

Not coincidentally, both the Federation, in the late 1970s and early 1980s, and several voting rights activists in the mid-1980s, were investigated by the FBI for alleged misuse of federal funds (by the Federation) and alleged vote fraud in the west Alabama Black Belt (Bethell 1982; Katz-Fishman and Scott 1986; Slaughter 1992). Despite these efforts by the federal government to disrupt and even destroy these coalitions, the government's extensive investigations found no evidence of misuse of funds or vote fraud.

Presently, three of the most active multiracial working-class-based coalitions in the South are the Southern Organizing Committee for Economic and Social Justice (SOC), the Southern Region Up & Out of Poverty Now! and the Southeastern Regional Economic Justice Network. All are rooted in the economic and environmental crises of the 1980s and 1990s and, though they include both middle- and working-class people, in the main, their agendas reflect the needs of those at the bottom and a significant proportion of their leaders are women of color.

SOC had its roots in the Southern Conference Educational Fund (SCEF) founded in the 1950s by Anne and Carl Braden, White southern middle-class activists, to bring together Black and White organizers and activists in working-class movements. One of its best known projects was the Gulf Coast Pulpwood Workers Association, which fought to organize Black and White pulpwood workers. SCEF was destroyed in the 1970s because of sectarian infighting among left formations. A section of those, under the leadership of Anne Braden, then formed the Southern Organizing Committee for Economic and Social Justice in the late 1970s, continuing the mission of SCEF. In response to environmental racism and its concentration in the South (Bullard 1994), SOC began to focus its work on the fight for environmental justice.

The Southern Region Up & Out of Poverty Now! Campaign (Southern Up & Out) had its origins in the growing permanent poverty, joblessness, homelessness and hunger spurred by the high tech economic revolution of the 1980s. The deepening crisis of survival and social dislocation in poor and working-class communities across color line— mostly Black but including some Whites, Latinos, and Native Americans —brought three grassroots organizations together in Philadelphia, in July 1989, to found the Up & Out of Poverty Now! Campaign. The National Welfare Rights Union, the National Union of the Homeless, and the National Anti-Hunger Coalition created an organization led not by service providers, advocates and policy analysts, but by the victims themselves, who cannot compromise on the solutions to their problems. Southern participants in the founding convention returned to the South and organized the Southern Region Up & Out. Headquartered in Atlanta, the Southern Up & Out has developed a network of organizations from throughout the region to provide support and strength to local and regional struggles, to develop joint or coordinated actions and to share information and communications through *Street Heat* in the broad anti-poverty fight in the South (Southern Region Up & Out Poverty Now! Campaign n.d.).

The Southern Up & Out is led primarily by Black working class women activists and some men, but also includes middle- and working-class activists who are White, Native American and Latino. Latino participation in the Southern Up & Out is primarily in Florida, Georgia and the Carolinas where migrant farm workers are part of the network fighting for economic justice. Project South: Institute for the Elimination of Poverty & Genocide emerged as the educational and research arm of the Southern Up & Out in 1991. It is also a multiracial organization of working-and middle-class scholar and grassroots activists—primarily women—who develop popular political and economic education and action research to address the organizing needs of those in the trenches.

It took roughly 100 years for U.S. industry to expand from North to South. It took less than 30 years to cross the borders to the rest of the hemisphere. With each southern stopping point, wages plunged and the quality of life and the environment deteriorated. Grassroots activists fighting for economic justice in the South in the 1990s had not heard of NAFTA and GATT a few years ago. Today, many have visited the *maquiladoras* and have learned much about the globalization and integration of the economy.

The right-to-work laws pervasive throughout the southern states have weakened the union movement as an institutional locus of the fight for workers rights and economic justice. In its place, are networks such as the Southern Up & Out and especially the Southeastern Regional Economic Justice Network (REJN)—which share a number of common member organizations. REJN was formed in 1991 as a regional network, initiated by Southerners for Economic Justice (SEJ), an organization in Durham, NC, which concentrated on North Carolina. REJN established itself as an independent organization in 1994.

REJN consists of worker organizations, a few unions and mostly community-based organizations at the front lines of the struggle for economic justice. Because of the rapid economic integration of the hemisphere and the need to develop ties across national borders, REJN also includes member organizations from Mexico and Canada. REJN is working-class led and is multiracial and multinational, including Blacks, Whites, Latinos, Native Americans, Mexicans and Canadians (SEJ 1993). U.S. Latino participation in the network is greatest in Florida and North Carolina where migrant farm workers are concentrated.

These economic justice and political democracy coalitions struggle daily to secure the necessaries of life for their members and a future for their children and youth, and to develop an understanding of the new realities confronting working-class women and men of all colors. There are no flashy victories and each day things get worse. Jobs move from one region to another or across national borders, and robots and computers replace workers everywhere. Human beings are increasingly superfluous to the production and distribution process.

Given current economic and political realities, there is no section of the ruling class unlike during some previous periods, that shares with working women and men of any race or nationality the desire to reform the political and economic system. Rather, both the governmental and economic sections of the ruling class are working to increase productivity with fewer workers and to balance the budget on the backs of the poor and near poor. The success of these new multiracial working-class-led coalitions is measured not so much by reforms won—since they are few or nonexistent—but by the expansion of the organizing efforts. Where southern organizing succeeds, the coalitions are led primarily by the working-class based in the South. They have no place to go—no options. They must stay and organize for economic and political justice no matter how great the repression. Their survival depends upon it.

WORKING CLASS–BASED MULTIRACIAL COALITIONS: THE DANGER AND THE CHALLENGE

Given the weight of southern history and the dominance of White supremacy both ideologically and structurally within economic and political institutions, long-lasting and successful multiracial coalitions in the South have been difficult at best. Historically such coalitions have fallen into two main types: one led by members of the working -class and the other by the middle class. Too often in these coalitions internal class divisions and/or disruption and destruction by the government have brought them to an end.

The first type is composed of Black, Native American, Latino and/or White working-class and some middle-class members, but no elite or ruling-class representatives, and is led by the interests of the working class. These coalitions include the Maroon communities, some of the Populist and later farm organizing efforts, the citizenship schools, and the most recent economic justice and political democracy movements. The Maroon communities were destroyed by the U.S. government through the Seminole Wars and the Trail of Tears. Some farm organizing efforts in the Populist movement broke up because of the different interests of the middle-class farm owner and the working-class farm laborer or sharecropper. In the early 1900s, other coalitions made up entirely of farm workers ended because of the government's violent actions, including the jailing and even killing of some organizers. The citizenship schools anticipated the modern civil rights movement, and, though attacks were made on individual leaders and the Highlander Center, they were allowed to play their preparatory role. The contemporary economic justice and political democracy movements represent a qualitatively new period in economic and social history—we will return to them below.

The other type of coalition has been mainly between the Black, Red, and Brown masses and the White middle-class and/or representatives of a section of the ruling class under the leadership of the middle class. The White coalition members have been primarily but not exclusively northerners. These coalitions include the abolition movement and the modern civil rights movement. Both were successful—for a limited time—reform movements within capitalist economic and political relations. In both instances there was a brief coincidence of interests between the Black, Red and Brown masses seeking freedom and equality and a section of the ruling class. In the abolition movement, the coalition's elite members primarily desired to transfer power from the slavocracy to northern industrial capital and to preserve the union. In the civil rights movement, the elite's interests would be served by expanding the economic base of U.S. industrial capitalism into the South and securing a position in the developing countries through support of their anticolonial struggles. In both instances, however, the victories of political and economic inclusion were not final. Jim Crow and southern apartheid replaced Reconstruction and today's permanent poverty and the prison industrial complex are replacing the civil rights gains.

Clearly, things are very different today than in the 1860s, the1890s, and even the 1960s. The high-tech revolution has fundamentally transformed the economic world. Workers—Black, Red, Brown and White—are increasingly superfluous to the production and distribution of goods (Rifkin 1994). The ruling class and the government will not concern themselves with the quality of life of workers they no longer need to exploit for economic gain, so currently there is no section of the ruling class whose interests coincide with those of the Black, Red, Brown, or White masses.

The working class's fight for survival has given rise in the 1980s and 1990s to the early stages of multiracial coalitions led by the demands of those in poverty, such as the economic justice and political democracy coalitions discussed above. Most of these budding coalitions are led by southern Blacks—largely women. As Latinos and Native Americans become more dispersed throughout the South, they too become important coalition partners. In the main, the White coalition members participate not out of a sense of morality or *do-gooderism*, but out of a sense of their own survival interests. These coalitions include no representatives of the ruling class since the interests of the workers and the poor are increasingly at odds with those of capital. Thus, they are without funding and other resources that supported earlier coalitions.

However, the history surveyed here suggests that these new multiracial working-class-based coalitions will be long-lasting, will challenge the weight of Southern history, and can succeed in fundamentally changing the economic, political and social system.

Past coalitions with sections of the ruling class have had some (although limited) success in gaining political equality, but have failed (and will always fail) to change the underlying, systemic condition of inequality in the U.S. We argue that, for the first time in history, conditions are ripe for multiracial coalitions among Black, Red, Brown, and White working-class women and men in the South. The new conditions of the global high-tech economy threaten the survival of a far greater *absolute number* of Whites than of Blacks, Latinos, and Native Americans in the South (and throughout the country). This should not lead us to underestimate the historic and institutional pull of White supremacy and the power of elite manipulation of the *race card*.

If the problems of those at the bottom of society—the un/underemployed, the poor, the homeless and the hungry, those in prison and on death row—are to be solved, working class coalitions across race lines must be forged. Unless coalition leadership is held by those at the bottom who cannot compromise, their demands will not be met. If the middle-class leads and if compromises are demanded, history suggests that this class will sacrifice the interests of those at the bottom, for example as did Northerners in the Compromise of 1877 and the White Farmer's Alliance during the Colored Farmer's Alliance strike in the 1890s. The middle class can participate in a meaningful way, but they must follow the program and support the demands of the most impoverished stratum of the working class. As the security of middle-class women and men is increasingly threatened by the new economy, their participation is more and more possible and probable. In contrast, when a section of the ruling class is a coalition partner, its command of resources through bribes and manipulation of the political environment allows it to commandeer the coalition and movement to serve their elite interests. Working-class and, increasingly, middle-class people of all colors lose.

After more than 500 years of the global expansion of the capitalist world system, U.S. workers, including southern workers of all colors and nationalities, are finally learning a hard lesson: the much heralded capitalist model of development does not benefit working women and men, their families, or the environment. This is true in the Black Belt South, in Appalachia, in the growing fields of Florida and Texas, and in the mills and offices throughout the South. It is also increasingly true in the North, the West, in Chiapas and Mexico City, and throughout the world. A touchstone for rethinking how the economy works, how politics and economy interconnect, and what kinds of coalitions and movements are needed for working people to win should be the recent round of capitalist maneuvers for the passage of NAFTA. The uprising in Chiapas on January 1, 1994, the day NAFTA went into effect in Mexico, was the opening round of the struggles of the future. Today's economic justice and political democracy coalitions in the U.S. South are an integral part of this new reality and new world.

NOTES

[1] Coalitions, by their nature, are situational alliances between groups who come together to accomplish certain objectives they cannot achieve on their own. Typically the coalition has objectives that are not identical to those of the partner groups. Thus tensions are inherent within coalitions from the beginning and are more pronounced the greater the disparities between group interests and the overall coalition objectives. Success can bring an end to coalitions as can external forces seeking to destroy coalition (Gomes and Williams 1992).

[2] For each of the coalitions, we consider (1) its location within the periodization of U.S. and global capitalist development; (2) its race composition; (3) its class composition; (4) the race, class, and gender make-up of the coalition's leadership; (5) its goals and objectives (e.g., various reforms within capitalist property relations and/or more direct challenges to capitalist relations); and (6) the conditions that gave rise to the coalition, the results of the coalition, i.e., its success or failure, and the length of its existence.

[3] This has been particularly true in the deep South where the legacy of chattel slavery has left even today a highly racialized society, an economically dependent region, and a political tradition of reaction and repression.

[4] While more than half of Blacks (54%) remain in the South, Latinos are highly concentrated in the West (45%) with another 30% in the South. The "rub," however, for Black and Latino urban coalitions is that "outside of Texas, Florida and the District of Columbia," the South's Latino population is "barely visible (less than 3%)" (Harrison and Bennett 1995:150). Further, the South remains the least urbanized region in the country (U.S. Bureau of the Census 1994:43).

CHAPTER 6

Displaced Labor Migrants or the "Underclass"

African Americans and Puerto Ricans in Philadelphia's Economy

CARMEN TERESA WHALEN

Southern African Americans and Puerto Ricans came to the Philadelphia area as labor migrants in the World War II era.[1] Employers and government agencies recruited them for food processing work during the war and for farm work after the war. Policy makers emphasized the seasonal nature of the work and expected migrants to return "home" when their labor was no longer needed. Government and industry looked at migrants as low-paid, seasonal laborers, not as permanent community members. But African Americans and Puerto Ricans viewed seasonal migration as a source of income or a stepping stone for permanent settlement. Philadelphia's postwar economy, however, was segmented by race and gender and migrants became clustered in certain sectors of the labor market. Moreover, during the 1970s, they found themselves displaced as the city's economy shifted from manufacturing to professional and other services. By 1990, economic change and residential segregation had created conditions of concentrated poverty for many of the African Americans and Puerto Ricans who made the city their home.

Social scientists, policy makers and journalists have used the "culture of poverty" and "underclass" constructs to interpret the experiences of African Americans and Puerto Ricans.[2] Both constructs are racial ideologies pointing to particular groups of people, emphasizing their "problems" and holding them culpable for their own poverty. They focus on the assumed behaviors of individuals, while downplaying migration histories and the roles of economic change, residential segregation and government policy. When government policy is addressed, assessments have centered on welfare and whether or not it creates "de-

pendency." In contrast, this essay examines government policies fostering labor recruitment, deindustrialization and residential segregation in
Philadelphia, from World War II to the 1990s. I include a preliminary
exploration of the "culture of poverty" and "underclass" interpretations
of African Americans and Puerto Ricans. Few historical works have addressed the World War II era migrations of these groups or the evolution
of racial ideologies from the "culture of poverty" to the "underclass."
Most scholarship treats these groups separately.[3] Yet, there are important parallels in their post–World War II migration histories, in the contemporary conditions they confront in the inner cities and in the
convergence of racial ideologies that define them. This brief and selective historical essay suggests the impacts of migration histories, structural change and racial ideologies in shaping conditions in the inner
cities, the debates that surround them and the challenges that Puerto Ricans and African Americans confront. It identifies the factors bringing
together these two communities in Philadelphia, as well as those driving
them apart.

RECRUITED LABORERS

During World War II, employers and government agencies recruited
southern African Americans and Puerto Ricans to southern New Jersey
for seasonal food processing, one of the lowest-paid war industry jobs.
The War Manpower Commission (WMC), the government agency most
directly involved with labor recruitment, made food processing plants in
southern New Jersey a priority and called for "full cooperation between
the canning industry and the Field Representatives of the War Manpower
Commission" (McNamee 1944a:1). Such cooperative efforts were necessary because food production was central to the war effort, yet it paid
less than other war industry jobs and it was seasonal. The WMC con-
ceded: "It is difficult for canneries to compete with other industries in
[the region] in the recruitment of labor on account of the differences in
wage scales" (McNamee 1944a:3).

Food processors were accustomed to seasonal labor shortages and to
migration from the southern states to meet them. The war, however, mag-
nified these shortages. The Campbell Soup Company, a large food-processing firm in Camden, New Jersey, exemplified labor recruitment and
cooperation between employers and government agencies. The company
was willing to use all laborers recruited by the WMC—Puerto Ricans,
African Americans from the southern states, foreign workers, prisoners

of war, local women—and was relentless in its own recruitment. In 1944, the WMC and Campbell intensified their recruitment.

Although migrants from Virginia, West Virginia, Florida, South Carolina, Washington, D.C., and Tennessee did respond, they had not met New Jersey's labor needs in 1943 and were not expected to meet them in 1944. To encourage migration, the WMC requested gasoline ration coupons and improved its clearance program, as in 1943 "employer representatives were able to discover labor pools in the same areas where public agency recruiting methods failed." The WMC and food processors turned to labor sources that had been effective in 1943—soldiers on furloughs, released war industry workers, civilians on vacation, and "housewives who do not normally work in any industry" (McNamee 1944a:2). Still anticipating a shortage, they looked for new sources of labor, including prisoners of war, "the surplus labor reported to be in the Island of Jamaica" and "the supply reported from Puerto Rico" (McNamee 1944b:n.p.).

With the support of the WMC, the Campbell Soup Company actively pursued the migrant labor force from Puerto Rico. Personnel managers held meetings with other canners and the WMC and went to Puerto Rico and Washington, D.C. The WMC noted that, "Porto [sic] Ricans are considered to be excellent workers. The importance of this labor pool, maintained by the government and allocated by the War Manpower Commission cannot be underestimated" (Costello 1944:3). Discouraged by the slow progress in recruiting them, Campbell reminded the WMC of the magnitude of their need for labor and of their contribution to the war effort.

Yet, labor migrants were wanted only on a seasonal basis. The status of Puerto Ricans as U.S. citizens meant that, unlike foreign workers, they could remain in the U.S. This concern outweighed WMC's assessment that they were "excellent workers." As the *Washington Post* explained: "Heretofore, Puerto Ricans have been bypassed in the farm labor importation program because of the fear they might want to remain in this country when the war is over." The benefit of employing Jamaicans, Mexicans and workers from Newfoundland, the article explained, was that they "could be returned because they are not American citizens" (Washington Post 1944:n.p.). Puerto Ricans were not recruited as agricultural workers, for the more limited purpose of working in food processing and the railroads. Between May and July 1944, nearly 2,000 Puerto Ricans were brought to the continental U.S. The Campbell Soup Company accepted 500 who joined the southern migrants and foreign workers already employed (Cross 1944:1).

The WMC encouraged African American and Puerto Rican migrants to return "home" when their labor was no longer needed. In contrast to foreign workers who could be deported, the WMC had little enforcement power over these U.S. citizens. In the case of southern migrants, food processors signed an agreement with the WMC stating, "I will use all reasonable efforts to insure the return to their homes, upon the agreed upon dates, of all workers recruited for me under this program" (WMC 1944b:n.p.). Employers also agreed to (a) notify the WMC if a worker was discharged or quit, (b) sever the worker on the specified date, (c) provide workers with free transportation home, and (d)deny them information about other jobs. The WMC criticized the canneries for high employee turnover, fearing that its expenses in recruiting laborers were not being recouped and that migrants were seeking better paying, permanent jobs in the region instead of making their way "home" (Doe 1944).

Puerto Ricans breaking contracts was one of the "typical problems" for the WMC, who instructed local offices to try "to dissuade" workers by reminding them of "the legal nature of. . . obligations under the contract" (Cross 1944:2). Workers were informed that if they broke their contracts, in addition to forfeiting free transportation and Selective Service deferment, they would become subject to employment stabilization plans and to an increase in tax withholding. Although local offices were required to report individuals who left, the WMC reminded them that "Puerto Ricans, as you know, are citizens of this country and have the same rights and privileges in regard to employment that obtain for other citizens" (WMC 1944c:2). The WMC knew it had little control over the migration patterns and employment choices of African American and Puerto Rican citizens. Such active recruitment of Puerto Ricans was short-lived, since foreign workers were preferred and solicited instead.[4]

After the war, the continuing demand for seasonal agricultural labor and increasing anti- communist sentiment fostered a shift from foreign to domestic labor recruitment. The March 19, 1952 issue of the U.S. Department of Labor's *Employment Security Review* made explicit the connection between the "defense" of the USA and the use of domestic labor, proclaiming as its title, "Farm Work Is Defense Work: Maximum Utilization of the Domestic Labor Force." Therefore, Southern African Americans and Puerto Ricans were recruited for seasonal agricultural work on Pennsylvania's farms. As during the war, labor recruitment was for the least desirable jobs—low wages, harsh conditions and seasonal work. The cooperation between employers and government agencies continued, as the U.S. Employment Service (USES) took over where the WMC left off. The labor recruitment of southern African Americans continued and that of Puerto Ricans increased dramatically.

Although Pennsylvania's farmers expressed a preference for local laborers, they turned increasingly to southern African American and Puerto Rican migrants. They regarded local adults "as good workers who presented no housing problems, no language barriers and who created no social or other tension in the community." The availability of manufacturing jobs, however, had reduced the local labor pool to school youth, "idle industrial workers, house wives and other persons not generally considered to be in the labor market" (Pennsylvania Bureau of Employment Security 1953:14–5). The USES instructed farmers to use local labor first and then Puerto Ricans, before foreigners. Puerto Ricans replaced Jamaicans, Bahamians and the German prisoners of war from the World War II Glassboro, New Jersey labor camp (US Department of Labor 1950). Southern African Americans continued their northward migration. By the late 1950s, Pennsylvania farmers relied on approximately 45,000 seasonal workers annually and a labor force that was 80% local, just over 10% southern African American, and less than 10% Puerto Rican (Pennsylvania Bureau of Employment Security 1954–1970).

The Pennsylvania State Employment Service oversaw the entire labor recruitment program. It stressed recruiting local workers, but also arranged crews of southern African Americans to travel north. Representatives from the Employment Service made annual trips to Florida to orchestrate the migration of crews. Crew leaders organized migrants, especially in Florida, and were paid by deductions in the workers' pay. The Employment Service sent farmers' requests for laborers to the appropriate Puerto Rican government offices, which recruited and screened workers and monitored labor contracts that were signed by the employer and the worker and approved by Puerto Rico's Commissioner of Labor (Handsaker 1953; U.S. Department of Labor 1950).

In contrast to the situation during the war, African Americans and Puerto Ricans were no longer able to secure food-processing jobs. Instead, local labor dominated these jobs, and African Americans and Puerto Ricans were concentrated in field work. Food processing offered higher wages, workers' compensation, social security benefits and better working conditions than field labor. In 1951, locals provided 79%, Puerto Ricans 3% and southern African Americans only 1% of the "man-days" of work at twenty-two processor plants. The 17% not reported were assumed to be mostly local workers, with some Whites transported daily from the surrounding areas (Handsaker 1953:38, 41). Employers preferred local workers and seemed to honor local workers' preferences for food processing over field work and for work in some crops over others.

Working and living conditions exploited seasonal field laborers, despite the government-sponsored labor contracts that were supposed to protect Puerto Ricans. In 1953, economist Morrison Handsaker found that Puerto Ricans "are not subject to some of the abuses, petty or major, to which an undetermined proportion of Negro workers are subject under the crew leader system" (1953:78, 139). Yet Puerto Rican workers had been stranded and "victimized in other ways," and hardships extended to all migrant laborers: "Persons are in many instances virtually compelled to live in places hardly fit for human habitation." By 1958, the Pennsylvania Farm Placement Program confessed, "Experience shows that the migratory farm worker and his family is perhaps the most easily exploited, the lowest paid and lives and works under more substandard conditions than any other single group in the labor force" (Pennsylvania Bureau of Employment Security 1958:7). Employers and state agencies continued to recruit African Americans and Puerto Ricans for the least desirable of jobs.

Given harsh conditions, migrants sometimes left the jobs for which they had been recruited, in search of better options. During the war, the WMC and food processors complained often of workers leaving before their terms expired, but seemed unable to slow the tide. The competing interests of migrants and recruiters surfaced in the debate over transportation costs. The government covered these costs for agricultural field workers, but the "canners have the privilege of deducting transportation and maintenance from the worker's wage." The WMC noted that these "workers demand the same free transportation permitted agricultural workers and, secondly, many workers disappear before full deduction can be made" (Costello 1944:2). African American and Puerto Rican migrants, it seemed, had agendas of their own. While some earned seasonal income and returned home, others confirmed WMC's fears and used labor recruitment as a vehicle for permanent settlement. In the postwar period, complaints about workers not fulfilling their obligations continued and social service workers expressed concern over farm laborers settling in the city. Although social service agencies reacted with alarm, the local economy provided jobs and sustained the immigration.

Thus, labor recruitment contributed to the growth of African Americans and Puerto Ricans in Philadelphia, shifting the city's racial composition. African Americans increased by 50% during the 1940s with the arrival of 90,000 migrants and by another 41% during the 1950s with the arrival of 65,000 more. Puerto Ricans grew from less than 2,000 in 1950 to more than 14,000 by 1960. As these groups came to the city, Whites moved to the suburbs: 92,000 left during the 1940s and another 340,000 during the 1950s. In 1950, African Americans were 18% of the city's total; by 1970, they constituted 34% and Puerto Ricans slightly over 1% (Philadelphia Commission on Human Rights 1961:1–2; Muller, Meyer and Cybriwsky 1976:12-14; U.S. Department of Commerce 1940–1970). Facilitated by government policies and agencies, labor recruitment interacted with the availability of jobs in the city and the migrants' own agendas.

DISPLACED LABOR MIGRANTS

Government policies fostered labor recruitment along with the shift to a post industrial economy and residential segregation. In the words of Katz (1993:457), the "underclass did not just happen; its emergence was not inevitable; like the postindustrial city of which it is a part, it is the product of actions and decisions over a very long span of time." Economic shifts combined with residential segregation to displace African Americans and Puerto Ricans from the city's economy and to concentrate them in deteriorating neighborhoods devoid of economic opportunities. As Massey (1990:352) notes, "In the nation's largest urban areas, these groups are the only ones that have *simultaneously* experienced high levels of residential segregation and sharp increases in poverty." In the postwar era, federal, state and local policies continued to contribute to the conditions of concentrated poverty that affected their lives in Philadelphia.

This impact of government policies and economic change was shaped by earlier employment patterns. As African American and Puerto Rican migrants came to Philadelphia, they encountered a labor market segmented by race and gender. Migrants, particularly women, became concentrated in certain sectors of the economy. By 1950, African American women were concentrated overwhelmingly in non-professional services—51% in contrast to only 8% of White women. Puerto Rican women similarly were concentrated in manufacturing— 53% in contrast to 36% of White women (see Table 6-1). Although the disparities in employment patterns for men were not as great as those for women, African American and Puerto Rican men were under-

Table 6-1: Industrial Classification of Employed Puerto Ricans, Blacks, and Total Population, Philadelphia, 1950 and 1970

	1950						1970		
	Puerto Rican Male	Puerto Rican Female	Black Male	Black Female	White Male	White Female	Puerto Rican	Black	Total Population
Number	90	34	103,837	67,757	889,217	375,526	6,270	232,192	763,520
Percent in:									
agriculture, forestry, fisheries	1.1	0.0	2.3	0.5	2.7	0.5	1.4	0.7	0.4
construction, mining	5.6	0.0	14.4	0.4	8.1	0.7	5.3	5.6	4.7
manufacturing	26.6	53.0	28.2	21.9	39.1	35.7	49.3	26.0	28.2
transport, communications, public utilities	11.1	0.0	11.6	0.8	9.2	5.2	4.3	6.6	6.5
wholesale, retail trade	27.8	11.8	17.3	10.1	19.3	21.6	17.9	15.2	20.1
finance, insurance, real estate	0.0	2.9	2.0	1.1	3.9	6.6	2.2	3.7	5.7
services - business, repair, personal, entertainment	21.1	26.5	11.3	51.3	6.5	8.4	9.4	13.4	8.9
professional and related services	(a)	(a)	5.1	9.8	5.3	16.2	7.8	18.8	17.5
public administration	5.6	5.9	5.8	2.4	4.7	3.1	2.4	9.9	8.0
not reported	1.1	0.0	2.1	1.7	1.3	2.1	...	...	...

Sources: U.S., Department of Commerce, Bureau of the Census, as cited in Appendix C in Philadelphia, Commission on Human Relations, *Puerto Ricans in Philadelphia* (April 1954); and U.S., Department of Commerce, Bureau of the Census, *U.S. Census of Population*, 1950 and 1970.

(a) All services combined.

represented in manufacturing and overrepresented in nonprofessional services.

Between 1950 and 1970, Philadelphia's economy shifted from manufacturing to financial and professional services. According to geographer Peter Muller, "Since Philadelphia was perhaps the most overindustrialized of the nation's large old cities, it is suffering more than others as its manufacturing plants continue to die or emigrate" (Muller, Meyer, and Cybriwsky 1976:55). Factories left the city for the suburbs, for other regions of the United States and for overseas. The federal government's procurement policies during World War II had shifted the growth of industry from the Northeast to the southern and western United States. The Highway Acts of 1944 and 1956 created more than 160 miles of federally funded highway in the Delaware Valley region between 1950 and 1973, facilitating the suburbanization of industry and people. State, county and municipal governments issued tax-free bonds to fund the acquisition of land and its development by industry (Oberman and Kozakowski 1976:93-94).

Within the city, redevelopment programs created more professional service jobs, determined their downtown location, and continued the trend toward increasingly polarized incomes at the top and bottom of the pay scale. City officials formed public–private partnerships with business leaders in the expanding service sector. One such alliance, the Greater Philadelphia Movement, established in 1949, challenged the earlier dominance of the Chamber of Commerce, which represented manufacturing interests. The 1950s became known as "the reform era," as civic and business leaders forged links with city government and began downtown renewal programs that dictated Philadelphia's economic development. Reformers organized an electoral coalition, comprising the city's business leaders, trade unionists, African Americans and Democratic Party ward leaders, that defeated the entrenched Republican machine in the mayoral elections of 1951 (Adams 1990:212–214). Rather than mitigating the negative consequences of economic shifts,"redevelopment can be seen to have helped to reinforce the existing dichotomy between the haves and the have-nots in Philadelphia"as Carolyn Adams et al. (1991:118) argue.

Aggravating the local economic situation, plant closings and job loss began during the 1960s and accelerated in the 1970s. The city claimed 61% of the jobs in the area in 1960, but only 48% in 1972. Industries remaining in the city were those with older plants that "because of long term plant investments and the need for cheap unskilled labor not available in the suburbs would simply find it too costly to move" (Muller, Meyer and Cybriwsky 1976:57). The textile and clothing industries were among the hardest hit by plant closings. Changes in clothing styles, relocation of industry, the increase in clothing imports and the growth of conglomerates played roles. Between 1950 and 1979, the number of textile workers decreased from 42,000 to 18,000 and the number of clothing workers in the union from 20,000 to 8,000 (Haines 1982:212, 216).

Manufacturing jobs decreased from 35% to 28% of the labor force between 1950 and 1970, with women's employment decreasing by 10% and men's by 4% (see Table 6-2). Professional services, in contrast, increased from 8% to 18% of the labor force. These trends continued during the next twenty years; manufacturing jobs declined from 28% to 14% of the labor force, while professional services increased from 18% to 30%. In a study of 173 firms that closed between 1976 and 1979, Hochner and Zibman (1982:207) found that multinational and conglomerate firms "were responsible for the overwhelming majority of jobs lost among the 173 firms." These were the largest and most successful firms that relocated in search of higher corporate growth rates. These authors (1982:199) concluded, "the decisions are the outcome not of the free market but of economic and political concentration which gives these enterprises great power and of federal and state government policies on taxes, subsidies, loans, defense spending, labor law, and economic development which favor the multinational and conglomerate firms."

African Americans and Puerto Ricans remained concentrated in declining sectors of the economy and were unable to gain a foothold in the expanding sectors. In 1968, PBES, the Pennsylvania Bureau of Employment Security (1968:4–5) claimed that, despite manufacturing losses, the "area managed to recoup its position because of heavy representation in the fast-growing service sector." Yet, the new professional services did not employ those most affected by manufacturing decline. Instead, professional jobs were filled by the new suburbanites, while manufacturing jobs in the suburbs were out of reach for African Americans and Puerto Ricans living in the city. For the former, the suburbanization of industry continued earlier patterns of exclusion. For the latter, manufacturing provided a brief period of employment followed by the loss of jobs. As this sector declined, African Americans increasingly gained a foothold and Puerto Ricans remained over represented. While professional services grew, the two groups remained concentrated at the lower end of the occupational structure, in low-paying jobs with little room for advancement (see Table 6-3). In 1970, the majority of African American (58%) and

Table 6-2: Industry of Employed Persons, Philadelphia, 1950, 1970, and 1990

	1950	1970	1990
Number	827,636	763,520	651,621
Percent in:			
agriculture, forestry, fisheries	0.2	0.4	0.5
construction, mining	5.6	4.7	4.5
manufacturing	35.1	28.2	13.6
transport, communications, public utilities	8.4	6.5	7.5
wholesale, retail trade	21.4	20.1	19.7
finance, insurance, real estate	4.3	5.7	8.2
services - business, repair, personal, entertainment	10.3	8.9	9.0
professional and related services	8.0	17.5	29.6
public administration	4.9	8.0	7.5
not reported	1.7	. . .	. . .

Sources: U.S., Department of Commerce, Bureau of the Census, *U.S. Census of Population*, 1950, 1970 and 1990.

Puerto Rican (66%) men worked as operatives, laborers and nonprofessional service workers, compared to 40% of all men. Most African American (54%) and Puerto Rican (63%) women were also in these occupations, in contrast to only 37% of all women. As sales and clerical work became the largest occupations of Philadelphia's women, African American and Puerto Rican women were left by the wayside.

Labor force participation shifted as the city's economy changed. Because of their greater concentration in certain sectors of the economy, the contrast among the city's women was greatest. As manufacturing declined and personal services remained a stable employer, African American women continued to enter the workforce while Puerto Rican women left it. Between 1950 and 1970, labor force participation for all women increased from 34% to 43% (see Table 6-3). The labor force participation of African American women increased more dramatically, from 40% to 59%, while that of Puerto Rican women decreased from 33% to 31%.

Table 6-3: Selected Economic Characteristics of Puerto Ricans, Blacks, and Total Population, Philadelphia, 1950, 1970, and 1990

	1950			1970			1990		
	Puerto Rican	Black	Total	Puerto Rican	Black	Total	Puerto Rican	Black	White
Number:	1,910	427,829	2,071,605	26,702	653,747	1,948,609	40,920	469,251	704,820
In labor force (a): male	58.4	72.0	77.4	73.8	72.2	74.1	62.2	63.1	69.4
female	33.4	39.9	33.9	30.8	59.1	43.3	36.4	54.2	50.4
Occupations: Professional/technical/managerial: male	10.0	5.7	18.4	5.8	10.2	18.3	13.2(b)	19.4	28.3
female	20.6	5.1	12.8	11.4	11.3	16.1			
Sale/clerical: male	6.7	9.0	17.3	14.7	21.6	29.2	27.5(c)	33.4	36.8
female	11.7	6.8	36.3	22.1	31.0	44.7			
Craftsmen: male	7.8	11.5	22.0	12.2	9.8	12.5	10.6	6.6	10.5
female	2.9	1.1	2.1	3.5	2.6	2.4			
Service: male	36.7	49.0	9.1	14.6	24.5	14.8	16.7	26.6	11.9
female	8.8	53.2	19.3	11.0	32.3	18.9	29.1	16.6	11.9
Operators/laborers: male	35.5	22.7	32.0	51.8	33.4	24.9			
female	55.9	32.3	27.9	51.9	22.3	17.7			
Farmers: male	1.1			0.8	0.6	0.2	3.0	0.4	0.5
female	0.0			0.0	0.5	0.2			
Not reported: male	2.2	2.0	1.2						
female	0.2	1.6	1.6						

Sources: Philadelphia, Commission on Human Relations, *Puerto Ricans in Philadelphia* (April 1954); and U.S. Department of Commerce, Bureau of the Census, *U.S. Census of Population*, 1950, 1970, 1990.

(a) Persons 14 years and older for 1950, and 16 and over for 1970 and 1990.

(b) Male and female combined.

(c) For 1990, technical is included with sales/clerical.

For men citywide, labor force participation decreased from 77% to 74% between 1950 and 1970; by 1970 the rates for African American and Puerto Rican men were comparable to the city totals. In spite of modest improvements in economic status during the 1960s, African Americans and Puerto Ricans remained poorer than their counterparts citywide. By 1960, Puerto Ricans earned only 59% and African Americans 73% of the total population's mean family income. Ten years later, Puerto Ricans still earned only 62% and African Americans 79% of the total family income (U.S. Department of Commerce 1960, 1970).

Between 1970 and 1990, economic shifts continued to have a negative effect on African Americans and Puerto Ricans. By 1990, they were still under represented in the growing sectors of the city's economy, as professional and managerial occupations employed 28% of Whites and only 19% of African Americans and 13% of Puerto Ricans (Table 6-3). Instead, African Americans were still over represented as nonprofessional service workers, with 24% of their employed workers in contrast to only 12% of Whites. Puerto Ricans were still over represented as operators or laborers, with 29% compared to only 12% of Whites. Economic shifts and earlier employment patterns continued to shape labor force participation rates. Men's overall rates decreased from 74% of all men in 1970, to 69% of White men, 63% of African American men and 62% of Puerto Rican men in 1990. For women, the disparities in labor force participation remained greater than those for men. Their labor force participation increased from 43% of all women in 1970 to 50% of White women and 54% of African American women, but only 36% of Puerto Rican women. The impact of deindustrialization was most evident among workers who had been most concentrated in the manufacturing sector— Puerto Rican women (Colon-Warren 1996).

Meanwhile, government policies and the actions of private investors fostered residential segregation. Postwar federal housing policies focused on home ownership, public housing, and urban renewal. The Federal Housing Administration (FHA) promoted home ownership through mortgage programs, but it limited mortgage loans to new housing, creating a housing boom in the suburbs and denying mortgages in the city. In addition, FHA relied on the 1930s guidelines for the Home Owners' Loan Corporation, which appraised housing in racial and ethnic terms and had restrictions against providing loans to African Americans in White areas. Mortgages were denied in the city's older industrial and streetcar neighborhoods, which were "redlined" based on explicitly anti-Black and anti-ethnic criteria. According to Bartelt (1993:133), these policies "ensured that the FHA subsidized segregation." Similarly, public housing policies, both large project construction and scattered site (or Section 8) placements in properties leased by the city, increased segregation as African Americans were placed in "Black areas." Summarizing the impact of federal policies, Bartelt (1993:151) concludes: "housing policies prior to the 1970s supported a predominantly White movement to the suburbs and a disproportionate allocation of home-ownership options to White families. At the same time, urban renewal and public housing policies hurt predominantly Black communities by displacing their residents and reinforcing de facto segregation." Although the scholarship focuses on African Americans, government policies had a similar impact on Puerto Ricans who were settling in the city.

Rather than improving low-income housing, urban renewal programs sought to attract private investment and led to gentrification and the redevelopment of commercial and business centers. According to Adams (1991:104), for Philadelphia's redevelopment officials, "Making the transition to a corporate service economy implied remaking the city to attract and retain the professional White-collar classes as residents and to downplay the presence of the poor and working classes." In the 1960 Plan for Center City, policy makers focused on housing for White, middle-class professionals. Gentrification was facilitated by federal tax policies, including the 1976 historic-preservation tax credits and the 1986 tax reform, reducing interest deductions except for those on mortgages and home equity loans. Other neighborhoods were crippled by disinvestment. As federal agencies disinvested, so did banks and individual owners—through building abandonment or deterioration. African Americans became concentrated in the city's older industrial neighborhoods and streetcar suburbs, areas north and west of Center City. Puerto Ricans lived in a narrow strip running north and south between Black and White Philadelphia. It was a settlement pattern shaped by racial discrimination, "White flight" and government policies.

Segregation within the city intensified, even as immigration and racial and ethnic diversity increased. By 1990, the city's population was 52% White, 39% African American, 6% Latino, and 3% Asian and Pacific Islander. Puerto Ricans were 4% of the total population and 76% of the Latino population. During the 1980s, Asians increased by 145% and the Spanish-speaking population by 40%, reflecting the impact of the 1965 immigration reforms, which eliminated national origin quotas and instituted preference categories based on family reunification and occupations. Yet, as the fifth largest city, Philadelphia ranked only sixteenth as the destination of new immigrants. By 1990, 72% of African Americans resided in census tracts that were 90% or more African American. Similarly, 80% of Puerto Ricans resided in 15 of the city's 364 census tracts (U.S. Department of Commerce 1990; Goode 1994:213-218; Goode and Schneider 1994:4). African Americans and Puerto Ricans were concentrated in areas of the city that experienced the loss of manufacturing jobs and that were not aided by public redevelopment funds.

The combined impact of economic change, residential segregation and government policy was evident. During the 1980s, "the region's income distribution became more unequal," and "the metropolitan area's poor became increasingly concentrated in the city" as Madden and Stull (1991:148, 97) note. In 1988, the poverty rate was 8% for the metropolitan area and 16% for the city. While the decade witnessed increases in average family and per capita income, significant gaps remained not only between the suburbs and the city, but also among racial groups. Average annual household income for African Americans was 61% and for Latinos 53% of that of White households. Similarly, employment increased for all groups during the second half of the decade, but remained lower for African Americans and Latinos. In short, "the incomes of the poorest quintile of families . . . substantially decreased relative to the incomes of the richest quintile" (Madden and Stull 1991:148), or put another way, the rich got richer and the poor poorer. As Madden and Stull conclude (1991:149), "the most prosperous residents of the metropolitan area became increasingly isolated, both physically and economically, from the least prosperous over the decade." By 1990, Philadelphia was ranked the worst of the fifty largest cities in terms of number of census tracts with high concentrations of the very poor (Adams et al. 1991:27).

Thus, African Americans and Puerto Ricans recruited to the Philadelphia area became displaced labor migrants after War II. As recent arrivals, they bore the brunt of the transition to a postindustrial economy. As Theodore Hershberg et al. (1981) write, "Today's Blacks inherit the oldest stock of deteriorated housing once inhabited by two earlier waves of immigrants, but the jobs that once were located nearby and that provided previous newcomers with avenues for upward mobility are gone." African Americans and Puerto Ricans also bore the brunt of residential segregation and "White flight," which transformed the racial composition and eroded the economic foundations of urban areas. These migrants-turned-residents became concentrated in urban areas that were devoid of economic opportunities. It was the combined impact of eco-

nomic change and residential segregation that created conditions of concentrated poverty.

"CULTURE OF POVERTY" AND "UNDERCLASS" PARADIGMS

From the World War II era to the present, African Americans and Puerto
Ricans have been perceived not as displaced labor migrants, but as people with "problems," who create "problems" for the community. As they
settled in Philadelphia, social service workers reacted with alarm. In
1949, one social worker contacted the Glassboro farm labor camp director, who assured her that he was "well aware of the problems that might
be created by Puerto Ricans coming to cities like Philadelphia" and was
"very willing to cooperate in any way possible that might solve the PR
problem" (Friese 1949:1, 2). In its 1962 study, the Pennsylvania Economy League wanted to provide information to "underprivileged newcomers," African Americans and Puerto Ricans, but feared it "might
make Philadelphia more attractive to such persons and that they would
migrate here in increasing numbers." That, according to the league,
would "be undesirable because Philadelphia has a surplus of unskilled
labor" and the majority of "nonWhite" and Puerto Rican inmigrants "fall
in the underprivileged category" (p. x). The migration and settlement of
African Americans and Puerto Ricans, thus, were perceived and discussed as a problem. As scholars and policy makers sought to explain
their assumed "problems," they relied on the "culture of poverty" paradigm, which encapsulated a set of assumptions underlying public perceptions and scholarly works and explained their poverty by blaming
their cultures. More recently, some scholars and policy makers have la-
beled those living in conditions of concentrated poverty as "the underclass." Both discourses have national and local dimensions.

In the postwar era, the experiences of African Americans and Puerto
Ricans were interpreted through the lens of the "culture of poverty."
Writing in 1965, anthropologist Oscar Lewis articulated the "culture of
poverty" and applied the concept to Puerto Ricans. Lewis (1963:xliii)
considered "poverty and its associated traits as a culture . . .with its own
structure and rationale, as a way of life which is passed down from generation to generation along family lines." He severed the culture of
poverty from the conditions of poverty, and presented it as a self-perpet-
uating culture. Migrating Puerto Ricans carried their culture of poverty
with them so that "many of the problems of Puerto Ricans in New York

have their origin in the slums of Puerto Rico" (1965:xxviii). For Lewis (1965:lii, xi), Puerto Ricans had a "relatively thin" culture marked by little integration with the larger society, little organization in the ethnic community beyond the level of the family, families that verbally emphasized unity but rarely achieved it and individuals with a high level of tolerance for pathologies (see also Lewis 1973). The same attitudes were ascribed to African Americans and were also termed "pathologies" (Katz 1993:13–14; Trotter 1991). From this perspective, African Americans and Puerto Ricans were deficient in their cultures, their families and their communal life.[5] Proponents of the "culture of poverty'" nonetheless, advocated social programs to ameliorate the "problems" of these groups.

In Philadelphia, "culture of poverty" perspectives appeared in the Pennsylvania Economy League's 1962 study (II-1, II-2), which viewed African Americans and Puerto Ricans as "underprivileged" migrants with a distinct set of "problems" stemming from their cultures—that should be remedied through "assimilation." It attributed their problems to immigration and the migrants' "rural or slum background," while also noting "those 'problems' which arise from poverty, ignorance or color and which are common to both immigrants and natives in the 'underprivileged' class."

The League (II-1) saw little distinction between migrants and "some native Philadelphians [who] display a similar ignorance," stemming only from "poverty, ignorance, or color." Here, it emphasized "cultural" explanations for social problems, rather than the disruptions of migration or the challenges of resettlement. The proposed solution was "assimilation," defined as "the adjustment by the immigrants to the laws of Philadelphia and to the social mores generally accepted by the majority of Philadelphians." The League stressed that it did not want a migrant to assimilate to "the standards which appear to prevail or do prevail in the neighborhood where he resides"— neighborhoods marked by "high degrees of social disorganization and consequent lawlessness and dependency." The League's use of the "majority of Philadelphians" implied a White, middle-class standard. The League wanted to make migrants "self-supporting and law-abiding." This emphasis on "assimilation" suggested that the migrants' "problems" stemmed from their own cultures and could be remedied by modifying individual and group behavior.[6]

Philadelphia District Health and Welfare Council's (PDHWC) 1960 study (6–8) revealed similar attitudes toward African American and Puerto Rican newcomers. The Council attributed the differences in two neighborhoods to the characteristics of residents. Kensington, a White ethnic area, was praised for its "strong community pride," "parochialism" and "stability." The report interpreted "parochialism" and "stability" as positive, even while noting that the boundaries maintained by the local council "serve not only to confine the Council's efforts geographically but deter communication with adjoining communities or with minority groups within its boundaries." The study found that, "Residents . . . fear possible racial change more than they do redevelopment and reportedly would rather have their houses torn down than to sell it [sic] to Negroes or Puerto Ricans—and anticipate 'real trouble' should such a move-in occur."

White residents moved out and, when necessary, redefined their western boundary, "which coincides with the drifting color and Spanish language line." In contrast, the study (p. 12) described east of Ninth, an area of first settlement "for Philadelphia bound southern Negro families and for new Puerto Ricans," as an area that "never seemed to have had any distinctive neighborhood identity." In east of Ninth, problems were caused, in part, by "rapid changes and inevitable social disorganization" (PDHWC 1960:20). Thus, for the Council, community "problems" came with the migrants and stemmed from racial change.

Based on its perceptions of residents, the Council defined solutions differently for the two areas. For Kensington, the study recommended a "neighborhood conservation program" and "above all, community organization techniques to bring residents into full participation in the program" with "block organizations and community councils" (PDHWC 1960:5). The Council assumed that these methods would fail in east of Ninth. Here, the problems were "fortified by the high proportion of people not yet accustomed to family and community life in Philadelphia and who have a minimum of the community social skills that are required for fruitful life here." Instead of residents' "full participation," the study advocated the intervention of those thought more capable—community "troubleshooters," a youth worker, social workers better trained in human relations, and business owners who no longer lived there. The Council was confident that what was needed was "the right kind of service," and recommended a focus on "immediate goals" rather than a "long-range effort." Social workers lacked faith in the abilities of "Negro and Puerto Rican" newcomers but retained faith in social programs (PDHWC 1960:20).

By the late 1970s, the national discourse no longer defined African Americans and Puerto as "newcomers" but as static minority groups that comprised the "underclass." For adherents of this concept, the "underclass" "a new social stratum, identified by a set of interlocking behaviors, not primarily by poverty, dominated the wastelands that were all that remained of America's urban-industrial heartland" (Katz 1993:5). While some use the term "underclass" for conditions of concentrated poverty, others use it to imply "pathological" behaviors. The criteria for the latter definition of the "underclass" mirrored Lewis' criteria for the "culture of poverty," including pathological behavior and a lack of integration with the larger society or social isolation. The "underclass" paradigm explained concentrated poverty by emphasizing the problematic behavior of those living in poverty, blaming social programs for fostering dependency and pathologies in these groups or, sometimes, claiming biological and genetic inferiority.

In his 1990 ethnography, Elijah Anderson (x) interprets the conditions of concentrated poverty in the "Black ghetto of Northtown" in ways that echo the culture of poverty. Although he mentions deindustrialization and the loss of jobs, ultimately he focuses on individual behavior, especially of young African American men, and the demise of the "community" as the central causes of poverty in the "ghetto." The problems, according to Anderson (1990:66), arise as youth "lose perspective and lack an outlook and sensibility that would allow them to negotiate the wider system of employment and society in general." These youth scorn subsistence jobs and unemployment results, in part, from "their inability or unwillingness to follow basic rules of middle-class propriety with respect to dress and comportment." Like the "culture of poverty," this "underclass" is marked by "antisocial behavior, "family disorganization" and the fact that residents are "only loosely anchored to conventional institutions." For Anderson (1990:237–39), there are "at least two distinct but overlapping cultures." The "middle-class culture" comprises "middle-class Whites, along with a small number of middle-class Blacks and others," whose "values are those associated with the 'great tradition' of Western culture." The second culture is that of the "large Black ghetto." This second culture fosters the "view of the area as an urban jungle," an area "thought to embody a 'little tradition' and [that] has the reputation of being economically depressed and beset by classic urban ills."

As with the "culture of poverty," the definition of the "problem" shapes the recommended solution. Anderson concurs with the view of the "large Black ghetto": "many characteristics of the jungle can indeed be found there" (1990:239). He blames the Black middle class for contributing "however unintentionally, to the construction of a local underclass" (1990:66) by moving out of the neighborhood and leaving "the poorer, uneducated Blacks without tangible role models or instructive agents of social control" (1990:60). The "poorer, uneducated Blacks" cannot be "role models," according to Anderson, and the residents of the "jungle" are incapable of improving their lives or their community. Hence, the Black middle class— not segregation, gentrification, or economic decline— is responsible for the increasing isolation of the "underclass." The solution is for the federal government "to enact policies that will give young people a serious stake in conventional society" through education, job training, and drug treatment, and to encourage the private sector to provide employment. Anderson's solution is, in large part, to change individual behavior (1990:253-254).

In his discussion of Philadelphia's "underclass," Roger Lane (1991:405) links the "underclass" with the "culture of poverty" by referring to "the behavior associated with an underclass 'culture of poverty'." He defines the "underclass" as people with no legitimate jobs or the ability to connect with the world of work due to handicaps such as lack of education and knowledge of the requirements of modern employers. Yet, "culture" plays a role as well. Defining "culture" as "a widely shared set not only of formal values but of attitudes, habits, and priorities," he concludes that the attitudes, habits and priorities of the underclass prevent people from living "up to these ideals" and that, "In addition to poverty itself, . . . the African-American experience has created a large number of people who are easily discouraged, unrealistic about the relation of ends to means, lacking pride in themselves and trust in others." He points to crime, drug addiction and family instability, as behaviors which may stem from long-term structural unemployment, but that also become obstacles for advancement. In contrast to Anderson, Lane devotes more attention to economic restructuring and the role of racism in excluding urban Blacks, "in Philadelphia and elsewhere" from the urban industrial revolution. Hence, for Lane, the "underclass" is the result of both "structural conditions which simply deny its members the chance to work," and "other 'cultural' factors within the group, which make its members unable or unwilling to take advantage of opportunities even when offered" (Lane 1991:376-379).

Lane's view of the "underclass" (1991:404) shapes his proposed solutions. He does not turn to those he describes as, "the great pool of 300,000 undereducated, sometimes hostile, poor Philadelphians who constitute the underclass." Like Anderson, he points to the Black middle class as part of the problem and as part of the solution. Middle class African Americans moved out of the poorest areas, leaving "no 'old heads,' no role models, no one to help in any way" (1991:378). Lane (1991:392) suggests the need for "formal voluntary action" to replace "the old neighborhoods and natural networks" and to provide "role modeling." Yet, because of his greater attention to "structural conditions," Lane also advocates the involvement of all levels of government and the corporate business community to increase jobs and improve education.

The continuities between the "culture of poverty" and the "underclass" paradigms lie in the targets of these labels—World War II migrants of color who were never considered migrants—and in their focus on the presumed "problems" of these groups. Although many Europeans were unwelcome during their own immigration, in retrospect, they have appeared in the scholarship and in the public imagination as hardworking, determined individuals who migrated to work and improve their lives and who succeeded in the "American dream."[7] Similarly, as historian Jacqueline Jones suggests, White Appalachian migrants encountered fewer obstacles in their new environments than did African Americans—whose obstacles were compounded by racism and discrimination—and have not been stigmatized with the "underclass" label despite urban poverty (Jones 1993). "Culture of poverty" and "underclass" interpretations continue to stigmatize African American and Puerto Rican migrants and blame them for their poverty.

CONCLUSION

With their focus on "deficient" cultures and "pathological" behaviors, "culture of poverty" and "underclass" perceptions have shaped public policies. Even though most "culture of poverty" proponents called for social programs and most "underclass" proponents are calling for their elimination, both have assumed the need to transform individual and group behaviors, with little attention paid to the larger forces that shape and impinge on those behaviors. Both paradigms ignore the history of migration, the role of the state and employers in recruiting migrants as cheap laborers, the structural changes accompanying the transition to a postindustrial economy, and residential segregation. In short, government policies, structural inequalities and racism are not viewed as central to the challenges confronting African Americans and Puerto Ricans. Perhaps, in the World War II era, these paradigms reflect the demise of biological racism, but they operate as more "culturally" based ideologies in marginalizing those who were wanted as laborers but not as community members. Instead of being viewed as displaced labor migrants,

African Americans and Puerto Ricans are still perceived as a "community problem."

At the same time, the negative perceptions of poor people of color embedded in the "culture of poverty" and "underclass" paradigms have influenced ideas about who is capable of addressing the issues confronting the urban poor. As Jackson suggests (1993:403), there has been historical continuity, as "reformist experts and policy makers debate and design programs that can be sold to the overwhelmingly middle-class electorate, without seeking to redress the class bias in the electorate itself, and without more directly involving the poor in transforming the conditions of their own lives." Both the "culture of poverty" and the "underclass" consider their subjects, African Americans and Puerto Ricans, incapable of intelligently shaping their own futures. As a result, these groups confront structural conditions of concentrated poverty and racial ideologies that render them responsible for and incapable of improving those conditions.

NOTES

[1] The author thanks John Betancur, Douglas Gills, the participants of the 1995 conference, and Jerma Jackson for their helpful comments on earlier versions of this essay; Victor Vazquez for his research assistance; and Kellee Blake of the National Archives— Mid Atlantic Region.

[2] For reviews of the literature, see Katz 1993, Trotter 1991 and Moore and Pinderhughes 1993.

[3] For example, Katz (1993) does not include Puerto Ricans or Latinos/as, while Moore and Pinderhughes (1993) begin with a discussion of the exclusive focus on African Americans and the applicability of the "underclass" to Latinos/as. For an exception, see Torres 1995.

[4] Between 1942 and 1945, 400,000 foreign workers—Mexicans, British West Indians, British Hondurans, Canadians, and Newfoundlanders—were employed in the USA (Henderson 1945).

[5] For an example, see Frazer and Moynihan 1963.

[6] For a discussion of social scientists equating culture with behavior, see Kelley 1994.

[7] For a preliminary discussion of the different treatments in the scholarship, see Whalen 1994, Chapter I.

CHAPTER 7

Pulling Together or Pulling Apart?
Black–Latino Cooperation and Competition in the U.S. Labor Market

CEDRIC HERRING
MICHAEL BENNETT
AND DOUGLAS C. GILLS

People of color in the U.S.A are currently confronted by several complex issues that threaten to halt the incremental improvements they have been making in their quality of life.[1] At the national level, these issues include attacks on affirmative action, with a potentially deleterious effect on economic mobility opportunities, welfare reform, which will likely increase their levels of poverty; and anti-immigrant initiatives that characterize immigrants as criminals and welfare abusers, indeed a drain on the U.S. economy. These efforts have been introduced into the political process with varying degrees of success. Unfortunately, all of them help foster a climate in which violence, hatred, and racism can fester. Without question, many policies important to Blacks and Latinos reflect the shift toward conservatism as the dominant political mood of Whites in power. In a climate in which there is greater resistance among Whites to programs that would reduce racial inequality and less collective activism between Blacks and Latinos, it is likely that many of the proposals now on the public agenda will do more harm than good for all peoples of color.

As real and threatening as these issues are for both Blacks and Latinos, they are not the entire story. While these two communities have been the victims of discrimination and subordination from the Anglo community, rarely have they coalesced to form partnerships and coalitions to contest their common foes, especially outside a few urban centers (as identified in other chapters in this volume). In fact, the levels of "social distance"—i.e., the level of unwillingness among members of one (racial) group to accept or approve and support common demands calling for collective efforts and interactions with members of another (racial) outgroup—historically has been great between Blacks and Latinos (Herring 1993).

To many analysts, the need for cooperation and coalitions between Blacks and Latinos is self-evident. In their efforts to find objective, and even subjective, bases for unity of action between these two groups in U.S. cities, many analysts ignore some of the real issues that divide them. Issues such as access to jobs in the shrinking U.S. labor market may produce increased competition between Blacks and Latinos and, therefore, generate more conflict between them.

If would-be coalition builders are sincere in their desire to have Blacks and Latinos unite around matters of common concern, they must be willing to take an honest and frank look at issues that potentially separate the members of these communities. This paper puts forth such an effort. It provides an assessment of (1) the social distance between Blacks and Latinos, (2) the effects of Latino population size on the earnings and employment rates of African Americans, and (3) the effects of African American population size on the earnings and employment rates of Latinos. The results of these analyses are used to assess the potential for cooperation between Blacks and Latinos in their quest to secure political and economic empowerment in the U.S. We discuss the implications of our findings for future research and policy directions.

BLACK–LATINO SOCIAL DISTANCE

In racial and ethnic relations, "social distance" reflects the degree to which members of racial and ethnic groups are disinclined to accept members of other racial and ethnic outgroups in varying social contexts. This notion of social distance has become closely associated with theories of interethnic relations and prejudice.

In the United States, the dominant explanation of interethnic relations has been the "assimilation" perspective. This perspective, associated with Robert E. Park, one of the first major American theorists of ethnic relations, suggests that intergroup contacts and relations regularly go through stages of a race relations cycle. This progressive and irreversible cycle consists of contacts, competition, accommodation, and eventual assimilation (Park and Burgess 1921; Park, Burgess, and McKenzie 1925).

Migration and exploration bring peoples from different cultures into contact with each other. Contact, in turn, leads to new forms of social organization for both the natives and the newcomers. Also, with the new interactions come economic competition and subsequent conflict between the indigenous population and the foreigners. In the accommodation stage, both groups are compelled to make adjustments to their new social situations so that relations might be stabilized. Finally, in the assimilation stage, there will be an inevitable disappearance of cultural and ethnic differences that distinguish these once rivaling ethnic groups.

The assimilation perspective argues that cultural differences between national-origin groups are passed on to later generations in progressively diluted forms and ultimately disappear in modern society. This belief rests on the assumption that the importance of ascriptively oriented relations wanes with increasing emphasis on universalism. As time passes, therefore, ethnic antagonisms subside and ethnic groups become increasingly similar in their world views.

The "Anglo-conformity" variant of the assimilation perspective (e.g., Gordon 1981) claims that to the degree that there is an identifiable "American culture," it is Anglo-Saxon (English). Further, it suggests that most ethnic groups have adapted to the core Anglo-Saxon culture. American ethnic groups will have some degree of consensus about which racial and ethnic groups are to be favored and which are to be disfavored: virtually all assimilated U.S. ethnic groups will favor those nations that most closely resemble Anglo-Saxon cultural forms.

Milton Gordon (1964) earlier explained assimilation as a series of stages through which various ethnic groups pass. He identified seven stages in the adaptation of ethnic groups to the host society: (1) cultural assimilation or acculturation, in which ethnic groups change their cultural patterns to more closely fit the patterns of the dominant culture in the host society; (2) structural assimilation, in which ethnic group members are granted extensive access into the social organizations and institutions of the host society; (3) marital assimilation or amalgamation, in which ethnic group members begin to date and intermarry with members of the dominant culture; (4) identificational assimilation, in which ethnic group members develop a sense of peoplehood based virtually exclusively on the tendencies of the dominant culture; (5) attitude receptional assimilation, in which members of the ethnic group are no longer the targets of prejudicial feelings from members of the dominant culture; (6) behavior receptional assimilation, in which members of the ethnic group are no longer the targets of any discriminatory practices from members of the dominant culture; and (7) civic assimilation in which there are no real signs of value or power conflict between members of the ethnic group and members of the dominant culture. Assimilation, in this view, is invariably unidirectional and progressive.

In contrast, the "cultural pluralism" variant emphasizes the persistence of cultural heritage as the basis of the continued importance of ascriptive groups (Abramson 1973; Greeley 1974). It argues that immigrant groups often remain culturally distinct from the dominant Anglo culture beyond the time frame predicted by the Anglo-conformity perspective (e.g., Glazer and Moynihan 1970; Greeley 1974). Through multicultural interactions in the schools and the homogenizing influence of the media and other institutions, ethnic groups do become more similar to each other (i.e., more "Americanized" not "Anglicized") over several generations. Analysts, however, point to U.S. pluralism and argue that a number of distinctive ethnic groups never assimilate to the Anglo-Saxon way of life. Instead, they argue, some immigrant groups migrated to America with cultural backgrounds that were already similar to that of English settlers. Thus, their apparent "assimilation" to Anglo ways is really nothing more than a continuation of patterns that existed prior to coming to the U.S. Other groups will retain certain distinctive cultural traits. Bona fide aspects of the heritage from their native lands will continue to thrive in America. Thus, according to this perspective, U.S. ethnic groups share a number of cultural traits with the general society, but also they retain major nationality characteristics from their homelands as well.

The cultural pluralism perspective suggests that U.S. ethnic groups will have varied opinions about which groups are to be favored and which are to be disfavored. If, for example, there is an ethnic group that is a historical enemy of Africa but an ally of Mexico, African Americans will be more likely to feel unfavorable toward the group whereas Mexican Americans will be more likely to feel favorable with respect to it. By the same token, contemporary hostilities between different ethnic groups within the United States can emerge, as different groups with no prior histories of antagonism develop antipathy for each other within the American context. Still, to the degree that there are people from nations that closely resemble the U.S. socially, politically, and culturally, there should be relatively more support for the people from those nations among all U.S. ethnic groups. Conversely, if there are people from nations that are viewed as being very dissimilar from the U.S., there should be relatively less support for them among virtually all U.S. ethnic groups.

A third group of theories that attempts to account for interethnic relations are "group conflict" theories. These theories start with the premise that economic forces are at the root of ethnic antagonisms. Subordination, exploitation and resource inequalities play major roles in ethnic stratification and interethnic relations. Variants of this paradigm include internal colonialism perspectives (Hechter 1975; Blauner 1972), segmentation theories (Bonacich 1972), and middleman theories (Bonacich and Modell 1980). These explanations focus on the special roles of "racial" ethnic groups who, unlike their "White" ethnic counterparts, have been excluded from aspects of U.S. society.

According to these perspectives, U.S. culture contains an arrangement of racial and ethnic images that supports the subordination of Asians, Africans, Latinos, and Native Americans (i.e., groups with so-called Third World nationalities). As a nation founded on the basis of Eurocentric images, the ideologies in force are those that purport the superiority of European cultural forms and promote the domination of non-Whites, non-Westerners. Because non-European, nonWhite ethnic groups do not share such world views, they are not likely to hold the same preferences as European ethnics. To the degree that any group empathizes with "Third World" peoples, group conflict perspectives suggest that U.S. ethnic groups will have varied opinions about which nations' citizens are to be favored and which are to be disfavored. According to these formulations, the primary distinction will be between those peoples favored by "racial ethnics" (i.e., nationalities[2]) versus those favored by White ethnics.

Of course other (nonracial) conflicts can exist, but non-Western ethnic groups will be more likely to favor non-Western nations than will European ancestry groups. Also, to the degree that there are nations that closely resemble the homelands of racial ethnic groups socially, politically and culturally, there should be relatively more support for the peoples of those nations among those ethnic groups. Conversely, if there are nations that are viewed as being antagonistic toward or very dissimilar from those nationality (or "racial ethnic") groups' homelands, there should be relatively less support for the peoples from such countries among those nationalities.

We seek to test these simple hypotheses using the available data of a national study, the 1990 General Social Survey, to examine patterns of social distance between Latinos and African Americans. Second, we consider urban regional, and city to city variations where Latinos and African Americans have been historically and are currently concentrated, relative to White population concentrations.

DO AFRICAN AMERICANS AND LATINOS GET ALONG? A LOOK AT SOME PATTERNS

The Data

The first data source for this paper is the 1990 General Social Survey (GSS). The GSS is an independent survey sampling English-speaking persons 18 years of age or over, living in the United States in noninstitutional settings (Davis and Smith 1992). Information from respondents who reported their ancestry and answered questions about sentiments toward contact with various ethnic and nationality groups were used to operationalize variables used in the analysis. These operationalizations and the variable labels (in italics) are presented below.

Operationalizations

In order to operationalize ethnicity, respondents were asked "from what countries or part of the world did their ancestors come?" Self-reported ethnic identifications include these groups: African (and West Indian), Asian (Chinese, Japanese, Filipino, Indian, and Arabic), European (English, Welsh, Scottish, Irish, Italian, French, German, Austrian, Danish, Finnish, Norwegian, Swedish, Polish, Czechoslovakian, Hungarian, Lithuanian, Russian, Yugoslavian and Rumanian) and Latino (Mexican, Puerto Rican, Spanish-speaking, and other Spanish). Respondents who reported that they were *Jewish* or were raised as Jewish were also coded for this ethnicity.

Three items were used to measure levels of assimilation and social distance. To measure resistance to integration in schools with Black children, respondents were asked whether they would be willing to send their children to schools in which up to half of the students were African Americans. To measure attitude/behavior or receptional assimilation, respondents were asked if their party of affiliation nominated a Black for President, would they vote for the candidate.[3] To measure relative social distance from various racial and ethnic groups, they were asked about how favorably they viewed living in a neighborhood in which about half their neighbors would be Jews, Blacks, Asians, Latinos, or northern Whites.

Results

Are Latinos any more willing to interact with African Americans than are people from other ethnic groups? Are African Americans any more willing to support interaction with Latinos than they are to support exchange with other ethnic groups? If differences on the magnitude of 20% are considered significant and those of 10% are considered nontrivial, then Figures 7-1 to 7-3 show that there are nontrivial and significant differences in how likely various ethnic groups are to interact with African Americans in several contexts. Figure 7-1 presents the relationship between ethnicity and unwillingness to send one's children to schools in which up to half of the students are African Americans. This graph shows that while only one out of ten (10%) African Americans are unwilling to send their children to such schools, nearly four out of ten (37%) Asian Americans report that they would be unwilling to send their children to them. Latinos are the group next to African Americans least likely to object to sending their children to predominantly Black schools, with only 16% objecting to such integration. Greater proportions of other ethnic groups raise objections; 25% of European-Americans and 27% of Jewish Americans object to having their children in such schools.

Figure 7-2 presents the unwillingness to vote for a Black presidential candidate by ethnicity. Again, there are nontrivial differences by eth-

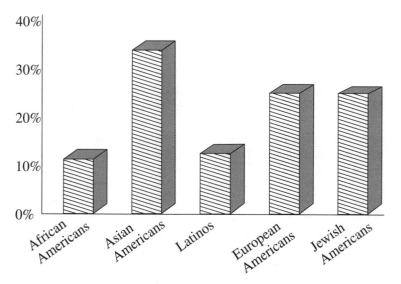

Figure 7-1. Percentage Objecting to having Their Children Attend Predominantly Black Schools by Race and Ethnicity

Source: Data derived from Davis and Smith (1992). General Social Survey.

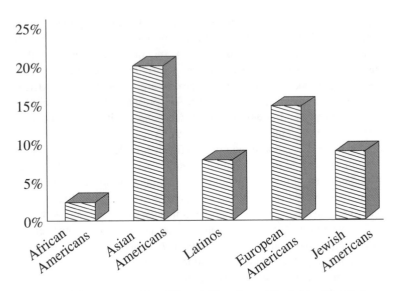

Figure 7-2. Percentage Unwilling to Vote for a Black Presidential Candidate by Race and Ethnicity

Source: Data derived from Davis and Smith (1992). General Social Survey.

nicity, with only 1% of African Americans saying they would be unwilling to vote for a Black presidential candidate, but 20% of Asian Americans reporting that they would be unwilling to vote for a Black presidential candidate nominated by their party. Less than 10% of Latinos say that they would be unwilling to vote for a Black candidate. This finding has major implications for coalition politics, as it suggests that more than nine out of 10 Latinos at least claim their willingness to vote for an African American.

Figure 7-3 shows the percentage of people from various racial and ethnic groups who are opposed to living in neighborhoods in which half the residents are White, Black, Jewish, Asian or Latino. With only a few exceptions, this chart shows that higher proportions of the ethnic groups report opposition to living among Blacks than among any other racial or ethnic group. Unfortunately for proponents of coalition building, Blacks appear to object to living among Latinos more than they do to living in any other kind of "ethnic" community. Also, about one out of five Latinos opposes living in "Black neighborhoods." While the levels of opposition to coexistence are generally not as great as the levels of social

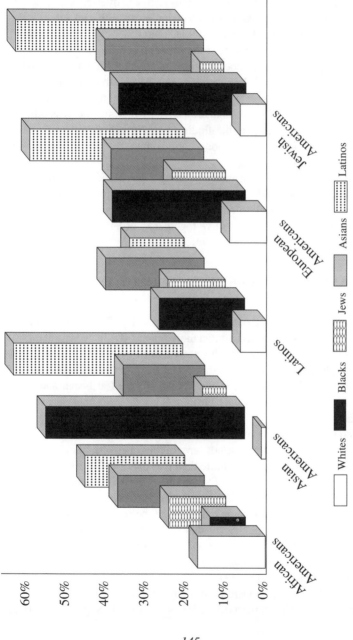

Figure 7-3. Percentage Opposed to Living with Various Ethnic Groups

Source: Data derived from Davis and Smith (1992). General Social Survey.

Whites | Blacks | Jews | Asians | Latinos

distance between Blacks and other groups, these results are not good news for those who seek allies, as both African Americans and Latinos express greater comfort with Anglos than they do with each other.

Overall, these results of the 1990 General Survey (Davis and Smith 1992) provide mixed support for the notion that African Americans and Latinos are close enough socially to form meaningful coalitions. While Latinos generally show less resistance to Blacks than do other ethnic groups, they express greater resistance to living among Blacks than they do to living among Whites and Jews. Even worse for the possibility of Black–Latino coalitions is the finding that African Americans express greater reluctance to living among Latinos than they do to living among any other group examined.

Coexistence is significant for building place-based coalitions. It may not be salient for building condition-based and interest-based coalitions and collaborations. Condition-based and interest-based coalitions do not require that their constituents live together in order to work together or even be on the same scenes to be effective.[4]

JOB COMPETITION BETWEEN LATINOS AND AFRICAN AMERICANS

The 1990 Census enumerated a total of more than 22 million Latinos in the United States. This constituted more than a 50% increase since 1980. Several factors contributed to this growth during the 1980s, most significantly a higher birth rate than the rest of the population and substantial immigration from Mexico, Central America, the Caribbean and South America (U.S. Bureau of the Census 1993a). In 1990, more than a third of Latinos in the U.S.A. were immigrants. Of the nearly eight million Latino immigrants, about half came during the 1980s.

Despite the fact that Latinos have higher rates of labor participation than the general population, more than two out of every 10 Latino families were living in poverty in 1990 compared with less than one of every 10 families in the general U.S. population. The median family income of $25,000 for Latinos was more than $10,000 below the median family income of $35,225 for all U.S. residents. This pattern reflects the fact that Latino workers are overrepresented as laborers, farm workers and service workers and are substantially underrepresented as managerial, professional and technical workers.

As of 1990, there were more than 30 million Blacks living in the United States. This comprised 12.5% of the total U.S. population (U.S.

Bureau of the Census, 1993b). Like Latinos, African Americans had higher than average poverty rates. More than one out of every four Black families had incomes that were below the poverty line. This is despite the fact that the educational attainment gap (measured as years of schooling) between Whites and African Americans had dwindled to less than half a year by 1990. Still, in 1990, Blacks had earnings that were less than 70% of those of Whites. The bulk of these earnings differences persists even after one takes educational attainment into consideration, as the earnings gaps occur for each educational attainment level. Even Blacks with college degrees earned only 70 cents to every dollar that their White counterparts received.

Labor market segmentation theory suggests that such earnings differences between Whites and people of color occur because the U.S. labor market is divided into two different sectors, the primary and the secondary sector (Doeringer and Piore 1971; Dalto 1987). The former tends to be part of a labor market governance structure that provides job security, upward mobility, and higher incomes and earnings. Primary sector jobs are posited to be more likely to be full time and to offer mechanisms that allow their incumbents to accumulate skills that lead progressively to more responsibility and higher pay.

In contrast, secondary sector jobs are more likely to be part time, low paying and to have reward structures that are not related to job tenure. Also, because rewards in this sector are not strongly related to experience and performance, workers have less motivation to develop attachments to their firms or to perform their jobs well. Thus, it is usually only those workers who cannot gain employment in the primary sector who are likely to work in the secondary sector. Because discrimination (not only by employers but, at times, by restrictive unions and professional associations) plays a role in determining who gets access to jobs in the primary sector, people of color are concentrated in the secondary sector.

Moreover, labor market segregation is reinforced by normative ideas about "White jobs" and "minority jobs." This framework suggests that reduced returns to educational attainment are a likely consequence of being employed in the secondary sector where returns on human capital investments are substantially lower than those in the primary sector.

To the degree that African Americans and Latinos are relegated to the secondary labor market, they work in jobs that carry lower rewards and benefits. Moreover, because these groups are largely excluded from employment in the primary sector, they often must compete with each other for the inadequate jobs in the secondary labor market.

While there has been much speculation about the effects of Latino immigration and population growth on the employment prospects for African Americans, there has been little systematic research. One notable exception is the work of Ong and Valenzuela (1995). These authors (1995:9) estimate "that there is a small positive impact of Latino immigration on earnings [of African Americans]" and argue that

> immigrants have a complementary effect for African Americans in public sector employment due to the increased demand in public services and agencies as a result of the growth of legal and illegal immigration. As the demand for public services, programs and personnel has grown due to the population growth, a large part of which comes from immigration, African American employment in this sector has increased.

Differently, a growing literature anticipates that the mechanisms underlying racial conflict involve both perceived and actual threats based on competition for scarce resources. Following Rifkin (1995), Alkalimat, Gills, and Williams (1995) argue that infusion of technologies in production and information processing will lead in the long run to reduced demands for labor. Moreover, Wilson (1996) argues that the attacks on the welfare state, reductions in income transfers for the poor, and the conservative thrust of the federal government will lead to fewer quality jobs.

The ecological tradition presents ethnic patterns that question the assertions made by Ong and Valenzuela about the relationship of Latino population size and access to opportunities in the labor market for Blacks. These studies repeatedly show that an increase in the relative size of minorities (i.e., Blacks) in local labor markets is likely to increase minority groups' economic (mostly occupational) disadvantage (Tienda and Lii 1987; Semyonov, Hoyt, and Scott 1984).

This literature offers two explanations of the positive association between minority size and socioeconomic subordination. The first contends that increases in minority size generate greater threats and fear from competition, and therefore hostility, antagonism and motivation to discriminate grow with the proportion of the minority in the labor market (Blalock 1967; Allport 1954). An alternative view suggests that increases in the size of the minority population expand the supply of cheap labor as a target for economic exploitation. Since occupational labor markets are organized across racial lines, the availability of subordinate minority workers increases the potential pool of workers for the less desirable low-status jobs. Consequently, race-linked socioeconomic inequality is likely to increase with increases in the proportion of the population that is minority (e.g., Glenn 1962; Semyonov, Hoyt and Scott 1984).

However, the ecological tradition does not consider reactions, strategies and the ability of minority populations to resist discrimination. Several authors have suggested that when the minority population is large enough and reaches a critical mass, it can mobilize resources and develop independent labor markets, or exert pressure (political or otherwise) for reallocation of resources (Frazier 1957; Lieberson 1980). Indeed, when the minority population is large enough and highly concentrated in a labor market, it can attain occupational positions even against the will of majority group members (Semyonov 1988; Lieberson 1980). In this regard, Lieberson (1980:297) has persuasively argued that "if the Black population is large enough, there will be support for Black doctors, Black clergy and so on, even if they remain totally unacceptable by others." This idea is also consistent with the enclave thesis (Zhou and Logan 1989; Wilson and Portes 1980) and with other studies on sheltered economies (Semyonov 1988; Semyonov and Lewin-Epstein 1994). There is reason to believe that if members of various minority groups work together, they can leverage their size and concentration into higher earnings and more jobs.

Below, data from the 1990 U.S. Census are used to examine the impact of African American and Latino population concentrations on African American and Latino earnings and employment. The data help to answer two questions. How does the presence of African Americans affect the earnings and employment rates of Latinos? How does the presence of Latinos affect the earnings and employment rates of African Americans? Table 7-1 presents the mean earnings of African Americans and Latinos by the proportion of residents who are African American, after controlling for the effects of race/ethnicity, gender, age, education, marital status, region and labor market sector.

Table 7-2 presents parallel results by the proportion of residents who are Latino. While not strictly linear, there is a general pattern of declining earnings for African Americans as their proportion in the population increases. Specifically, when less than 1% of the population is African American, they have average weekly earnings of $329.85. As the proportion of African American residents exceeds 20%, the mean weekly earnings of African Americans decrease to $201.77. There is a similar pattern among Latinos. Meanwhile, when Blacks are less than 1% of the population, Latinos average $290.54 per week, but when the proportion of

Table 7-1 Adjusted Mean Earnings of African Americans and Latinos by Proportion of Residents Who are African American*

% African Americans in Population	Adjusted Mean Earnings African Americans	Latinos
<1%	329.85	290.54
1–5%	337.96	282.55
5–10%	250.72	178.57
10–20%	307.87	247.24
20–50%	201.77	162.12
>50%	223.25	190.84

*Results are based on Ordinary Least Squares Regression Analysis that controls for race/ethnicity, gender, age, education, marital status, region, and labor market sector, and then stratifies the analysis by the proportion of the population that is African American.

Source: U.S. Bureau of the Census 1993. Census of Population and Housing Public Use Microdata Sample 1-Percent Sample (I-Percent PUMS); U.S. Census Bureau. 1993a. *We the American Hispanics.* Washington, DC: U.S. Government Printing Office. U.S. Census Bureau. 1993b. *We the American Blacks.* Washington, DC: U.S. Government Printing Office.

African Americans exceeds 20%, weekly earnings for Latinos drop to $162.12.

Table 7-2 shows that when the focus is on the proportion of the population that is Latino, there are some very different patterns. In particular, there is a general tendency for an increase in the earnings of African Americans and Latinos as the proportion of the population that is Latino increases. When Latinos constitute less than 1% of the population, African Americans average $199.42 per week earnings. As the proportion Latino exceeds 50%, African Americans earn an average of $520.67 per week, a 260% increase. There are similar, but less dramatic improvements for Latinos as well. When they are less than 1% of the population, they earn an average of $316.90 per week, but when Latinos comprise more than 50% of the population, they earn $498.10 per week on average, a 157% increase.

The patterns in Tables 7-1 and 7-2 suggest that Latino increases have

Table 7-2 Adjusted Mean Earnings of African Americans and Latinos by Proportion of Residents Who are African American*

% Latinos Americans in Population	Adjusted Mean Earnings	
	African Americans	Latinos
<1%	199.42	316.90
1–5%	236.73	238.80
5–10%	160.67	90.44
10–20%	388.21	349.17
20–50%	410.66	335.49
>50%	520.67	498.10

*Results are based on ordinary least squares regression analysis that controls for race/ethnicity, gender, age, education, marital status, region, and labor market sector, and then stratifies the analysis by the proportion of the population that is Latino.

Source: U.S. Bureau of the Census 1993. Census of Population and Housing Public Use Microdata Sample 1-Percent Sample (I-Percent PUMS); U.S. Census Bureau. 1993a. *We the American Hispanics.* Washington, DC: U.S. Government Printing Office. U.S. Census Bureau. 1993b. *We the American Blacks.* Washington, DC: U.S. Government Printing Office.

no adverse effects on the earnings of Blacks and, in fact, are associated with higher earnings. Higher percentages of Blacks, however, are associated with lower earnings for both African Americans and Latinos.

Table 7-3 presents the employment rates of Blacks and Latinos by the proportion of residents who are African American, after controlling for the effects of race/ethnicity, gender, age, education, marital status and region. Table 7-4 presents corresponding results by the proportion of residents who are Latino. Table 7-3 shows that there is no clear relationship between the proportions of African Americans in communities and the employment rates of African Americans. (The multivariate results did, however, suggest that there is a positive relationship between the proportion of African Americans in communities and the probability that an African American resident will be employed.) There also appears to be little systematic relationship between the percentage of African Americans in communities and Latino employment rates.

Table 7-3 Adjusted Employment Rates of African Americans and Latinos by Proportion of Residents Who are African American*

% African Americans in Population	Adjusted Employment Rate African Americans	Latinos
<1%	74.2%	66.5%
15%	59.3%	61.8%
5-10%	56.3%	64.3%
10-20%	57.6%	60.8%
20-50%	60.1%	74.1%
>50%	59.1%	70.7%

* Results are based on logistic regression analysis that controls for race/ethnicity, gender, age, education, marital status, and region, and then stratifies the analysis by the proportion of the population that is African American.

Source: U.S. Bureau of the Census 1993. Census of Population and Housing Public Use Microdata Sample. 1-Percent Sample (1-Percent PUMS); U.S. Census Bureau. 1993a. *We the American Hispanics*. Washington, DC: U.S. Government Printing Office; U.S. Census Bureau. 1993b. *We the American Blacks*. Washington, DC: U.S. Government Printing Office.

Table 7-4 shows that there is a slight tendency for the employment rates of African Americans to increase as the proportion of Latinos in the population increases. Among Latinos, in contrast, there is a decrease in employment rates as the local proportion of Latinos increases.

The results in Tables 7-3 and 7-4 suggest that increases in the Latino population are associated with slightly higher employment rates for African Americans. Higher percentages of Latinos, however, are associated with lower employment rates for Latinos.

DISCUSSION AND CONCLUSIONS

This paper began with three central concerns: (1) the degree of social distance between Blacks and Latinos, (2) the effects of Latino population size on the earnings and employment rates of African Americans, and (3) the effects of Black population size on the earnings and employment rates of Latinos. These issues were examined to identify the objective

Table 7-4 Adjusted Employment Rates of African Americans and Latinos by Proportion of Residents Who are African American*

% Latino Americans in Population	Adjusted Employment Rate African Americans	Latinos
<1%		
1- 5%	58.3%	76.4%
5-10%	57.2%	64.6%
10-20%	53.1%	66.2%
20-50%	59.7%	63.4%
>50%	62.0%	58.1%

*Results are based on Logistic Regression Analysis that controls for race/ethnicity, gender, age, education, marital status, and region, and then stratifies the analysis by the proportion of the population that is Latino.

Source: U.S. Bureau of the Census 1993. Census of Population and Housing Public Use Microdata Sample. 1% Sample (I% PUMS); U.S. Census Bureau. 1993a. *We the American Hispanics.* Washington, DC: U.S. Government Printing Office; U.S. Census Bureau. 1993b. *We the American Blacks.* Washington, DC: U.S. Government Printing Office.

and subjective conditions that either favor or limit cooperation and collaboration between Latinos and Blacks.

Overall, the analysis of the degree of social distance between Latinos and Blacks provided mixed support for the idea that these groups are close enough socially to form meaningful coalitions. Latinos generally showed less resistance to Blacks than did other ethnic groups, but even Latinos expressed greater resistance to living among Blacks than they did to living among Whites and Jews. Even worse for proponents of Black–Latino coalitions was the finding that African Americans expressed greater reluctance to live among Latinos than they did to live among any other group examined. This finding is balanced by the point that condition- and interest-based collective action efforts are not necessarily contingent upon Blacks and Latinos sharing places of residence and physical proximity. As noted in Chapter Two in this volume, such spatial concentration and proximity may increase the potential, even the objective circumstances necessitating joint initiatives between Latinos and Blacks in urban centers.

The effects of African American and Latino population concentrations on earnings and employment exhibit some intriguing patterns. Increases in the Latino population had no adverse effects on the earnings of Blacks and, in fact, were associated with higher earnings for Blacks. Higher percentages of Blacks, however, were associated with lower earnings for both African Americans and Latinos. Increases in the Latino population were also associated with slightly higher employment rates for African Americans but with lower employment rates for Latinos.

Combined, these results suggest that, up to this present juncture in society, higher concentrations of Latinos in communities are, if anything, beneficial to African Americans in terms of employment and earnings. With the collapse of the welfare state, attacks on affirmative action, constraints on immigration patterns and devolvement of the national governments role in urban and social development, these trends may not continue.

Nevertheless, we also found that Latinos appear more receptive than other racial and ethnic groups to interactions and cooperation with African Americans. Yet, African Americans appear to resist interaction with Latinos more than they do with any other racial or ethnic group. This is despite the fact that the presence of higher proportions of Latinos is associated with higher earnings and employment rates for African Americans, but higher concentrations of Blacks are associated with lower earnings for Latinos. Perhaps, this is due to the historical lack of familiarity with Latino culture and heritage and relative ignorance of Latinos. The main forms of information about each other that Blacks and Latinos have are through prejudicial media representations and the social policy discourses, dominated by White elite institutions and their agents.

These findings suggest that for Black–Latino coalitions to succeed, African Americans must recognize the common plight that they share with Latinos. They must begin to challenge popular sentiment that would have them blame their problems on Latino immigrants. They must realize that Latinos are similarly situated victims of discrimination, disadvantage and exclusion. They are both among communities experiencing the backlash of "angry White men."

The prevailing racialized climate should act as a glaring indication that people of color are in the same boat and should not blame each other for being there. Rather, all people of color should be concerned about attacking the underlying racism that unfairly concentrates them into sectors of the economy where they clash over a shrinking job base. Forming workable coalitions will not mean that African Americans and Latinos should gloss over the real issues that divide them. It means that they will need to confront these issues head-on and devise strategies for resolving them so that larger issues can be attacked jointly.

NOTES

[1] An earlier version of this paper was presented at the "Black and Latino Relations National Working Conference on Strategies of Contention and Collaborations, Chicago, IL, September 7-9, 1995.

[2] A further distinction from the "melting pot" hypothesis is the distinction made between European ethnics identifying with the supra nationalism of oppressor nations and the nationality and nationalism of oppressed peoples and nations. This leads to a distinction between such European-based ethnics who are relatively more assimilated into U.S. cultural and social life than are the nationalities that have continued to be racially and culturally oppressed and excluded. The latter tend to retain their cultural traits and traditions preferring not to be culturally assimilated but politically and economically integrated without regard to the imposition of racial ascriptions. We refer to these "racial ethnic" groups as the new "nationalities" or peoples of color. The importance of the distinction is that oppressed nationalities tend to be more inclusivist, tolerant of differences than are Eurocentric ethnics in their relations with outgroups. See Peoples College Collective, *1977, Introduction to Afro-American Studies,* 2 volumes; also Alkalimat and Associates 1984 & 1989.

[3] Note: it would have been "politically correct" to ask the question: "Would you vote for a Latino (Asian, Jewish, Native American) president, were he/she qualified for the job?"

[4] Gills and Betancur (1995) and Chapter 2 in this volume identify three forms of *community* that have been salient in generating change-based mobilizations among insurgent or outsider forces within the urban political process. They are *communities of place,* organized around the neighborhood; *condition-based communities,* organized around real and presumed oppression, discrimination and exclusion; *and interest-based communities,* organized around economic circumstances. Accordingly, these motions relate to the *Three D's*: the promotion of material and social *development,* the extension of *democracy;* and struggles to promote *diversity* (or to affirm *difference*).

CHAPTER 8

Can't We All Just Get Along?
Interethnic Organization for Economic Development

REBECCA MORALES
MANUEL PASTOR

By the year 2000, African Americans and Latinos will constitute together nearly one-fourth of the nation's population, and an even larger share of the population in major urban areas. While the ongoing economic crisis of urban areas, particularly the dismantling of social programs, has created a basis of common interest, the ability of these two groups to engage in joint interethnic action may prove elusive. In part, this is because they have experienced the economic transformations of the past decade in different ways: deindustrialization has eliminated the usual paths of upward mobility for working class African Americans and second- and third-generation Latinos, while reindustrialization has fed a tremendous demand for low-wage, immigrant, often Latino labor. The ensuing sense of labor market competition has fueled the division between African Americans and Latinos.

This paper explores organizing strategies being used to move beyond division and build common ground between African Americans and Latinos on economic development issues. We first examine the trends that have structured the changes in economic opportunity for these communities in urban America as well as the general problematic of interethnic unity efforts. We then turn to case studies of organizing projects, including (1) two in Los Angeles, one conducted by the United Neighborhoods Organization (UNO) and the Southern California Organizing Committee and the other by the Coalition of Neighborhood Developers; (2) one in San Antonio, Project QUEST, conducted by the Communities Organized for Public Service (COPS)/Metro Alliance, and (3) one in East Palo Alto, undertaken by the Congress of Community Organizations (COCO). We specifically compare the effects on process and outcome of: (1) *coalitional* strategies that tend to bring together established groups, often from disparate and conflicting communities, for ad hoc policy efforts; and *(2) organizational* strategies to construct a permanent ongoing organization that largely ignores divisive sub- issues in the interest of sustaining a common front. We conclude that organizational strategies may be more effective for achieving concrete economic gains. While they have shortcomings in the realm of process, or community building, they perform reasonably well in this area also.

ECONOMIC TRENDS, ETHNIC TENSIONS, AND ORGANIZING STRATEGIES

In contrast to other countries that have responded to restructuring by retaining wage, income and social policies to support displaced and/or low wage workers and their families, the U.S.A. has sharply retreated from its welfare commitments, thereby accelerating trends toward growing inequality and poverty.[1] This economic transformation and the accompanying political responses have had their sharpest effects on minority communities. Such hardships could create a basis for Black–Latino unity; with more stringent welfare regulations and a diminished social safety net, the prospect of Blacks and Latinos in urban areas are increasingly comparable, and, over the last two decades, each group's unemployment experience has become more like the other's (see Figure 8-1).

Still, there is the general perception that Latinos, particularly immigrants, have been wage-reducing substitutes, rather than employment-expanding complements in the labor market. Moreover, there are other areas of divergent interest. Bilingual education is essential for Latinos, but in an era of scarcity, it arguably reduces education resources available to African American schoolchildren. Latinos have been under represented in public employment but demands for hiring more threaten the role government employment has played in Black economic advancement. Public money allocated to one neighborhood is essentially taken from another when the fiscal pie is shrinking.

The question is, given this complex panorama of economic trends can Latinos and Blacks build a common set of interests and an effective interethnic alliance? In examining issues over which these groups have coalesced at the national level, Vigil (1994) found that, during the 1988 presidential election, Latinos shared similar positions with Blacks on national health insurance, federal day care funding and social program re-

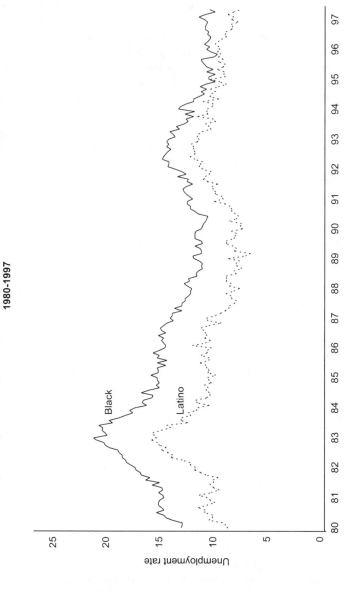

Figure 8-1 The Convergence of Black and Latino National-Level Unemployment Rates 1980-1997

tention. They were not united on issues of amnesty to Central American refugees, bilingual education, English as an official language and abortion rights. In fact, the issues uniting nationally elected Latino officials were generally those in which they were at odds with Blacks. For example, the Congressional Hispanic Caucus, created in 1976, at its peak in 1985 could only reach unanimous agreement on immigration reform and the need to contest English as an official language, issues around which Blacks either took opposing positions or gave only weak support. This hardly seems like the recipe for forging a new permanent minority consensus on economic development.

What could create the basis for interethnic cooperation? Contemporary social analysts have focused on the power of "social capital" as a basis for collective action and democratic communities. Social capital is defined as "features of social organization, such as trust, norms and networks, that can improve the efficiency of society by facilitating coordinated actions;" it is, in short, the set of values embraced by a community as expressed through its relationships and social networks (Putnam 1991:7). Part of this capital develops through collaboration: after multiple and mutually satisfactory interactions, people develop trust that can translate into more mutually beneficial economic and social actions. Thus, this social capital can be cumulative in a sort of virtuous circle—or can unravel in a cycle of distrust and tension. For our purposes, the key issue is how best to develop social capital across racial lines.

The construction of social capital is the essence of community organizing. Strategies to build community and promote development can be broken into those that involve either *coalitional* strategies focusing on bringing together different groups, *or organizational* strategies involving common issues and ignoring and de-emphasizing ethnic-specific divisive sub-issues in favor of sustaining an ongoing permanent organization. The effects of such multiracial organizing around economic development can be evaluated on two criteria: (1) *process*: whether or not it builds a sense of joint interests and community (that is, constructs new social capital), and (2) *outcome*: whether it has an actual economic development impact (that is, enhances physical, financial or human capital). Figure 8-2 presents a framework for evaluating the success of each organizing approach with regard to process and outcome.

While many groups employ some combination of coalitional and organizational approaches, the two strategies differ in the ways they deal with consensus, collaboration and competition. Coalitional strategies seek to define clearly competitive areas, such as the electoral realm, then

Figure 8-2 Framework for Evaluating Organizational Strategies

Columns: Strategy Rows: Measures of Success	Primary Strategy: Coalition	Primary Strategy: Organization
Process: "Community-Building"		
Outcome: "Economic Development"		

identify specific, limited areas of consensus. Collaboration in this framework is tentative and generally based on previous success in achieving consensual objectives; each success raises the trust level and expands the possible realm of collaboration. The hope is that such collaboration will lead to a sustainable alliance (but not necessarily a new, independent and permanent organization) over the medium- term and, therefore, develop improved relationships and superior economic outcomes.

Organizational strategies start with points of consensus. They often explicitly steer clear of conflicts and avoid definitions of competitive areas; instead, they seek to define group identity around consensual issues. The result is organization building since the organization becomes the primary identifier rather than an individual's ethnic group.[2] Alinsky-style[3] groups are clear proponents of this approach. As Skerry (1993:156) notes, "The Alinsky emphasis on process over substance is particularly evident when organizers tell members: 'Issues don't really matter.' Indeed, the *idée fixe* of Alinsky and his heirs is that issues are only the means to the end of building up and maintaining 'the organization.'"

To evaluate the strengths and weaknesses of these different organizing methods, we examine four prominent instances of multiracial organizing around economic development issues in three cities: Los Angeles, the nation's second largest city; San Antonio, the tenth largest; and East Palo Alto, one of the nation's smallest cities. As shown in Table 8-1, all three have large minority populations, with both Los Angeles and East Palo Alto being majority minority. All three cities are also poorer than the nation as a whole (Table 8-2). Indeed, among the nation's fifteen largest cities, San Antonio was second, behind Detroit, in the percent of persons below the poverty level. Each of these cities experienced major shifts in their economic base in recent years (Table 8-3). Los Angeles and

San Antonio, for example, saw a decline in manufacturing and the emergence of employment in trade and services; East Palo Alto, a city chartered in 1983, needed to build its economic base. In 1990, Each of the cities suffered from substantially higher unemployment than the nation on average, especially East Palo Alto (Table 8-4). Although these objective conditions created potential for interethnic tension, the cases discussed here demonstrate that groups sometimes can develop social capital and organize across racial lines for positive economic development outcomes.

CASE STUDIES OF ORGANIZING AROUND ECONOMIC DEVELOPMENT

Los Angeles

Economic difficulties in Los Angeles stem from long-term processes of de- industrialization and re-industrialization—the expansion of nondurable manufacturing and low-skill service employment, often based on low-wage, largely immigrant, employees. The most serious negative ef-

Table 8-1 Demographics, 1980 and 1990

| | National | | Los Angeles | | San Antonio | | East Palo Alto | |
	1980	1990	1980	1990	1980	1990	*1980	1990
Total Population (000's)	226,546	248,710	2,967	3,490	785	966	NA	24
Non-Latino (percent)	79.8	75.1	48.3	37.3	38.0	36.2	NA	12.1
Black (percent)	11.7	12.1	17.0	13.0	7.3	6.8	NA	41.5
Latino (percent)	6.4	9.0	27.5	40.2	53.7	55.6	NA	36.4
Asian (percent)	1.5	3.0	7.0	9.2	0.74	1.1	NA	9.2
Other (percent)	0.6	0.8	0.6	0.3	0.3	0.3	NA	0.8

*NOTE: Not applicable (NA) to East Palo Alto because the city was chartered in 1983.

Source: 1980 and 1990 U.S. Census, Bureau of the Census, U.S. Department of Commerce; for Los Angeles, from the City of L.A. Demographic Research Unit.

Table 8-2 Income Statistics, 1980 and 1990

	National		Los Angeles		San Antonio		East Palo Alto	
	1980	**1990**	**1980**	**1990**	**1980**	**1990**	**1980***	**1990**
Per Capita Income ($)	9,521	14,420	8,431	16,188	5,734	10,884	NA	9,968
Percent Below Poverty Level (All families)	9.6	10.0	13.0	14.9	16.9	18.7	NA	14.7

*Note: Not applicable to East Palo Alto because the city was chartered in 1983.
Source: 1980 and 1990 U.S. Census, Bureau of the Census, U.S. Department of Commerce

fects of this restructuring—higher unemployment and reduced wages—have been felt most sharply among minority subpopulations and neighborhoods.

In 1990, for example, the poverty population was 15% Black and 57% Latino; in contrast, in the population whose household incomes were twice or more that of the poverty level, African Americans were less than 10% and Latinos less than 27%. As for the unemployed, 15% were African American and 47% percent were Latino even though these two groups represented only 8% and 37% of the labor force.[4]

This congruence of economic suffering—that is, relative overrepresentation of Blacks and Latinos in the poor and unemployed—would seem to augur well for coalition-building, particularly in light of the growing presence (and hence potential political power) of minorities in the various municipalities that comprise the Los Angeles County. However, the differential experiences of Latinos and Blacks also create a material basis for division.[5] While both groups are poor, they have experienced this regional restructuring in very different ways: for African Americans, the problem is mostly joblessness resulting from deindustrialization while for Latinos it is mostly low-wage employment resulting from reindustrialization.[6] Ethnic competition surfaced, for example, in the scramble for rebuilding resources in the wake of the 1992 civil unrest.[7] Nonetheless, there have also been numerous efforts to jointly organize African Americans and Latinos (as well as other ethnic

Table 8-3 Selected Employment, 1980 and 1990
(Percentage of Paid Employees by Selected Industries)

	National		Los Angeles		San Antonio		East Palo Alto	
	1980	1990	1980	1990	1980	1990	*1980	1990
Manufacturing	22.4	17.7	23.0	18.4	11.9	9.0	NA	19.80
Wholesale & Retail Trade	22.5	21.2	19.9	20.2	24.5	23.9	NA	16.7
Finance, Insurance and Real Estate	5.7	6.9	No data	8.1	No data	8.6	NA	2.5
Service	19.8	8.4**	20.1	7.1**	21.2	9.4**	NA	11.1**

*Note: Not applicable to East Palo Alto because the city was chartered in 1983.
**Note: These figures are for health-related services only.
Source: 1980 and 1990 U.S. Census, Bureau of the Census, U.S. Department of Commerce.

groups) around issues of economic development. The focus here is on two: the organizational approach of the Industrial Areas Foundation and the coalitional efforts of the Coalition of Neighborhood Developers.[8]

The Industrial Areas Foundation (IAF)

The Industrial Areas Foundation (IAF) in Los Angeles consists of several allied organizations, the most prominent of which are the United Neighborhoods Organizations (UNO) and the South Central (now the Southern California) Organizing Committee (SCOC).[9] UNO is based

Table 8-4 The Unemployment Rate, 1980 and 1990
(in Percent)

National		Los Angeles		San Antonio		East Palo Alto	
1980	1990	1980	1990	1980	1990	*1980	1990
7.1	6.7	7.4	9.0	6.8	7.1	NA	10.6

*Note: Not applicable to East Palo Alto because the city was chartered in 1983.
Source: 1980 and 1990 U.S. Census, Bureau of the Census, U.S. Department of Commerce.

primarily in East Los Angeles and has a predominantly Latino member-ship. SCOC is based in South Central and includes African Americans and Latinos. Both organizations are rooted in churches, but especially in the Catholic Church. They are explicitly committed to Alinsky-style or-ganizing and, in keeping with that approach, are staff-driven in their agenda and tactics. Moreover, they tend to focus on cross-ethnic issues of common concern. They are, in short, a classical example of the *organizational* strategy.

Between 1987 and 1995, the IAF engaged in at least two major eco-nomically-oriented initiatives: the Moral Minimum Wage Campaign and the Nehemiah West housing effort. The former was conducted in 1987 and succeeded in raising California's minimum wage above the federal level of $3.35 an hour to $4.25 an hour.[10] To push for the increase, IAF members were mobilized for protest activities, including 2,000 who showed up in Los Angeles for an October 1987 meeting of the California Industrial Welfare Commission, the state agency empowered to raise or not raise the minimum salary. Using a strategic analysis of business, IAF organizers also attempted to secure the support of retail food chains, not-ing that they would benefit from the increased buying power of the poor while suffering few costs (since most of their own workers were union-ized and paid well above minimum). The IAF therefore asked the head of one major chain (president of the California Retailers Association) to support a minimum wage hike. When he refused, the IAF selected one of his stores for a "shop-in" designed to tie up check-out lines (for example, by paying for all purchases with pennies), and quite quickly he agreed to issue a statement supporting an unspecified increase in the minimum. The IAF also worked to solicit support from the Catholic Church, key Democratic politicians, and unions. The end result was success—the minimum wage was increased and an estimated $1 billion in income was transferred to the working poor.

Soon after the minimum wage victory, the Los Angeles IAF organi-zations borrowed a strategy from sister IAF organizations in New York and pursued the building of owner-occupied low-income housing under the label of *Nehemiah West*. To implement this project, the IAF groups set up a separate spin off corporation, the Nehemiah West Housing Cor-poration (NWHC), with a board consisting of an equal number of repre-sentatives from the Latino-dominated UNO and Black-dominated SCOC (and a few others).[11] The President and the lead organizer for NWHC were both African American but both fought hard for building the first project consisting of 126 units in Bell Gardens, a largely Latino city.

More than 90% of the first occupants were Latinos. In Compton, a majority Black city and one of the Nehemiah target sites, the President of NWHC backed a Latino over a Black candidate for City Council on the grounds that the latter would actually be better for NWHC. This was a bold move in a city in which Blacks have been reluctant to share power with the burgeoning Latino population. The Compton project (which, in spring 1995, opened 32 projects and had another 131 under construction) houses a majority Black clientele, but the ability of NHWC to put ethnic interests and simplistic interethnic solidarity on hold for the sake of the overall goal of building Nehemiah housing speaks to the high level of interethnic cooperation.

While this would suggest a positive rating on *process*, the record may be more mixed. Although the IAF has been able to mobilize forces and maintain a great deal of interethnic cooperation within its constituent groups, it does not work well with other organizations. The IAF prefers to work on its own and not in coalitions because its focus is on *building the organization*. This has led to significant tensions with traditional Black leaders and politicians. As a result, SCOC, based in South Central Los Angeles, has made few inroads with the more mainstream African American religious institutions (Skerry 1993:206). Some in Los Angeles also criticize the "over representation" of White organizers in the IAF groups (although this has changed through the years) and lament the strong role of staff vis-a-vis community leaders.

The essential thrust of the two strategies reviewed—increasing the minimum wage and developing owner-occupied low-income housing—favors Latinos who are disproportionately represented in the working poor. Without also focusing on employment, this strategy may not alleviate the material basis of interethnic tension. Still, in terms of actual *outcomes*, the IAF has been extremely successful: the minimum wage campaign generated a significant redistribution of income to poor workers, and the housing projects, while hardly sufficient to meet the needs of an overcrowded Los Angeles, provide models for similar efforts.

The Coalition of Neighborhood Developers

The Coalition of Neighborhood Developers (CND), a diverse alliance of over 50 community-based development corporations (CDCs) and other related groups, was formed in 1990. After the 1992 Los Angeles uprising, it significantly expanded its membership and was incorporated as a freestanding, nonprofit organization.[12] CND's constituent

CDCs served ten communities in south, east and central Los Angeles, all of which have been severely affected by the economic restructuring of the past 15 years and many of which were hard-hit by the 1992 civil unrest.

The Coalition of Neighborhood Developers, as its name suggests, was a classic coalition seeking to develop a common agenda from the sharply defined interests of its various members. The major effort of CND was the creation of a composite planning document, *From the Ground Up: Neighbors Planning Neighborhoods,* which was an attempt to identify common policy issues and development objectives across neighborhood "clusters." In generating the document, each cluster wrote separate Neighborhood Plans articulating the area's needs and potential opportunities. The common themes that emerged included promotion of home ownership, creation of economic linkages between regional employers/businesses and local residents, development of youth services and enhancement of the image of the various neighborhoods (CND 1994). CND, as the umbrella group, was then to lobby for overall policy changes that would make each cluster's strategy easier to achieve. As part of this, CND worked with the City of Los Angeles in the development of its application for a federal Empowerment Zone designation.

While the central goal of the planning process was to have the constituent CDCs in each cluster create both a mutually supportive relationship and a common policy agenda, there were a series of problems of structure and vision.[13] First, the founding members were mostly located in African American communities, a fact that made the Latino and Asian-based CDCs incorporated in the post-uprising expansion feel like junior partners. Second, CDC's are by definition spatially rooted and tend to compete for limited funds for "their" neighborhoods; this competition was never fully abandoned in the planning process (in sharp contrast to the Nehemiah West process outlined above) and so power sharing was difficult.[14] Third, in order to maintain control—an imperative which may have resulted from the somewhat suspicious relationship between CDCs—CND opted for a strong board/weak staff structure, quite the opposite of the strong staff leadership provided by Alinsky-style organizations. Fourth, CND never fully articulated a strategy beyond the development of a "composite planning document." It was not clear whether the next step would be joint development, advocating for policy change, or step-by-step development in which one cluster would be the first target of development efforts, fully supported by others waiting in the queue for scarce funds.

Thus, despite the hopeful beginnings and the innovative framework for uniting CDCs, CND floundered. Its entire small staff either quit or was fired, and its major alliance with the city government on the Empowerment Zone bore no fruit since L.A.'s application was denied.[15] Relations among CND board members became fractious. While CND continues to exist, it is sharply reduced in scale, scope, and effect. In short, its record on outcomes has been meager: while individual relationships between some constituent groups continue, the construction of overall "social capital" between CDCs was on the whole unsuccessful.

San Antonio

Like Los Angeles, San Antonio has experienced a traumatic shift in the local economy. Once home to a diverse industrial base and a number of military installations, the city lost over 14,000 jobs in manufacturing, textiles, transportation and construction during the 1980's, followed by the reduction in military jobs. At the same time, new jobs were opening up both in low-wage sectors that require few skills and have little employment stability, such as the tourist industry, as well as in high-wage sectors that require extensive skills, such as health, education and business services.

Two affiliates of the Industrial Areas Foundation in San Antonio, the Communities Organized for Public Service (COPS) and the Metro Alliance, decided to tackle the problems induced by these broad economic changes.[16] COPS is the flagship organization of the IAF and is the outgrowth of community organizing in San Antonio's south and west sides, primarily poor, Latino and Catholic. However, the organization had difficulties expanding into other parts of town that were also poor, but not Latino and Catholic. Therefore, the IAF established a sister organization, the Metro Alliance. Incorporated in 1989, the Metro Alliance covers San Antonio's central city and east and north sides, and represents a broader cross section of the population, containing proportionally more Blacks, Whites, and non-Catholics who hail from the organization's roots in the Baptist, Lutheran and other community churches. Together, COPS and the Metro Alliance have forged a strong union but they still maintain separate identities and formal structure and are based in different racial communities.

COPS and Metro were catalyzed to act on the issue of employment and economic development by the 1990 decision of Levi-Strauss to shut down operations in San Antonio, a move that would have cut 2,000 jobs.

By the end of 1991, the two groups began developing the political support necessary to launch a new type of job training program and, in 1992, incorporated Project QUEST (Quality Employment through Skills Training).

Many consider QUEST to be the region's most effective training program for placing welfare recipients in work, with its graduates earning much more than welfare recipients trained by other, and specifically short-term, programs.[17] Most recently, QUEST received an Innovations in American Government Award from the Ford Foundation. Thus, any assessment of these IAF organizations would conclude that they have had a relatively positive economic impact on the material conditions of Blacks and Latinos, both in terms of overall neighborhood improvements and in terms of Project QUEST itself.

As in Los Angeles, however, the IAF has not been so successful in coalition building. Blacks and Latinos were united through their base organizations but the fact that separate organizations had to be put together (e.g., COPS had to support the formation of the Metro Alliance rather than simply absorb new members) suggests the difficulties in constructing a single multiracial polity. Moreover, collaboration among these two groups occurred within the IAF structure, but *not* across organizational boundaries—that is, collaboration did not include non-IAF organizations. Whether this is a first step toward building the sort of broad "social capital" necessary to sustain inner city neighborhoods, or whether the IAF will continue to go its own independent way, remains a key question.

East Palo Alto

East Palo Alto (EPA) was only incorporated in 1983. The city was born out of the population left behind when the more affluent San Francisco Bay Area Palo Alto and Menlo Park communities captured the wealthy areas and productive industrial base. In contrast to the surrounding communities, which are largely White and highly educated, EPA is heavily poor and minority. While the mean household income in San Mateo County is $63,672, East Palo Alto's corresponding income is $38,152. Drug trafficking and violence have been so pervasive that, in 1992, EPA had the highest murder rate per capita in the country. However, by 1993, the situation was beginning to turn around, largely due to the efforts of coalitional organizing under the aegis of the Congress of the Community Organizations (COCO).

COCO had its genesis in the meetings of the "Just Us" organization, a neighborhood group established to document the problem of drug sales and to report its findings and recommendations back to the community. The group soon realized that the only way realistically to stem the drug trade was to build a strong economic base. Toward this end, they organized a meeting of representatives of community-based organizations, churches, public agencies and local government to create a unified front for dealing with the economy and other challenges. The result of this meeting was the organization of COCO in October of 1991.

At the first meeting of COCO, the participants agreed to organize neighborhood block clubs. Each block club brought together residents, sometimes for the first time. Although some of the blocks were racially uniform, others were not, and collaboration required overcoming cultural differences and sometimes language barriers in order to come together as neighbors. The early organizers recall that many meetings were required before their common interests surfaced sufficiently to transcend differences and develop a clear focus.

The primary impediment to their efforts was neither the racial nor the cultural differences between individuals and neighborhoods, but rather a lack of financial resources. COCO began meeting with philanthropic organizations, as well as with corporate and business groups, to secure funding for (1) elimination of poverty and (2) development of strong families. During this time, the City of East Palo Alto was also conducting elections. The newly elected Mayor came out of COCO and had a strong background in community-based organizations. Faced with meager city resources, the Mayor began to meet with COCO to see if, through their coordinated efforts, they could jointly apply for funding to secure services in the city. To address local needs, they created the Dialogue Group.

This liaison forged a partnership between COCO and—by extension—the City and the community groups. The city and COCO received local funding that was then leveraged for preparing an application to the federal government as a federal Empowerment Community. As a result, EPA created its own police force (previously it was serviced by the county sheriff) and improved community relations such that crime dropped by 82% within a two-year period. Moreover, the city began to work with businesses to attract jobs and initiated the development of a major shopping center. The center opened in Christmas of 1996 and alone has created 1,200 jobs—to which EPA has attached a first source hiring policy.[18] After a decade and a half of existence, EPA is showing major advancements despite overwhelming odds against it.

COCO did not evolve from a sophisticated analysis and plan for community organizing but rather from grassroots efforts. From a consensual base developed through block clubs, COCO and the City were able to achieve not just job creation but actual economic development, as well as active community involvement in decisions affecting governance of the city. The relationship to municipal authorities has been close, as evidenced by the election of a COCO leader as mayor and subsequent efforts to work together on a citywide master plan. While the organization has had only minor regional impact—East Palo Alto is, after all, a small city in the large and dynamic Silicon Valley region—COCO was very successful at promoting collective work across ethnic lines.[19]

This success at transcending racial differences, identifying common purposes and building alliances with city authorities was due in part to the desperation of EPA's situation: with nowhere to go but up, the city of EPA and the constituent elements of COCO had to join together to achieve anything. Yet, it is also a function of the decision to organize on the basis of block clubs. Unlike the community development corporations of the Los Angeles Coalition of Neighborhood Developers, these block clubs were not competitive since they were not already in the development "business"; thus, they could more easily become the building blocs for democratic participation in new institutions. This is an impressive, if modest, performance: economic outcomes have been positive, new alliances have been formed, and the overall strategy has been organically rooted in neighborhoods.

CONCLUSIONS AND IMPLICATIONS FOR ORGANIZING AND POLICY

All of the cases examined illustrate instances of Black–Latino joint organizing around economic development. Looking at the results as a whole, the most classic coalition—the CND, which was cobbled together by first defining interests and then by looking for commonalities—scores low on both process and outcome. At the other extreme, the classical organizational model of the IAF (in Los Angeles, UNO/SCOC and in San Antonio, COPS/Metro) has had a significant impact on development and built consensus within its membership—but not in collaboration with other organizations. East Palo Alto's COCO harnessed grassroots support to successfully (re)build the local economy and its community organizers worked effectively with local government. Like COCO, CND worked with local government but with less success. Meanwhile, the

IAF groups tended to leverage government programs, seeking to affect policy (such as an increase in the minimum wage).

A review of the cases suggests that some organizational strategies may be more effective than others at reaching sustained economic development goals (see Figure 8-3). This is partly because of the nature of economic development efforts themselves. Such efforts often fall into one of two categories: people-based or place-based. People-based development focuses on building human capital or skills, increasing individual and community capacity and connecting residents to jobs (or improving their working conditions) wherever they may be. Because of this latter feature, such development is necessarily regional in impact and often scale, as both Project QUEST in San Antonio and the IAF's Minimum Wage Campaign in California demonstrate.[20] By contrast, place-based development focuses on revitalizing particular neighborhoods/places, hoping that such revitalization will attract business and jobs and thereby stir economic development. This is generally the mission of community development corporations (which provide housing and neighborhood-based services). These CDCs always risk adopting the zero-sum mentality associated with "bidding for business" or fighting for scarce funding for their efforts. In Los Angeles, the derailment of CND by its wary constituent CDCs exemplifies this tension.

At the same time, the difficulties of geographically based constituents can be overcome by proper organizing. The Nehemiah West project in the Los Angeles area was able to craft an alliance in which two separate ethnic communities were able to lobby together for housing development, despite the highly localized character of housing construction and the fact that one development inevitably would occur before the other. COCO in East Palo Alto was able to build a coalitional approach from grassroots units; it was further able to translate this into tangible economic development results, partly because of its close relationship with local government. Indeed, all the successful groups somehow leveraged government programs—QUEST became a vehicle for job training funds while Nehemiah West made use of local land use policy, and the Minimum Wage Campaign influenced state regulations—a pattern which suggests that the best efforts, be they organizational or coalitional, may require a relationship with government and state power.

These cases do not exhaust the realm of possibilities; also, they are not randomly drawn. Nonetheless, they do indicate that, despite the problematic economic conditions confronting U.S. minorities, Black and Brown unity can be achieved, particularly when one either takes an orga-

Figure 8-3 Ranking of Organizational Strategies of Case Studies

Ranked highest to lowest in category		Coalition	Organization/Consensu
Process: "Community-Building"	(+)	COCO: strong base for developing future policies	San Antonio and Los Angeles IAF: significant trust and community-building within organiza-tion; tensions with other organizations and general refusal to work in coalition
	(-)	CND: initial concept strong; strains due to ethnic and geographical tensions and "failure" may impede future efforts	
Outcome: "Econ. Development"	(+)	COCO: development of retail complex, provision of social services, insti-tutional capacity build-ing	SA IAF: model employ-ment and training program; revamped community college courses
	(-)	CND: minimal outcome (planning document) but constituent CDCs doing active development	LA IAF: strong results on minimum wage campaign; housing effort modest relative to need but at least in place.

nizational approach or carefully crafts a coalition. Such concerted efforts are warranted for several reasons. First, the current economic and social circumstances facing urban America are likely to heighten divisions be-tween Blacks and Latinos unless we engage in the building of new social capital between and within communities. Second, such community em-powerment and organizing are critical to the successful achievement of economic development objectives; without a population which is both ready for development and well-represented in the decision-making process, urban revitalization will remain a distant goal. Thus, the road to successful economic development and social equity lies in community organizing, and it is up to both researchers and activists to fully under-stand, and act on, the lessons from these and other experiences of in-terethnic action for economic empowerment.

NOTES

[1] See Bluestone and Harrison (1982), Harrison and Bluestone (1988), and Morales and Bonilla (1993).

[2] Skerry (1993: 157) notes, for example, that despite a strong base in Mexican American communities, neither Communities Organized for Public Service in San Antonio nor United Neighborhoods Organization in Los Angeles pursued issues traditionally associated with ethnic politics (such as bilingual education).

[3] The Industrial Areas Foundation, to which both COPS and UNO belong, was founded by community organizer Saul Alinsky in 1940, and is meant to be a network linking grassroots efforts. The "Alinsky-style" is very specific, involving, as noted in the text, a focus on building the organization, using paid staff, avoiding issues that might divide relevant constituencies, building a base in local institutions (particularly churches), and developing grassroots leaders. For a brief description, with a focus on COPS and UNO, see Skerry (1993: 144-174.

[4] Data from the Public Use Microdata Sample (PUMS), 1990 Census of Population and Housing, U.S. Bureau of the Census, Washington, D.C.

[5] The relationship between the growth of ethnic, particularly non-Black populations in electoral politics in Los Angeles is reviewed in Jackson and Preston (1994) and Saltzstein and Sonenshein (1991). Our focus here is on the broader "politics" of community organizing and development.

[6] On deindustrialization and African Americans in Los Angeles, see Johnson et al. (1992a, 1992b). For general and specific views of Latinos and reindustrialization in Los Angeles and elsewhere, see Melendez (1993), Morales and Ong (1993), Pastor (1993), and Wolff (1992).

[7] Pastor (1993:19–24) and Sonenshein (1993:254) discuss conflicts over jobs and resources after this. See also Miles (1992).

[8] There have been many other worthy interethnic efforts, including The Ethnic Coalition (which consisted mostly of professionals whose objective seemed to be the diversification of various governmental agencies), the New Majority Task Force (which brought together minority urban planners and community activists), and the Labor/Community Strategies Center, a leftist grouping that has been fairly successful at fund-raising and has a very clear regional and organizing strategy, particularly around transportation issues. Space precludes a full analysis of these groups although it is important to note that only the last group remained active as of late 1996. For a review of these and other groups involved in interethnic alliances in Los Angeles, see Regalado (1994).

[9] The IAF also includes the East Valleys Organization (EVO) and Valley Organized in Community Efforts (VOICE), which cover the San Gabriel and San Fernando Valleys respectively.

[10] For more on the minimum wage, see Industrial Area Foundation (1988).

[11] Indeed, the President and Vice-President of the Nehemiah board were former chairs of SCOC and UNO respectively.

[12] The only explicit criterion for CND(Coalition of Neighborhood Developers) membership was that the relevant neighborhood-based non-profit group place a "clear priority on the development of permanently affordable housing and community economic development" (CND 1994: 9). Organizations that did not primarily work in the field of neighborhood development were also welcome to join the CND's efforts as long as they made "positive contributions" toward the betterment of the coalitions' client-communities.

[13] One informant also suggested that CND's formation and expansion may not have been "organic" but rather due to an external catalyst of funder interest in developing the organization in the post-uprising atmospherics of Los Angeles. Indeed, tremendous hope was placed by many in Los Angeles in this effort since cross-neighborhood organizing has not been common in Los Angeles (in contrast to the experience of many Eastern cities). As a result, the CND process was generously funded by the James Irvine Foundation and received start-up capacity-building help from the Los Angeles office of the Local Initiatives Support Corporation (which mostly serves as an intermediary between community housing developers and funders and financiers). Unfortunately, when the funding for the separate umbrella organization began to decline, so did the group.

[14] Many of the individual groups and leaders do work together on development projects but some interviewees suggest that these would have occurred anyway and that very few such efforts occurred "inside" the CND process.

[15] This is particularly striking since the Empowerment Zone legislation was developed as a response to the L.A. uprising and Los Angeles was considered quite likely to receive Zone support.

[16] For more on the IAF in San Antonio and elsewhere, see Cortes (1993).

[17] For a discussion of QUEST's history, structure, and success, see Morales (1996).

[18] First source hiring implies that a developer or business must first attempt to employ a local resident.

[19] Indeed, promoting such interethnic work was one of their stated objectives. See Document of the Congress of Community Organizations, n.d:6.

[20] Although the Nehemiah West efforts may be place-based, they are emerging from a people-based framework, targeting the working poor. Moreover, the organization behind them, NWHC, is not attached to a specific place but rather to the goal of owner-occupied low-income housing in Southern California. Another interesting combination of place- and people-based strategies is embodied in the Dudley Street Neighborhood Initiative in Boston (see Medoff and Sklar 1994).

CHAPTER 9

Building Networks to Tackle Global Restructuring

The Environmental and
Economic Justice Movement

TERESA CORDOVA, JOSE T. BRAVO, JEANNE GAUNA, RICHARD MOORE, AND RUBEN SOLIS

We have a system of apartheid here in the United States. Particularly in places like where you find yourselves today, where us, 70% of the population, are dominated, exploited and repressed by a minority. A minority that continues sustaining a system of apartheid where 4.2 million agricultural workers have to suffer the use of pesticides for the simple reason that the majority are Mexicans. This is to provide profits to a group of food processing corporations which show no interest in the harmful effects to the land, the water, the air and even less to the agricultural workers. (Carlos Marentes, President of the Border Agricultural Workers Union (UTAF), El Paso, Texas)

And they are knowing in Washington in the medical field. They have records since the beginning of time about the effect of these toxics. Before they use them, they know what they will do. You will not find this in the aristocratic parts of town. But they will come to your area and they will put in on your border and they will tell you that they want to help you. Now that's racism. They know that they are going to destroy you and you are not counted. Well maybe this is kind of harsh, but I think you need to know this and you can't call it anything else but racism. That's all. Plain old racism. (Reverend R.T. Conley, New Waverly Baptist Church, West Dallas, Texas)

The U.S. government has entered into many agreements and treaties with the indigenous peoples of America, yet when the U.S. negotiated the North American Free Trade Agreement, which is an agreement between sovereign states, the indigenous people and our tribal governments were not invited to the negotiating table. We were not consulted. There were no open and respectful dialogues of the various impacts both pro and con of the free trade agreement; no consideration of the possible negative impacts to our fundamental human rights; nor to the protection of our natural resources, culture, aboriginal self-determination or sovereignty rights . . . Indigenous territories are sought or values for our raw trade good and materials such as timber, minerals, water, and non-renewable energy producing extractions such as oil, gas, coal and uranium. The industrial countries' energy policies are at the expense of our indigenous people. This is environmental injustice. (Jackie Warledo, Indigenous Environmental Network, Tulsa, Oklahoma)

Restructuring is dramatically shifting the processes of capital accumulation and enabling corporations to extract more profit from production (Castells 1989). The result is a widening gap between the rich and the poor, the exacerbation of all forms of inequality and the poisoning of neighborhoods and workplaces (Bluestone and Harrison 1982; Sklar 1995). People of color throughout the world have been especially hard hit by this restructuring (see Chapter 2).

Grassroots activists within the environmental and economic justice movement are confronting the exacerbated inequality and environmental degradation that accompany this restructuring. In this chapter we[1] present insiders' views of the consciousness, organizational structures and mobilization strategies of a grassroots movement's response, as defined by people experiencing the injustices. Through an assessment of the Southwest Network for Environmental and Economic Justice (SNEEJ or the Network), we identify significant characteristics of the environmental and economic justice movement and provide the grist for further analysis of grassroots challenges to global restructuring. The analytical, organizational and strategic elements of the Network suggest that grassroots activists have created an avenue and arena to challenge the most localized impacts of global restructuring. The main vehicle is the formation of networks of grassroots organizations. The case of the Southwest exemplifies globalization processes, their localized impacts and community responses to environmental racism.[2]

We begin with an analysis of the concept of networking within SNEEJ and how it developed to illustrate how people's organizations can respond to changes in the structures of exclusion and abuse. Next, we describe the impact of networking on the ideological and strategic methods of this form of organizing. We then address how this method of organizing facilitates the coming together of racial and nationality groups—e.g., Blacks, Latinos, and others—and how these collaborations, in turn, facilitate challenging localized impacts of global restructuring. Finally, we identify significant lessons for Blacks and Latinos in urban settings.

IDEOLOGICAL BASIS OF ORGANIZING THROUGH NETWORKS AND THE FOUNDING OF THE SOUTHWEST NETWORK FOR ENVIRONMENTAL AND ECONOMIC JUSTICE

The concept of networking stems directly from our political activism during the Chicano Movement of the late 1960s and 1970s. It evolved both from the experiences of the struggle and changes in the political economy. By the late 1970s, we were questioning the effectiveness of organizing methods employed during the Movement. The old methods were not working. They lacked the flexibility, inclusiveness, and adaptability that seemed necessary to address a changing environment and our own internal limitations. Our frustrations led to infighting and splits.

During this early period, there were three major organizational forms: committees, coalitions, and pre-party formations. Committees were formed around single issues. Coalitions comprised groups coming to the table with their single issue agendas. These approaches often led to fighting between positions over issues. In turn, this led to fragments in coalitions. It was difficult for everyone to feel autonomous in these coalitions. Often organized under national umbrellas, pre-party formations were very rigid and dogmatic. Their ideological platform and the centralized organizational structure preempted democracy and inclusiveness as working concepts and did not provide for more pluralistic relations and ownership. Many of us believed that the answers were contained in the platform and that organizing was a matter of taking this *conciencia* to the people. The ideological rigidities deprived us of the wealth of feedback and expanded actions that a more inclusive and democratic approach might provide.

Meanwhile, restructuring brought a new set of challenges related to capital mobility, the global reach of corporations and international agencies. This has resulted in negative impacts for our people and their ability to shift locations, has set people of color against each other, and has allowed corporations to bypass local organizing through increasingly flexible structures of operation.

We developed our concept of networks as an ideological, organizational and strategic response to progressive pre-party formations. It proved particularly flexible and responsive to the new challenges of restructuring. Incrementally, we were able to develop a new structure of intervention that proved effective and far reaching. We began to understand that ideological underpinnings of previous movements had prevented an appreciation of the knowledge people have of their own situations. People do not need imposed ideologies but rather structures to bring forward their voices and enable their participation. In 1979, we began our search for more effective organizing methods. Building on this insight, in the early 1980s, we built local organizations such as the Southwest Organizing Project (SWOP) and the Southwest Workers Union. Throughout the 1980s, the idea of networking was realized informally through the many connections being made regionally, nationally and internationally between organizations.

In 1990, SWOP convened the People of Color Regional Activist Dialogue on Environmental Justice. More than eighty activists from nearly twenty-five organizations met and discussed patterns and trends in the Southwest as well as new avenues for addressing them. The continued extraction of mineral resources and the growth in minority labor pointed to the region's significance as a resource colony and a strategic location for the global economy. We could observe the impact that changes were having on our communities of color. The best way to fight them, we thought, was to collaborate in a network led by people of color, for people of color. The result was the formation of the Network.

These efforts led to the 1991 People of Color Summit in Washington, D.C. At the Summit, the rallying cry became, *we speak for ourselves*:

> **WE, THE PEOPLE OF COLOR,** gathered together at the multinational People of Color Environmental Leadership Summit to begin to build a national and international movement of all peoples of color to fight the destruction and taking of our lands and communities, do hereby reestablish our spiritual interdependence of the sacredness of our Mother Earth; to respect and celebrate each of our cultures, languages and beliefs about the natural world and our roles in healing ourselves; to insure environmental justice; to promote economic alternatives which would contribute to the development of environmentally safe livelihoods; and to secure our political, economic and cultural liberation that has been denied for over 500 years of colonization and oppression resulting in the poisoning of our communities and land and the genocide of our peoples, do affirm and adopt these Principles of Environmental Justice.

We united around seventeen principles deriving from our connection to Mother Earth and threats to it.[3] Each group could identify with the overall covenant because it was inclusive and comprehensive. With these principles as a basis, we joined forces to confront the multilocal, flexible arrangements of globalization. Democratic organizational structures enabled our unity. Networks were the tools through which we could transcend ideological rigidity and to construct a concrete platform of action emerging from an organic, evolving process of dialogue and action. This process was flexible and patient, allowing for differences in views, beliefs and structures. It gave us a powerful mechanism for information gathering, multilocal intervention, and coordination of actions that, at the same time, included local initiative and self-determination.[4]

By collaborating and sharing information grounded in experience, we provide ourselves with the analysis needed to tackle environmental racism and to shift strategies toward what we call *a politics of engagement.* This politics is implemented through linkages: between local issues and the global economy; between economic and environmental issues; between workplace and community; among local organizations connected through a network; between labor and consumers; through communications across international borders; and among various racial and ethnic groups. Next, we describe in more detail the main elements of the Network.

ORGANIZATIONAL STRUCTURE ALLOWS PARTICIPATION OF DIVERSE VOICES

SNEEJ strengthens the work of local groups and harnesses the power of communities of color to influence local, state, regional and national policies on the environmental and economic justice issues important to them. It includes more than 82 grassroots groups from Texas, Arizona, Oklahoma, New Mexico, Colorado, Nevada, and California, as well as four states in Mexico—Baja California, Chihuahua, Coahuila, and Sonora—and organizations from Native Nations in the region. "The first network of its kind in the U.S., SNEEJ is challenging the myth that people of color are unconcerned with environmental issues" (Environmental Health Coalition 1993:15).

SNEEJ's primary purpose is to strengthen poor communities and organizations of color under stress from environmental degradation and economic injustice. It comprises groups that are organizing themselves to fight for their human rights. Its base is diverse.[5] It includes farm workers affected by pesticides; communities exposed to increased health risks from industrial pollution; garment workers impacted by plant closings; Native Americans threatened with or already paying the costs associated with uranium mining and militarism; Asian, Latina, and Pacific Islander *high tech* workers being poisoned on the job; indigenous communities fighting toxic incinerators and landfills; and Chicano and Black communities suffering from severe lead poisoning. SNEEJ is organized internationally and confronts issues that epitomize global restructuring. The Border Justice Campaign, for example, brings together communities from both sides of the border to confront environmental and economic racism at home and at work.

A major organizing premise is to build on diversity without excluding the special concerns of constituents. We accomplish this through our organizational structure and our decision making processes that allow for the full participation of all partners. Ownership of a process is critical to our efforts. If the organization is owned by its members, then, it creates a democratic, *bottom up* process. A bottom up approach takes longer but, in our opinion, is the clearest way of ensuring the efficacy of the Network and a movement true to those who participate in it. Accountability and responsibility drive the process. Based on our identities and experiences as people of color, we have developed a model to help us build real democracy.

ORGANIZATIONAL DECISION MAKING AND AGENDA SETTING

At its annual gathering, SNEEJ affiliates from each state select a representative to sit on the Coordinating Council, the executive body of the Network. The Network sponsors campaigns, which are the mechanism for organizing activities. Each of our campaigns has as its basic organizing unit a core group with seven to ten organizational representatives. This group makes the decisions regarding direction—goals, objectives, tactics—which are, in turn, reported as recommendations to the Coordinating Council. Currently, the campaigns include high tech, border justice, sovereignty, EPA accountability, youth, and workers' justice.

The Network's strength depends on the strength of local organizations. SNEEJ provides development support to local groups. It provides organizing and technical skill training along with infrastructure development relevant to the history and cultures of the Southwest and Mexico. It emphasizes leadership development and training of people of color. The

Network also hosts training activities in collaboration with others, increasing the capacity of affiliates to participate in decision making in order to overcome parochialism and cultivate comprehensive leadership.

COLLABORATIVE STRATEGIES

The process of collaboration works like this: people give voice to their experiences; from these voices emerge the analysis, the agenda and the strategies of the Network. We understand the impacts of restructuring through our local experiences. Our combined knowledge of local forces is the basis for our vision and strategic thinking. We are able to combine our knowledge, for example, to track particular corporations moving from one site within the Southwest to another, usually along the border. We are also able to share knowledge about the workings of public agencies, especially the Environmental Protection Agency (EPA). Our joint collaboration and communication allow us to respond to local manifestations of global restructuring.

Our strategic orientation has seven main characteristics:

1. We build strategies on analyses that emerge from people's experiences, e.g.,with North American Free Trade Agreement (NAFTA).
2. We develop regional perspectives to address environmental degradation and other social, racial, gender and economic justice issues.
3. Our work links issues of environmental, economic and social justice to local, regional, national and global forces.
4. We seek practical strategies that bring success and a sense of victory; the Network provides grassroots organizations in the region with a means of sharing local successes and organizing ideas as well as promoting solidarity with one another.
5. We promote the concept of accountability of industry and government. Government has become increasingly acquiescent to the needs of capital; we believe that it should be accountable to people. Unharnessed industry, which uses public resources, also needs to be accountable to the public. This is a major organizing principle.
6. We developed a bi-national organization bringing together community, labor, human rights, youth and student grassroots organizations based in the U.S.A. and Mexico.

7. We engage with other regional networks in campaigns and strategic efforts. For example, SNEEJ has joined with five other networks to develop an Environmental Justice Fund. It collaborates with other national activists by participating on the National Environmental Justice Advisory Council (NEJAC) of the EPA. Recently, SNEEJ brought representatives of the various environmental justice networks to join a partnership with the Oil, Chemical and Atomic Workers Union. The partnership is part of *Just Transition*, SNEEJ's campaign directly challenging the effects on labor of global restructuring.

Based upon our examination of the implementation of these strategies through collaboration, we can construct a theory and praxis of globalization and its relation to environmental racism, internal colonization, and the grassroots pursuit of justice.

GLOBALIZATION OF THE SUNBELT SOUTHWEST— ECONOMIC RESTRUCTURING, INTERNAL COLONIALISM AND ENVIRONMENTAL RACISM

Despite the accelerating polarization wrought by economic restructuring, patterns of inequality are a continuation of historical processes that have systematically relegated minority populations to an unequal status (Betancur, Cordova, and Torres 1993). While restructuring may be accelerating the environmental degradation of communities of color, environmental racism is most likely rooted in historically shaped processes of structural inequality.

The histories of communities of color in the United States are rooted in patterns of exploitation and expropriation of their labor and resources. In the case of Chicanos, for instance, countless studies document the process of conquest and domination (Acuña 1988; Chavez 1984). Appropriation of land and other resources, destruction of local economies and cultures and forced labor segmentation characterize the Chicano experience since the immigration of Europeans to the Southwest. Mario Barrera (1979) documents the political economic history of Chicanos in the Southwest suggesting that this history lays the foundation for the continued socioeconomic subordination and unequal status of the Chicano people. After an examination of several theories of racial inequality, Barrera favors the explanatory power of the theory of internal colonialism. Building on the work of Robert Blauner (1972), he argues that the process of establishing structural inequality in the Southwest bears characteristics of colonialism, despite the fact that the internal colony exists within the boundaries of a dominant colonial power.

> Colonialism historically has been established to serve the interests of merchants, industrialists and would-be landowners and of the state which ultimately safeguards the interests of the dominant classes. Internal colonialism is no exception to this rule. In addition, this model is consistent with the bulk of the material . . .on the role of agricultural and industrial capitalists in the nineteenth-century continental expansion of the United States, and in structuring the subordinate labor force that came into existence in the Southwest on the basis of various racial minorities (Blauner 1972:212).

Environmental racism, augmented by economic restructuring, is the continuation of this historically structured inequality.[6]

DEFINING THE OPPOSITION: AGENTS OF RESTRUCTURING IN THE REGION

We observed what was happening to us—and we asked why. We became aware that we, as people of color, were being poisoned by the dumping of deadly chemicals in the air, water and soil in our communities and the indiscriminate use of toxins in our workplaces. This compelled us to develop a focused analysis. People are dying after only a few years of exposure to poisons, particularly in high tech and defense industries. Farm workers and their families have tragically high rates of cancer and birth defects linked to pesticide exposure. Uranium spills have contaminated Native American lands. In the borderlands, children are being born without brains (SWOP 1993). The poisoning of communities of color is, in essence, genocide.

We asked who was poisoning us. We realized that the forces of U.S. capital drove these genocidal policies. We also needed to know how the various institutions and entities carried out these policies. We identified five major actors: the U.S. military, industry, agribusiness, governments at all levels and the mainstream environmental movement.

In the Southwest, the U.S. military has lived up to its reputation of being the world's largest polluter. New Mexico, often described as a military colony, is home to two out of the three U.S. national labs. The research and development, testing and storage of nuclear weapons has had extremely negative impacts on our communities (Race, Poverty and the Environment 1995). Texas has five military bases in San Antonio alone. Plans for temporary and permanent nuclear waste facilities complete this deadly cycle. President Clinton's recent call for military assistance to Mexico demonstrates the U.S. military role in globalization. The U.S. military will be used to deal with Mexico's current internal struggle when U.S. corporate investments are threatened.

Governments at all levels have also played a major role. Land use policies facilitate the disproportionate placement of polluting industries, municipal dumps, sewage treatment facilities and industrial waste sites in our communities (United Church of Christ 1992). Albuquerque's sewage facility is located in the South Valley, a mostly Chicano community. Yet, these residents do not have full access to sewage systems, storm drainage and clean water. The Department of Energy's proposal to dump nuclear waste water in Albuquerque's sewer system is an example of how the federal government places the burden on local communities (SWOP 1995a).

Corporations have a history of plundering human and natural resources with poisonous emissions and toxic exposure to workers. Throughout the Southwest giant high tech firms, such as Intel and Motorola, are operating (SWOP 1995b). Fleeing more stringent environmental standards and higher labor costs in California, they have set up shop in Arizona, Texas, New Mexico, and Puerto Rico. Intel, the largest microchip producer in the world, has received huge tax breaks to build its flagship plant in Rio Rancho, New Mexico. Along the way, it has expropriated scarce water resources and contaminated the air with toxic emissions.

Many workers at the Intel plant near Albuquerque are concerned that the massive amount of chemicals used in micro chip production may be impacting their health. They remember how GTE-Lenkurt, an Albuquerque-based high tech firm, poisoned at least 200 women—many of them Chicanas. Some of the women have died; many are ill and can no longer work; some have had children with birth defects. Known as a company with one of the worst cases of industrial poisoning in the USA, GTE-Lenkurt fled to Ciudad Juarez, Mexico, where environmental standards and labor protections are not enforced due to the lack of an adequate infrastructure.

U.S. agribusinesses are also guilty of contaminating the environment with and exposing workers to deadly pesticides. Farm workers are among the most exploited throughout the region. In Southern New Mexico, the chile barons use undocumented workers from Mexico to pick their crops. Their tenuous legal status forces many farm workers routinely to accept jobs picking crops in recently sprayed fields; many have developed skin and other diseases (SWOP 1993).

Recent changes to the Mexican Constitution promoted by pro-NAFTA forces allow for the privatization of communally owned land throughout Mexico. U.S. agribusiness, and others, such as the Japanese corporate giant Mitsubishi, are buying up the ejidos. This land too will now belong to those with capital (Beltran 1995). Such changes, instituted to facilitate the expansion of global capitalism, often create serious local problems. The Zapatista uprising, in our view, was due, in part, to the dismantling of the constitution and repeated human rights violations.

U.S./Mexico border communities devastated by unregulated agriculture and industrial development have found no remedy in NAFTA's environmental and labor sidebar agreements. Although consenting to these agreements, U.S. labor unions and some mainstream environmental groups now find themselves fighting simply another layer of bureaucracy. The borderlands are an environmental disaster and our people pay the price, increasingly, with our lives (SNEEJ 1994).

The U.S. mainstream environmental movement also played a role in the poisoning of communities of color. Often many of these well-funded, and mostly White-male-led, groups have promoted environmental policies that protect their environment at our expense. For example, The Clean Air Act allowed for lower standards in the inner cities where people of color live and work, in exchange for higher standards in the suburbs. The Environmental Defense Fund's pollution credit legislation allows for less polluting industry to trade pollution credits with companies exceeding standards (The National Law Journal 1992). Its three-pronged strategy of "lobbying, litigation and legislation" (Dowie 1995) makes it particularly vulnerable to cooptation by industry and government. Corporate funding is a large part of their budget and influences their priorities. The beautiful Southwest has been a refuge for "the middle class looking for middle earth" for decades. In New Mexico, the Sierra Club successfully promoted legislation turning the Acoma Pueblo's sacred land into a national park (SWOP 1990).[7]

Identifying the enemies enables us to act. The forces of globalization, as represented by supranational corporations more powerful than (and unaccountable to) nation states and by governments and political forces rolling over to capital, have compelled us to organize ourselves as peoples of color across international borders. The environmental and economic justice movement provides evidence that people of color can resist toxic poisoning of workplaces and communities that are the result of unregulated global economic activities.[8]

THREE EXAMPLES OF BLACK–LATINO COLLABORATION

In West Dallas, a community of Blacks and Latinos, high levels of pollution from a lead smelter company were poisoning adults and children and contaminating houses and businesses. Reverend Conley of the Wavery Baptist Church visited the company to complain; the company denied any wrongdoing. He then took his concerns to the City of Dallas, which also claimed that "nothing was wrong." A door-to-door survey by residents confirmed the extensiveness of the health problem. Although many residents were initially hesitant to sign petitions, an information campaign built a strong base of support—both Black and Latino. An alliance between Lead Better, a Latino group, and the Black Waverly Baptist Church led to the formation of the New Start Organization. After multiple demonstrations, news coverage and pressuring of government agencies, the company relocated to Tijuana, leaving behind a polluted community with high levels of lead and arsenic.

Residents sought help in the clean up from EPA, to no avail. EPA asked for evidence. The community eventually worked out an agreement with the city to test the children. The results became the basis for two successful lawsuits against the lead smelter company.

SNEEJ joined the struggle in 1992 and worked with the community to get the attention of EPA. Through its connections to the National Environmental Justice Advisory Council to the EPA, SNEEJ secured hearings on Texarcana and West Texas, thereby calling further attention to the issues. Demonstrations and marches to the local EPA office further helped to focus the attention on the plight of the community, but clean up still remains a major issue. This experience helped SNEEJ to share its knowledge and organizing strategies with communities in Tijuana who continue the struggle against the company.

The second case is the fight of the Concerned Citizens of South Central Los Angeles, a SNEEJ member, against the siting of a toxics waste incinerator in the community. Residents became aware of the proposal in mid 1985, when the city announced it for the first time. After nearly three years of groundwork without community input, the proposal was brought to the City Council. Three Black sisters from the community attended the meeting and raised questions. The city responded with an Environmental Impact Review developed without community input.

Afraid of the potential local impacts of the incinerator, the sisters worked with other residents in an extensive community and citywide campaign to defeat the project. They formed the Concerned Citizens to preside over the effort. Local organizing took place across race and place. The campaign brought immense attention to the issue. A petition drive was enormously successful. Organizers attended every possible forum in which they might raise the issue. They disclosed the financial contributions of the builders of the incinerator to City Council members. After two years of intense opposition the project was defeated.

Along the way, the community learned about the uneven distribution of Community Development Block Grants between affluent and low income neighborhoods. The process of community-building around the incinerator was followed by pressure on the city for community development funds. Concerned Citizens has organized the Black and Latino communities, block by block. They have engaged in fights for traffic lights, job training, housing and have sponsored recycling programs. Block clubs have been crucial in this work, allowing people to "get stuff out in the open." They have brought Blacks and Latinos together around their common problems while providing them with the opportunity to address their concerns and fears face-to-face.

Through SNEEJ, Concerned Citizens has been able to share its experiences with other organizations and influence the direction of the Network—e.g., one of its members attended the regional meeting leading to the formation of SNEEJ and is a former Co-chair of SNEEJ.

Our third case is from West County in Richmond, California, a community of working class African Americans and Chicanos with increasing levels of Laotians, Mexicans and other Latinos. Suffering from an array of pollution-related health problems, the community formed the West County Toxics Coalition (WCTC) to tackle Chevron Corporation, the largest polluter in the area. The Coalition conducted a door-to-door organizing campaign and compiled an inventory of problems. They took twenty experts, including hygienists and members of the National Toxics Campaign, for an inspection of the refinery. On this basis, the Coalition developed a list of fifty proposals to eliminate pollution, which it gave to the company and released to the media. The company denied all the allegations claiming that the Coalition was just out to make trouble.

The Coalition then sponsored a series of demonstrations and protests, took the case to the stakeholders meeting and engaged in Earth

Day celebrations and attended meetings of the Citizens Better Environment to draw attention to the issue. Finally, Chevron agreed to meet with the Coalition and make changes to improve the situation. The Coalition also formed a partnership with long shore and boat men and successfully promoted pollution prevention measures. While WCTC was the main organization responsible for this work, it learned and obtained support from other SNEEJ organizations. SNEEJ was particularly involved in pressuring the EPA to step up its enforcement activity and force Chevron to abate emissions. According to the founder of the Coalition, SNEEJ is the leading organization in the country in coordinating the work of communities of color. By facilitating the ability of communities to work together, it provides the connections necessary to help resolve problems. "Isolated and separated," one of the Coalition founders told the authors, "we don't have a movement and cannot tackle the problems affecting our communities."

The Coalition obtained a major victory for a small community overwhelmed by the polluting practices of Chevron. Through its outreach efforts, and working in coalition with leading forces in each group, it gained the support of Blacks, Latinos, and other local groups.

In all three cases, the networking approach worked for these Black and Latino community movements. The grounded and shared analysis was the basis for going after companies. Different races and nationalities were able to work together to resolve common problems. Along the way, they had the opportunity to learn about each other, to feel comfortable with each other and to realize the potential of their collaboration. Organizing around environmental issues, they moved together to other economic development fronts. Sharing of strategies and support through the SNEEJ network enforced the local efforts of member organizations.

SNEEJ was particularly helpful in tying local efforts to regional and national forces, providing legal assistance and facilitating networking with other organizations which had experience in similar undertakings. It was the vehicle for strengthening local efforts by connecting them to external forces. Through our local experiences, we make regional connections and observe the patterns of corporate and government behavior. We then wage accountability campaigns to demand environmental and economic justice. Institutional racism comes together more clearly when we view the border and the extensive poisoning and exploitation taking place across communities of color. The ideological, organizational and strategic characteristics of the Network were successful in approaching this kind of work.

While the global economy may be complex at the corporate level, it is not difficult to see how it lands on the shoulder of the poor: leverage buyouts, swindling loans and the war of capital have direct impacts on them. For example, when the stock market went down in the mid-1990s, there was a 10% drop in wages on the border. Restructuring has meant cutbacks in working and living conditions. We see plants move from one side of the border to another looking for cheap labor and lax regulations. These connections become the basis of collaborations between racial groups and between labor unions and community groups.

Yet, it is the organizing at the local level that is most significant. According to the leaders of these initiatives, building relations with everybody— networking—expands your power, resources and reach across races and spaces. In the words of Reverend Conley, "when society sees people working together, that is power."

IMPLICATIONS AND SIGNIFICANCE OF GRASSROOTS ACTIVISM WITHIN THE SOUTHWEST NETWORK FOR LATINO AND AFRICAN AMERICAN URBAN COMMUNITIES

Activists in Latino and Black communities concerned with worker safety, international trade policies, toxic contamination, industrial tax incentives, the semiconductor industry, air and water regulations, youth development and a host of other issues can find the SNEEJ approach useful. Below we summarize basic SNEEJ principles and processes that we believe are effective methods of working for social change.

First, the primary vehicle for mobilization is through the formation of local groups tied together through regional networks. This is in contrast to organizational structures in which there is an umbrella organization with several local chapters that follow the direction of the central power structure. In SNEEJ, local groups define their own agendas. Networks of these organizations define campaigns and give direction to the activities. Through local groups, strategies are employed to directly confront the source of injustice in their communities.

Second, the level of knowledge and understanding is sophisticated and extensive. Activists in an urban-based environmental and economic justice movement will be able to provide an explicit understanding of what is happening in communities and why, and can then identify the impacts of environmental racism and who is responsible. Knowledge emerges directly from grounded experience enhanced by both an awareness of trends in the world economy and their local impacts and an understanding of government processes, from policy making to enforcement. In addition, the problems we confront require us to have access to very specific information about a number of complex issues, such as water management, tax structures and chemical composition.

Third, the values and principles within the movement stem directly from shared experience and are formed in opposition to ideologies of domination. To reach a level of consciousness that promotes action, we must first articulate our set of principles and values, and then clearly identify our opponents and their conflicting values. We know, for instance, that our belief that land, environment and people have use values is contradictory with the corporate concept of exchange values. Latinos and Blacks (overwhelmingly working people and displaced workers) can learn much from SNEEJ's experiences with collaboration based on diverse groups. Environmental justice activists have a cultural, regional and global identity as people of color coalescing around a common ground and shared experience.

Fourth, principles of democracy provide the basis for organizational structures and processes. Within the organization we make decisions from the bottom up, and we pressure corporations and governments to incorporate this model in their policy making: *Call us to the table while decisions are being made—not after.* Policy and regulation *can* come from the bottom, as they did in the case of the Executive Order on Environmental Justice. We recognize that the knowledge within communities is essential to every decision making process and that leadership development is fundamental if communities are to speak for themselves.

Fifth, the shared experience of bearing the brunt of the negative impacts of globalization creates the common ground for multiracial organizing. Common issues are the basis for unity—people of color are being poisoned. By understanding this SNEEJ creates opportunities not only to share its experiences with grassroots activists from African American and Latino communities, but also to bring them together with Indigenous Peoples and Asian/Pacific Islanders, despite a system that does everything possible to keep us at odds.

Sixth, cross-border organizing requires the development of international networking among grassroots activists. Concurrent with the increasing internationalization of the economy, activists from the Network are building bridges with activists worldwide. In the process we are learning more about the interconnected impacts of global restructuring. Cross border organizing between the Southwest and Mexico involves an intimate understanding of "free trade" policies and their consequences, particularly for indigenous peoples. Increasingly, grassroots activism is becoming internationalized through such networks, rather than single umbrella organizations.

Three other points are worth noting as they relate very specifically to African American and Latino political relations and work in the policy arena in cities. First, environmental and economic issues are inseparable elements of environmental racism and the fight against it. For people of color, environmental degradation is tied to economic processes.

Second, the economic and environmental justice movement demonstrates that resistance can exist even at a time when forces of domination seem overwhelming. The movement brings this resistance together while making sure that people do not feel alone. The movement succeeds by building on our consciousness, principles, unique organizational structures and effective mobilization strategies.

Third, *the politics of engagement* characterize the politics of grassroots activism within the Network. Rather than shunning *the enemies*, as in previous organizing styles, environmental justice activists directly confront them by inserting themselves into discourses of power and into decision making tables. We emphasize having control of our space and, thus, of our future. People of color have a history of confrontational, direct action, social movement involvement.

The environmental and economic justice movement might be viewed as an insignificant mobilization—if we see social change only as a massive turnaround in the logic of capital. But, if we view social change as the outcome of a protracted process of conflict (Córdova forthcoming), the environmental justice activists, within and outside the Black and Latino communities, who are in it for the long haul, may be providing an important set of principles and strategies to challenge corporations and colluding governments during an era of restructuring and global change.

CONCLUSION

SNEEJ is a network of linkages bringing together several issues and organizations. While local activists work in collaboration with other groups, we maintain a specific cultural and regional identity. Again, the collaboration is only as strong as each of the organizations. This suggests that collaborations are more effective when they are based on localized identities: the stronger these identities, the stronger are the bases for the collaboration. It is, then, localized actors, connected through regional, and international networks, that become the basis for confronting the impacts of global restructuring. Through the formation of networks for justice, grassroots activists of color challenge the global networks of dominance that are being formed at our expense. Through the politics of engagement, we directly resist the corporations and governments who dare to endanger our communities.

Grassroots activists, using the analytical, organizational and strategic elements of the Network, have created an avenue and arena to challenge the most localized impacts of global restructuring. Networks allow us to hear the voices of people with knowledge coming from their life experiences. Through networks we can share analyses and collaborate on strategies that directly confront the agents of environmental racism and maximize our effectiveness. Our approach to networking also shapes our ideological, organizational and strategic methods. By avoiding ideological rigidity or narrow political agendas, we allow for organic processes that are dynamic and flexible. Through processes of organizational formation that instill a sense of ownership, our method facilitates racial groups coming together to challenge the shared problems we are facing in our communities. These collaborations among racial groups, in turn, open the door for productive opposition to localized impacts of global restructuring. Our shared experience is the basis and strength for our collaboration. The *politics of engagement* through networks provides the ideological, organizational and strategic impetus to insert ourselves into the struggle to define the future of our communities.

NOTES

[1] The authors are four movement activists and an activist researcher. Jeanne Gauna and Richard Moore organized the Southwest Organizing Project (SWOP) in Albuquerque. Ruben Solis laid the foundation for what later became the Southwest Workers Union. Teresa Cordova is an activist researcher at the University of New Mexico. The authors are involved in multiple capacities in the environmental and economic justice movement particularly through Southwest Network for Environmental and Economic Justice(SNEEJ).

[2] Unequal environmental consequences of economic restructuring on communities of color constitute environmental racism. Industrial and agricultural toxins are disproportionately concentrated in the communities and workplaces of people of color. Research conclusively establishes race as the single most significant predictor in the location of incinerators, landfills, toxic industries and haz-

ardous treatment, storage and disposal sites (U.S. General Accounting Office 1983; United Church of Christ 1987; Bullard 1990; Bryan and Mohair 1992). People of color are disproportionately employed in highly toxic industries and occupations. In addition, government enforcement of environmental policies systematically ignores communities of color (The National Law Journal 1992).

[3] These principles affirm the sacredness of Mother Earth; demand public policy based on mutual respect and justice; assert our right to ethical, balanced and responsible uses of land and renewable resources; call for universal protection from nuclear and hazardous waste; affirm fundamental rights to self-determination; demand the cessation of production of all toxins; call for full decision making participation including assessment, planning, implementation, enforcement and evaluation and the right of workers to safe and healthy work environments; assert the right of victims to full compensation; the declaration of governmental acts of environmental injustice as violations of international law; demand recognition of Native Peoples sovereignty and self determination; call for policies to clean up communities; call for enforcement of policies which prohibit experimentation on peoples of color; oppose destructive operations of multinational corporations and military occupation and repression; urge education on social and environmental issues; and commit consumers to make choices which protect Mother Earth.

[4] For example, the Network has helped us understand patterns of activities of firms and government agencies, hence helping confront them more effectively.

[5] Projects and organizations include: toxic impacts from landfills and medical incinerators (Concerned Citizens of Sunland Park); construction of garbage incinerators (Concerned Citizens of South Central Los Angeles, Mothers of East Los Angeles); treatment and disposal plants (Native American communities, Kettleman City, California); pesticide fumigation, racially motivated zoning practices, unwanted industries (San Diego's Barrio Logan); and toxins in the workplace (Asian Women's Advocates, Southwest Public Workers Union). Groups are also confronting use of pesticides in agriculture (Union de Trabajadores Agricolas Fronterizos-UTAF, Lideres Campesinas), high tech (SWOP, People Organized in Defense of the Earth and Her Resources-PODER, Tonatierra), the contamination of bays, land and rivers (Environmental Health Coalition), lead contamination (Newstart, PODER), chemicals in the water (Tucsonians for a Clean Environment), worker health and safety (Fuerza Unida, Korean Immigrant Worker Advocates, Toxins Coalition), uranium mining (Havasupai Nation) and land and water issues (Tonantzin Land Institute). In Mexico, organizations fight contamination and labor issues at maquilas (Casa de La Mujer, Grupo Factor X, Centro Informacion Solidaridad Obrera—CISO, Centro Obrero de Acuña, Servicios Desarrollo y Paz—SEDEPAC).

[6] The globalization process is evidenced by examining dynamics of environmental racism in the Southwest and Mexico. NAFTA, for example, is seen in the environmental justice movement as the economic takeover of Mexico, a new stage in the history of colonialism in this region. Environmental activists in the Southwest define issues based on direct experiences with environmental racism and with those they have observed to be directly responsible.

[7] In the case of NAFTA, some mainstream environmental groups cut deals with governments on both sides, so that they could keep their projects in Latin America. Sierra Club is currently debating an anti-immigration stance that promotes population control and restricted immigration.

[8] For reasons of space, we cannot include here a list of the numerous involvements and accomplishments undertaken by SNEEJ activists. Many of them have great salience for Black and Latino collaborations in the cities where they are concentrated. For a list of them the reader can contact SNEEJ directly.

CHAPTER 10

Black and Latino Coalitions
Means to Greater Budget Resources for Their Communities?

STEPHEN ALEXANDER

In the City of Chicago, many groups and individuals in low-income communities, especially those that are predominantly African American and Latino, believe that municipal programs designed to deliver resources to neighborhoods and special needs communities are not reaching sectors with the greatest needs for public services. A survey of residents conducted by the *Chicago Sun Times* and Northwestern University in four different neighborhoods showed that perceptions of quality of services and the equity of their distribution varied according to income and race (Brune 1994).[1] Of those surveyed, more than half from communities with higher median family incomes and lower percentages of people of color (more than 85% White) rated public services to be "good" or "very good," while more than half from communities with lower median family incomes and higher percentages of people of color viewed city services as "very poor" or "fair," with only 25% believing that services were "good" or "very good."

These class- and race-based perceptions of fairness in the quality and the distribution of publicly funded programs and services need to be explored for several reasons. First, we must determine whether or not government-funded programs are inequitably distributed to low-income groups and communities of color as compared to middle- and upper-class Whites. Second, federal government retrenchment has produced significant changes with very damaging effects on African Americans and Latinos. Federal efforts to dismantle the welfare state, to restructure government through economic deregulation, and to return more decisions to state and local governments and communities create concerns about the ways in which local units of government raise their resources and decide how to spend them. Third, dramatic losses of quality jobs in the private sector, especially manufacturing, and in government services are forcing many heads of families and households into low-wage employment or out of the job market altogether. As a result, the poor, working class people and communities of color, who increasingly reside in big cities like Chicago, are affected most dramatically by distributional issues related to municipal budgets.

This essay reports the initial findings of research conducted by the author in Chicago. Specifically, it examines (1) the relationship between African American–Latino coalition and budget distribution; (2) findings from a comparison between the budget and management policies of the Harold Washington/Sawyer (1983-1989) and the Richard M. Daley regimes; and (3) implications for future research on the role of municipal budget policy processes and their relation to low-income residents and communities of color. Research and analysis are developed from a community empowerment and development perspective.

BUDGET THEORY/PHILOSOPHY

Public funding is critical for Black and Latino neighborhoods to adequately address many of their priority needs. The availability of public resources for these priorities is the result of the budgeting process.

Governments attempt to serve diverse constituents through the budget process by translating financial resources into human purposes. In every government budget, revenues are taken from the public and redistributed as programs and services. Conflict can arise over distribution of resources because of the wide variety and scope of needs. Thus, government should never represent the desires of any single group—it must attempt to represent the needs of many (Wildavsky 1986). It is important to understand that resource constraints normally do not allow governments to address everyone's needs. Therefore, conflicts and tradeoffs are inherent in budget-making. Budgets are the operational expression of priorities in the public sector.

If low-income communities and their elected representatives have priorities that need to be addressed through publicly funded programs, they must be prepared to deal with competing demands of communities and groups with different preferences. Affluent communities generally prioritize basic services such as police and fire protection, garbage removal, street cleaning and maintenance. In contrast, low-income communities with high rates of poverty and unemployment have additional social and economic needs such as access to quality jobs, affordable housing, adequate food and a vibrant neighborhood economy. Perceptions regarding fairness may vary according to income status and the associated level and type of need. The question that needs to be answered, thus, is whether or not the concerns of residents living in moderate and low- income communities of color about fairness and equity are justified.

In theory, governments develop budgets to allocate benefits and services that the public needs. Public policies reflect the preferences that are most powerfully expressed by individuals or groups. Preferences for certain policies are promoted by groups representing various sectors such as business, the middle class, low-income citizens, labor, persons of color. Ideally decision makers would balance the interests of these different groups. However, political leaders generally respond more to the priorities of those who are members of organized and politically powerful groups.[2]

Preferences of individuals and communities vary widely and, since resources are scarce, competition over which preferences get included and, conversely, which ones are excluded, is often very intense. Therefore, those individuals and organizations who are the most competitive and aggressive are the ones who are most likely to obtain resources to address their needs.

The political culture, within which government operates, dictates in part the response to requests of residents of communities whose needs are not addressed sufficiently. If a government operates under a fiscally conservative culture, then resource constraints can make equitable distribution of funds difficult. On the other hand, if elected officials are more socially conscious and are willing to raise sufficient resources to address serious problems, the priorities of low and moderate-income communities are more likely to be addressed.

Several types of political cultures have been observed over the last 30 years. They can be generally classified into three categories (Clark and Ferguson 1983:33-36):

Fiscal and Social Conservatism. Under this approach, government programs are eliminated or drastically reduced. The taxpayer is seen as the primary constituent. Reducing taxes is considered more important than providing government programs. The private market is considered more efficient than government. Social issues such as poverty, homelessness and health care are considered an individual, not a public responsibility.

Fiscally Conservative and Socially Liberal. This policy seeks to reduce tax burdens on the individual taxpayer and the middle class, while attempting to maintain programs that address the needs of the poor and disenfranchised.

Fiscally and Socially Liberal Government. Under this approach, government funds programs adequately and equitably, and actively engages issues of poverty, unemployment, public health and discrimination.

Typically, stable middle- and upper-income communities and businesses have supported a conservative approach to government. Low- and moderate-income communities have valued a fiscally and socially liberal form of government. Thus, if the needs of the Black and Latino communities require leadership that embraces a fiscal and socially responsive form of government, the question is: can Blacks and Latinos achieve their goals without being unified? A second question would be whether it matters if the elected political leader: (a) responds by carrying out the preferences of the two communities and uses the budget process to fund economic and social programs to address their needs; or (b) institutes his or her own priorities as opposed to those expressed by the two communities by embracing a social and fiscal conservative budget policy. These two questions will be examined below by comparing the Harold Washington and Richard M. Daley periods in the City of Chicago.

BUDGET POLICY AND RACE

In theory, if a mayor is socially and fiscally liberal, conditions for Blacks and Latinos should be better. Such a mayor would encourage Black–Latino unity because it would provide her/him with the political and community support needed to justify her/his socially liberal budget policies and priorities. On the other hand, if a mayor is socially and fiscally conservative, she or he should discourage Black–Latino unity because she or he does not want a politically powerful coalition that would hold her/him accountable for disbursing budget resources equitably to various communities.

The hypothesis is, then, that a socially aggressive budget policy is more compatible with a strong Black–Latino coalition in jurisdictions where they form the political majority. A socially and fiscally conservative policy is more likely to be successful in the absence of a Black and Latino coalition, even when they form a political majority or a significant political minority. To examine this hypothesis, I compared budget information and policies put in practice during the Harold Washington period to those set up by the Richard M. Daley regime.

Since current theory barely addresses whether or not the race of an elected political leader affects his or her ability to adequately respond to Black and Latino priorities, this study's findings and conclusions should be used cautiously. In this case, did the fact that Harold Washington was African American encourage his political opponents to obstruct the efforts of his administration to strengthen economic opportunities for Blacks and Latinos? Race as a factor is significant because opponents realize that if Blacks and Latinos receive greater resources as a result of forging a coalition, then they will become economically, socially and politically empowered. Thus, it is in the best interest of opponents to frustrate efforts of Blacks and Latinos to coalesce to improve their communities. Their failure would also send the message that a Black–Latino coalition will not work. Therefore, we first ask if race was a factor in the allocation of public sector budget resources in Chicago.

Robert Mier (1993), Director of Development for Mayor Washington, observed that race was a powerful aspect of most planning situations in urban activities. Yet, he added, race was too often the last way a problem or a crisis was framed (Mier 1993).[3] Two issues that occurred during Harold Washington's administration provide examples of why race is a crucial factor.

The first example involves a struggle over the way Community Development Block Grant (CDBG) funds were to be distributed by the Washington Administration. CDBG is a federal program specifically designed to fight poverty and improve conditions for moderate and low-income families and communities. Chicago's entitlement share of CDBG during Mayor Washington was approximately 100 million dollars.[4]

In 1984, the Washington Administration instituted an eligibility criterion based on individual standards of need rather than on traditional citywide income standards for CDBG-funded projects. The new criteria led to a confrontation with the Chicago City Council spearheaded by 10th Ward Alderman Vrdolyak. The Council majority (known as the "Vrdolyak 29") did not like this change, mostly because it would decrease funding to constituents in their wards.[5] Mayor Washington vetoed the CDBG budget for fiscal year 1985 because the City Council majority insisted on including some ineligible activities. Consequently, all employees funded by CDBG sources were laid off until the City Council relented and passed Mayor Washington's budget (Mier 1994). Unfortunately, many employees were Blacks and Latinos. Washington's opponents hoped that those who were laid off would blame the Mayor, but it backfired because most blamed the "Vrdolyak 29."

The interpretations of Mayor Washington's actions suggest that race played a key role. The popular and, in some cases, scholarly view was that Mayor Washington was using his power to reward African Americans and punish others. While all of Mayor Washington's City Council allies represented moderate and low-income communities, including those with the highest rates of poverty and housing problems, many in the majority represented more affluent communities (mostly White). Most observers ignored the fact that most of the poor were African American and Latino and, therefore, were eligible for CDBG funds. In their minds race, not poverty, was the main motivation behind Washington's actions (Mier 1994:237).

Another example in which race played a major role is the Washington administration's attempt to set up a targeted hiring program. The goal was to have businesses that received public subsidies provide job benefits to those who needed them most—unemployed and underemployed Blacks and Latinos. Efforts to develop targeted hiring programs in other cities were explored, with Portland, Oregon having the best model. Oregon's program, called "First Source Hiring," required businesses that received public assistance to enter a contract with job placement organizations to give them first opportunity to fill new jobs.

Attempts to carry out this program also created controversy. The program was cast as a patronage tool for Mayor Washington. The patronage image prevailed in spite of Mayor Washington's efforts, such as granting civil service or collective bargaining rights to 40,000 municipal employees, most of them White, to abolish the patronage practice that existed before he took office. Resistance to the program was especially harmful to the Black–Latino coalition because a targeted hiring program would have addressed one of the highest priorities of Blacks and Latinos—employment.

THE HAROLD WASHINGTON AND RICHARD M. DALEY PERIODS

African Americans and Latinos, along with progressive Whites, formed a powerful coalition that led to the election of Harold Washington as Chicago's first non-White mayor. Most press accounts emphasized the success that the Black–Latino political alliance had in crippling

Chicago's old political machine. More importantly for Blacks and Latinos, however, the sharing of power would enable them to make significant economic improvements as a result of a more progressive approach to Chicago's budget policies and priorities. Unfortunately, Harold Washington's death in November 1987 led to the resurgence of Chicago's political machine and ended the already tenuous alliance between Blacks and Latinos (see Chapter 4).

Does a coalition between Blacks and Latinos benefit each of these communities? Is the potential for the Black and Latino communities to receive greater shares of public resources during a coalition period than during a period when no coalition exists? A comparison of policies during the Washington and Daley periods, using political and budget theories as a guide, helps us better understand and predict the potential benefits of a coalition between Blacks and Latinos as well as the potential costs from the absence of a progressive coalition that has as its foundation a unity between Blacks and Latinos.

To begin to address these issues, this study asks whether there is evidence that Mayor Washington's budget and management policies reflected the priorities of the Black and Latino communities. A comparison of Washington's and Daley's record reveals several policy differences and suggests that the Harold Washington, Black–Latino coalition period offered greater potential for economic and social gains than the current Daley period.

The first policy difference involves approaches toward community development. Because of his explicit commitment to neighborhood development, Washington separated responsibility for economic development into two departments. His Planning Department was responsible for downtown projects, while his Department of Economic Development (DED) served the neighborhoods. This separation was designed to signal community leaders and residents that one major city agency was responsible for and accountable *only* to neighborhood economic development. This was evident since DED's budget was exclusively used to administer community development programs.

In contrast, the Daley period does not show such a clear commitment to community development. In fact, in 1991 Mayor Daley eliminated the Department of Economic Development by combining it with the Planning Department to form the Department of Planning and Development (DPD). This creation of a new, so-called "super agency" confounded the commitment of resources to the neighborhoods since DPD's budget contains resources for both downtown and the neighborhoods.

Under Daley's policy, the neighborhoods do not have a single agency or budget devoted exclusively to their community development. The argument for combining the two agencies was based on efficiency, but the question that needs to be addressed is whether this efficiency led to lower resource allocation to communities. Available evidence points in this direction. Daley's priority is downtown development, as opposed to the neighborhood emphasis of Harold Washington (see Chapter 2).

The second major policy difference involves the two mayors' commitment to job creation—an especially critical need in Black and Latino communities. Harold Washington sought to address this concern through the "first source" hiring policy described earlier. In addition, Washington assigned job creation policy to the community-focused DED, one of his key agencies. Under the Daley Administration, there is no single department whose primary mission is to create jobs. The Washington Administration explicitly engaged in efforts to ensure that low-income persons and city residents be given high consideration for jobs created through government contracts, loans to businesses, subsidies or other assistance. In contrast, the Daley regime has never made this a priority.

Furthermore, public statements by Mayor Daley reveal the City's, at best, minimum commitment to job creation. In his 1995 budget statement, he made his position clear: "Government can't create private sector jobs;" it can only create a better climate for businesses to expand and remain in the City.[6] This is a significantly different approach to employment policy, a major priority of Blacks and Latinos. Meanwhile, all levels of government clearly retain and create jobs through the provision of billions of dollars in contracts that directly benefit private businesses.[7] In addition, Mayor Daley's claim that the role of the city is the creation of a "better climate for business" might imply that this is his primary mission for economic development, as opposed to the job creation priority of the Washington period.

A third difference, not as obvious as the first two, involves policies for increasing minority and women participation in city contracts that both Washington and Daley support. However, a close examination of specific policies reveals important differences in contracting opportunities for Blacks and Latinos. Harold Washington was the first mayor to establish an affirmative action contracting policy in Chicago through an *executive order* that set the *minimum* for minority and women participation in city contracts at 25% and 5%, respectively. Washington further showed his commitment by establishing a very strong monitoring and enforcement system, overseen from the Mayor's office. This system required all departments to comply and submit regular updates on progress toward meeting the Mayor's goals. If progress was unsatisfactory, the head of each department had to explain his or her failure to the Mayor.[8]

Mayor Daley adopted Washington's policy and pressed for its adoption in City Council as an ordinance (a legislative act of local government). However, Washington's policy offered greater opportunities to persons of color and women because it included *all types of contracts,* that is, construction and professional service contracts. In contrast, Daley's ordinance focuses only on construction contracting. Since minorities and women face greater barriers to entry in the construction industry, opportunities for significant progress for Blacks and Latinos will be minimal unless the Daley administration takes actions to remove these barriers. Moreover, unlike Washington, monitoring and oversight from the Mayor's office does not exist in the Daley administration.

Another major difference is the affirmative action hiring policy of the two mayors. Budget resources for personnel are a very important part of the budget process and make up a substantial part of City budget funding. Washington's insistence on equality of representation in city jobs for all groups residing in Chicago was well publicized. He started one of the most aggressive affirmative action hiring programs in the nation (*Chicago Reporter* Annual Reports on Minority Hiring and Contracting, 1980–1995). This policy was very significant not only because it produced economic opportunities for Blacks and Latinos, but also because it led to increased investments in the neighborhoods. When Blacks and Latinos are employed, their taxes benefit their communities (as well as all of society). Their income provides for their families, maintains their homes, and helps local community businesses.

The Daley administration did not maintain Washington's affirmative action hiring policy and has not shown an interest in carrying out an effective policy. Currently, his administration takes little responsibility for affirmative action: given that his administration is committed to privatization, it is the responsibility of private sector firms to maintain minimum acceptable standards of minority inclusion in public sector contracts. Scrutinizing the practices of contractors receiving awards to provide city services is difficult. Moreover, the hiring practices of the Daley period have not received the same degree of scrutiny as those of the Washington period. The movement is more diffuse; the political climate is less intense (see Chapter 4 in this volume for a discussion of the relative employment and contracting practices of Blacks and Latinos under the two regimes.)

In 1983, the City of Chicago funded 35 community-based economic development organizations (CDCs or CDOs) as "delegate agencies."[9] Based on Mayor Harold Washington's philosophy of encouraging development in the neighborhoods, the delegate agency program was expanded by DED and, within two years, the number of delegate agencies grew to 100, an increase of 185% (Mier and Moe 1991). By 1989, there were more than three hundred nonprofit delegate agencies under the program, as it was extended by Mayors Washington and Sawyer (Gills 1991).

In contrast, during the Daley period, the number of community-based, not-for-profit delegate agencies funded by CDBG has decreased from their levels during Mayor Washington period. The current administration has preferred to deal with fewer community development organizations, in particular and community-based delegate agencies, overall (see Chapter 4). Furthermore, when adjusted for inflation, CDBG resources directed to community-based groups have declined significantly from their levels during the Washington and Sawyer period (Alexander and Theodore 1994). Decreases for CDBG-funded delegate agencies hurt Blacks and Latinos more than any other communities. Also, under Daley, Corporate (budget)-funded[10] delegate agencies' budgets have increased by more than 200% since the initiation of this program in 1985. Since Corporate agencies, with very few exceptions, are found in middle-income, White communities, the effect of Daley's policy is to increase funding for middle-income Whites while allowing funding for Blacks and Latinos to decline (Alexander and Theodore 1994).

EMERGING TRENDS

Besides the policy differences discussed above, several trends strongly suggest that current budget policies and practices are affecting low-income and Black and Latino communities. Again, analysis of Chicago provides important clues.

First, the Corporate Fund, which covers basic city services, has consistently increased over the last several years. For example, estimated revenues were projected to increase from 1.69 billion dollars in 1992 to 2.11 billion in 1997[11] in order to provide additional city services, in particular to hire more police personnel, and to improve fire and sanitation services. It also has been used for the installation of impressive infrastructures in the CBD and in areas targeted for development of middle income housing. Simultaneously, Mayor Daley achieved his primary revenue policy goal by cutting property and business taxes by more than $65 million from 1993 to 1996 (Chicago Budget Revenue Estimates).[12] This simultaneous growth in the Corporate Fund revenue and reduction of property and business taxes required increases from other revenue sources to make up the difference. In 1996, property and business taxes combined made up less than 10% of the Corporate Fund! The other 90 plus percent came from various revenue sources such as sales, utility, income, transportation and recreation taxes, and also non-tax sources like fines and forfeitures.

The question is: Who carries the burden? Revenue sources such as sales taxes and fees are highly regressive and, thus, place a higher burden on moderate and low-income groups. We need to examine thoroughly whether the burden is shifting ever more toward low and moderate-income individuals and families, where African Americans and Latinos are disproportionately represented. In other words, are Black and Latino families shouldering a larger share of the burden than most people perceive? Also, is the current trend to reduce property taxes helping or hurting those who are not property owners, low-income persons? These questions need further research before they can be adequately answered; however initial analysis of Chicago's budget suggests that this is definitely the case (Alexander 1995).

Second, the City's budget philosophy is to rely almost exclusively on federal, state and foundation grants (which are decreasing) to address the economic and social needs of low income populations and communities, while using locally raised (and increasing) Corporate Funds to provide basic services (police, fire, streets, sanitation). For example, in 1997, 67% of the Health Department, 90% of the Department of Housing, 93% of the Departments of Human Services and Planning and Development and almost 100% of the Mayor's Office of Employment and Training budgets came from grants (City of Chicago 1997 Budget). This trend will likely increase economic distress in low- and moderate-income communities.

While the City of Chicago's *total* budget (local revenue plus federal and state grants) has increased marginally over the last several years, the size and percentage of the grants' share of the total budget steadily increased from 550 million dollars or 14% of the total budget in 1992 to 910 million dollars or 27% of the total in 1995, but dropped to 802 million or 22% of the total in 1996, and to 750 million or 17% percent of the

total in 1997 (City of Chicago 1997 Budget). These trends are apparently
due in part to the impact of Congress' devolution policy. Unfortunately,
this downward trend in grant funds is likely to continue. This is because
Congress and President Clinton have agreed on a goal of balancing the
federal budget by the year 2002. This is to be done by reducing funding
for urban and social programs important to moderate- and low-income
persons. If the budget cutting trends embraced by elected officials at the
federal and state levels continue, Chicago will likely experience extreme
difficulties in meeting the enormous health, human service, and economic development needs of its low-income populations—Blacks and
Latinos in particular.

IMPLICATIONS FOR RESEARCH

Analysis of the Chicago situation suggests research areas that could have
salient implications for urban social policy and social action. The agenda
includes: municipal budgetary policy and program research as it relates
to the distribution of services to low-income urban communities and, especially, to low-income communities of color; urban public policies regarding municipal budgetary decision making processes; and social
action strategies that might be deployed by activists in low income and
nationality communities, particularly African Americans and Latinos
concentrated in big cities.

In particular, this analysis suggests two directions for continuing research. First, it is important to collect and analyze longitudinal data on
budget trends with desegregated categories by types of revenues and by
kind of municipal program expenditures and their distribution by income
and communities of color. Second, there is a need to explore comparative
municipal budget data on large cities with significant concentrations of
Latino and African American populations. It is desirable to pursue both
longitudinal and comparative data analysis in order to establish conclusively the trends observed in this study of Chicago's budget process
(Alexander 1995).

Moreover, to establish a definitive relationship between the apparent
race and class character of municipal budgetary allocation decisions and
patterns of distribution to urban communities, such as the one we identified for Chicago, more detailed comparative data both on budgetary
processes and revenue and expenditure distributions in a city are needed.
Of course, the possibility exists that the Chicago budgetary process is
unique, in any number of respects. More comparative analysis between

cities should be conducted to learn if the findings for Chicago represent a common, macro-systemic pattern, linked to national, and even global political-economic factors. To establish relationships and the directions of association between federal devolvement, restructuring of the economy, local government restructuring efforts and increasing demands of marginalized and disadvantaged communities for participation in municipal budget decision making and distribution of public benefits, a comparative study of so-called U.S. global cities is needed.

This is an ambitious research agenda requiring substantial funding and collaboration among researchers in various cities—exchanging data and findings and pursuing funded and unfunded research along the same lines of this research. Ideally, such projects would agree to use a common approach—for comparative purposes.

URBAN POLICY IMPLICATIONS

Although this study is preliminary, some patterns are worthy of note. One is the finding that property tax revenues are a declining portion of Chicago's Corporate Fund; a growing proportion of the city revenues are generated from sales taxes, fees, fines and forfeitures. (City of Chicago Consolidated Budgets 1991-1997). Due to the regressive nature of these revenues, the poor contribute higher proportions of their incomes to the City Budget than do middle-and upper-income residents. Moreover, since Blacks and Latinos are over represented among low-income persons and families, a greater proportional tax burden falls upon them. In fact, as sales taxes become a larger portion of city revenue, the poor will pay an even greater proportion of their incomes to support local government services. Thus, their claims to special needs are likely to become more legitimate. Right now, their claims and needs for services and benefits are not satisfied or recognized in the City's Corporate budget to the extent that those claims of the middle and upper income status groups are.

Actions that poor and disadvantaged income groups should be engaged in to secure more effective programs and a greater share of services should be studiously assessed. Middle and upper class claims to a greater voice in public affairs and to a disproportionate share in public services often are based on the arguments that poor and working class residents do not pay taxes and have less of a stake since they often do not own property. Property taxpayers, on the contrary, are seen to have legitimate privileges in the public policy process by virtue of this presumption of a greater tax burden. The famed "bureaucratic decision rule" and similar public administration corollaries have further legitimated the middle and upper class biases of public policy makers and administrators in the distribution of public services. If the pattern of revenue generation from sources other than property and business taxes observed in Chicago prevailed in other cities, this claim must be discounted and new, more equitable criteria established.

SOCIAL ACTION AND PUBLIC POLICY INTERVENTION STRATEGIES

Two major objects of social action research are to (1) provide research analysis from a popular and interested point of view, and (2) provide assistance to disadvantaged groups exploring alternative strategies to effect a progressive public policy in this area. These aims are directed to the examination of the social bases of revenue generation and public services allocation, vis-a-vis the municipal budget process. To realize new progressive revenue and public service allocation practices, popular education and grassroots intervention in the establishment of allocation policies are required. The extent to which such informed intervention counteracts racial- and class-based biases in the determination of these policies, the local decision-making process is likely to become more democratic, egalitarian and equitable. African Americans and Latinos, with other poor and disadvantaged segments of urban societies should lead the struggle to open up local budgetary processes. By doing so, they can likely produce increased flows of social and public resources for community, human and personal development.

CONCLUSION

The comparison of policies and budget practices of the Harold Washington and Richard M. Daley periods suggests that the potential for improving Black and Latino economic and social conditions is greater when they form coalitions, especially when the coalition produces a political majority. Without such a coalition an agenda or issue affecting both communities will likely get little attention. The demand for an alternative budget process, addressing the needs of low and moderate-income communities, can encourage coalitions between Blacks and Latinos, and also between these groups and Asians, American Indians and progressive Whites. A social action strategy focused on an alternative budget process, and a community-sensitive budget would:

- Empower working people with information and knowledge about how the city allocates resources.
- Encourage local elected officials, city administrative staff and community organizations to work more closely together to produce a fair budget process.
- Increase resources, technical capacity and improve equity in resource allocation to disadvantaged communities, especially communities of color.
- Open the budget making process for more voice from communities before final legislative passage by City Council.
- Develop policy and advocacy strategies that are based upon "best practices," the results of research and planning done with community constituents and civic groups.

New, progressive community politics are required for a new city fiscal and expenditure policy. A social action process, grounded in popular outreach and education, would increase low-income and working residents' understanding about how public resource allocation decisions affect their lives and communities. Involvement in such a process would empower constituents of disadvantaged and marginalized communities, showing them how they interface with others in similar conditions, and how they can participate in setting priorities for social programs and public services that could improve their standard of living and life quality.

The Black–Latino community coalition under Harold Washington was instrumental in opening up the process of participation in designing local policy to traditionally excluded groups. Lessons from that experience (and that of other cities) suggest that race-based politics can sustain minority nationality empowerment and development in multinational, global cities (see Chapters 4 and 5). The experience suggests that local government is most likely to promote such progressive budget policies and outcomes, addressing needs and priorities of Black and Latino communities in cities where they form an allied political majority.

NOTES

[1] The communities surveyed were Lincoln Park (85% White), Portage Park (89% White), Lower West Side (88% Latino), and Roseland (98.5% African American).

² Policy makers can respond in several ways: (1) by implementing preferences of citizens and communities; (2) by instituting their own priorities; or (3) by doing a combination of the two.

³ Robert Mier was a Professor of Urban Planning and Public Administration at the University of Illinois at Chicago and served as Commissioner of the Department of Economic Development during the Washington administration and as Director of Development for the City for Mayors Harold Washington and Eugene Sawyer.

⁴ The determination of entitlement share is based on the concentration of persons below the poverty rate and the age and deterioration of an area's housing stock.

⁵ Mayor Washington was generally opposed by a coalition of 28 White and 1 Latino aldermen until a special election was held in 1986. He was supported by 19 African American and 2 White aldermen and, therefore, had enough votes to uphold a veto.

⁶ Remarks of Mayor Richard M. Daley. *1995 Budget Speech*. Chicago, Il: City of Chicago. Office of the City Council Clerk (October 13).

⁷ Evidence that government funds create wealth and jobs is obvious when one evaluates the U.S. Defense Department's contracts to industries where large corporations such as Boeing, Martin Marrietta, Grumman, Lockheed, etc. receive billions of dollars from the federal government to produce defense goods and conduct research. At the local level, developers and construction companies are the prime recipients of funding for physical improvements, housing and commercial development.

⁸ The author served as Deputy Commissioner of Administration in the Department of Economic Development (DED) for eight years, five years plus under the Washington/Sawyer period and over two years under Daley. He was responsible for DED's affirmative action hiring and contracting policy and reporting under Washington.

⁹ Community development organizations (CDOs or CDCs) strive to improve economic conditions of the communities they serve through a variety of job creation, business development and infrastructure improvement programs. They include business associations, community development corporations, and industrial commissions.

¹⁰ The Corporate Fund or "Corporate Budget" is that part of the Chicago City Budget derived from tax revenues, fees and forfeitures. Corporate-funded agencies are funded out of the Corporate-budget—as opposed to those funded through "grant" revenues. The budget director under Mayor Washington, Ron Picur, explained to the author that, in 1985, the Mayor had agreed to the use of Corporate Funds for agencies that did not qualify under the HUD low-income area criterion for CDBG. (See previous section.) Thus, the Corporate Fund pro-

vided a "hidden" mechanism for funding organizations in middle income areas and addressing local needs not covered by HUD's CDBG benefit criteria. The practice was maintained by Daley; in fact it has been extended by his administration. While support funding for agencies servicing HUD-eligible areas and low-income recipients is declining due to retrenchment and federal cutbacks to urban development, local Corporate funding has been more stable. In fact, cuts experienced by agencies serving low-income areas and recipients could be attributed to decreasing funds from the federal and other units of government while denying the use of corporate funding to those groups. This is, apparently, what the current administration is doing. As a result, funding for low-income agencies, mainly serving Black and Latino constituents, has decreased while resource to HUD-ineligible areas has increased or remained stable.

[11] The Corporate Fund, which is the City's general operating fund, typically supports basic city services like police, fire, health, streets and sanitation, and some infrastructure activities. For sources of estimates, see City of Chicago. Consolidated Budgets 1991-1997. Office of Budget and Management. City of Chicago. Also, see Alexander (1995).

[12] This is the centerpiece of his administration for two main reasons: his most solid voting block consists of middle- income residents and owners of property in the city; similarly, the main contributors to his campaign are CBD businesses, developers and the real estate industry. Furthermore, his development policies are geared to additional growth of the central area of the city (the CBD, the lake front and adjacent communities) with the ultimate goal of securing the place of Chicago as a world quality city.

CHAPTER 11

Community Economic Development and the Latino Experience

EDWIN MELÉNDEZ AND
MICHAEL A. STOLL

Over the past two decades, concentration of Blacks and Latinos in segregated and impoverished urban communities has increased, thus making them more vulnerable to the negative effects of urban restructuring. In many ways, easing their plight, and that of the urban poor in general, depended on urban initiatives aimed at such communities. In this paper, we argue that the success of urban economic development largely depends on the articulation of such initiatives within communities and, in particular, on recognizing the role that racial and ethnic networks play in mobilizing resources around an economic development agenda. In other words, it is the convergence of race and class interests that provides the basis for economic development at the community or neighborhood level. Examples of economic development in Latino communities demonstrate how the understanding of race and ethnicity may contribute to more effective public policy and community strategizing.

The term *community economic development* refers here to a process whereby local actors, such as business, government, or community groups, enter into relationship with other actors, either private or public agencies, to stimulate social, economic and, to a lesser extent, physical development activity that is spatially-based. Typically, this activity includes job creation, housing development, and small business incentives, sometimes in conjunction with instituting or improving public goods such as city services and transportation. The central goal of community economic development, then, is to foster the potential of local institutional, physical, and human resources endogenously and to link them with regional economic development processes.

We review the Latino experience to examine whether or not an understanding of race and ethnicity contributes to more effective public policy, in this case economic development policy. Since poverty in urban centers is highly concentrated in ethnic and racial minority areas, the impact that ethnic and racial solidarity may have on economic development is of foremost importance. Ethnic and racial identity, solidarity, and mobilization are important determinants of social and neighborhood organization. They often become a form of *social capital,* defined as the ability of individuals or groups to successfully negotiate with formal institutions in meeting their goals, with positive effects on community economic development (Swanstrom 1993). To the extent that new policy strategies provide a mechanism to link expanding industry and business to the job and business opportunities of ethnic and racial minorities, the closing of the racial inequality gap may be achieved without resorting to race-specific policies. In the present political climate of opposition to race-conscious policies, the enhancement of such business linkages can play an important redistributive role.

SPATIALLY-BASED "PEOPLE" POLICIES AND URBAN POVERTY

Urban policies are generally considered a subset of antipoverty strategies. In this paper, we identify three major antipoverty strategies: spatially-based "people" policies, pure space policies, and pure "people" policies.[1] We consider the first two urban because they target specific urban areas.

The term *spatially-based people policies* refers to economic programs that target specific areas. In large part, these policies are designed to shift resources to areas where impoverished people are concentrated, to spur economic development within those areas, and to promote a more equal distribution of income in society. The type of community economic development as we define it falls under this strategy.

Pure spatially-based policies primarily involve economic revitalization efforts through physical improvements to areas or buildings in impoverished areas. These policies, which generally target blighted areas of central cities where few people live, are, in part, enacted to affect people beyond the geographic area of development. That is, pure spatially-based policies may foster job growth in a particular area, but primarily people from outside the area may benefit from the increased employment opportunities (e.g., downtown development).

In contrast to these area-specific policies, other antipoverty policies target the poor, either by providing direct assistance to individuals and/or families or by enhancing their ability to gain employment to support themselves. Direct assistance to the poor may take the form of cash transfers or allowances for food, housing, or other needs. Employment programs provide skills training, government employment, or private-sector placement. Policies of this type can be classified as pure people policies. However, some direct assistance and employment policies have a spatial dimension as well, since the poor and unemployed tend to be concentrated in specific areas. In fact, many of the funding allocations for employment programs are specifically linked to an area's unemployment rates.

Despite the importance of direct assistance to the poor, employment programs for local areas and pure physical development of blighted areas, we argue that to achieve successful economic development spatially-based people policies must be emphasized over other strategies and promoted and implemented in combination with other pure people and space policies. Furthermore, the ability of local governments to design effective spatially-based people policies will largely determine the success of any urban agenda.

Spatially-based people policies with a particular emphasis on community economic development have certain advantages over other antipoverty strategies. First, they can provide flexibility in responding to globalization and restructuring. By facilitating the retraining of displaced workers, developing small- to medium-size businesses, or forming community organizations to negotiate with companies planning to relocate out of the community, such policies may lessen the local impact of restructuring. Second, they are better able to promote the growth of *social capital* by providing organizations in spatially targeted areas with opportunities to join with one another to achieve particular goals. The resulting networks can create long-term relationships that may make the pursuit of future projects or goals more efficient and effective. Third, spatially-based people policies might mitigate potential conflict over who receives federal funds because such an approach obscures the fact that one group of people may be in conflict with another. Funding for these policies can be allocated on the basis of seemingly "objective" criteria of places, rather than, for example, racial background, while minority communities still might benefit if the criteria are carefully constructed (Edel 1980). This point gains importance because of increasing contention within the federal government over race–based policies.[2]

Fourth, such policies facilitate the articulation of economic development with racial and ethnic issues that are unique to each community.

Given the above discussion, what can we learn from the Latino experience in community economic development? In the following sections we propose that community economic development is an effective way to address racial equality and collaboration. Evidently, most antidiscrimination policies take the form of people-based programs. Through time, however, civil rights initiatives have been criticized for favoring one group of economically disadvantaged individuals over others. By definition, spatially-based people policies target economically disadvantaged populations, which are disproportionately racial minorities in most urban areas, bypassing stricter racial categories.

Empowering local actors (such as residents, community-based organizations, small businesses, and school administrators and teachers) has the added benefit of promoting racial harmony by focusing on solutions to problems that are of common interest to many groups. Community economic development offers the vehicle to establish this common ground by developing bridges between ethnic and racial groups. However, collaboration need not be at the expense of racial and ethnic identity-based organizations and solidarity. It is indeed important to recognize the role that racial and ethnic identity play in the mobilization of low-income communities, particularly regarding economic development (Swanstrom 1993). The Latino experience illustrates how public policy and programs can take advantage of existing ethnic networks to promote successful interventions.

ANTIPOVERTY APPROACHES IN HISTORICAL CONTEXT

Antipoverty initiatives during the last three decades have shifted emphasis from one type of policy approach to another and from the federal government to the states and cities. During the 1960s, the War on Poverty programs had a clear emphasis on skills acquisition, or people-based policies, and civil rights. But spatially based people policies occupied center stage with the enactment of the Model Cities program in 1966. This program aimed to provide direct economic assistance to poverty-stricken areas by channeling funds through community-based organizations (Levine and Williams 1992; Heilbrun 1981). The funding of social services and employment programs through community-based organizations created a vast institutional base in distressed communities throughout the country.

Community development corporations (CDCs) have been an important part of community economic development since federal programs first began to favor them. They promote neighborhood-based economic development in areas such as housing, small business, branch plants, commercial revitalization, and employment and training.[3] In a way, CDCs integrate and promote at the local level many of the urban policies presented above. They, however, need continuous external support, mainly because a vast proportion of their resources are devoted to affordable housing, which requires enormous subsidies. CDCs also concentrate on providing support to small businesses, whose failure rate is high and, hence, also require substantial external support to be successful. These problems have limited the impact of CDCs in neighborhood economic development (Blakely 1989; Heilbrun 1981).

Housing development has been the dominant activity of CDCs.[4] Although job creation has been less impressive than housing development, CDCs have the capacity and the experience to be successful job developers and employment trainers (Harrison, Weiss and Gant 1995). Recent reports suggest that more and more CDCs are turning to economic development strategies (Mazarakis 1994) other than housing.

Another urban economic development policy aimed in part at poverty alleviation is the promotion of small business. This policy came to the forefront of the national urban agenda when President Nixon created the Small Business Administration (SBA). The strategy became known as *Black capitalism.* It promoted Black-owned businesses in order to expand employment opportunities in the inner city. However, SBA programs and other state and local initiatives that promote small businesses are more beneficial to entrepreneurs with experience and venture capital than to the typical minority entrepreneur (Heilbrun 1981). Because there is relatively little technical assistance to compensate for the lack of entrepreneurial experience and because of the unavailability of local venture capital, these initiatives have had a negligible impact in economically distressed communities. More recently, substantial budgeting reductions to the SBA have resulted in a dramatic decline in the share of Black-owned businesses receiving guaranteed loans (Shao 1993; Fainstein and Fainstein 1989).

In the next sections, we examine the Latino experience in community economic development, with an emphasis on CDCs and small business promotion, to illustrate how ethnic networks facilitate the creation of linkages between urban economic development policies and programs and the targeting of these programs to areas of high poverty concentration. First, we discuss the Cuban enclave in Miami. Although the Cuban experience in Miami is in many ways unique and not "replicable" from a public policy point of view, it offers numerous lessons for the strengthening of ethnic-based business networks. From this discussion, we examine how successful programs assisting Latino businesses share some of the same elements, in terms of taking advantage of ethnic identity and solidarity, as the Miami enclave economy. The following section examines the Latino experience in housing and community revitalization and provides examples of CDCs that have succeeded in the implementation of spatially-based people policies.

THE CUBAN ENCLAVE OF MIAMI

In many ways, the Latino experience in economic development and public policy resembles the dichotomy between business-oriented programs and efforts directed at poverty alleviation. Indeed, most of the academic literature on this topic focuses on the enclave economy and the adaptation of Cuban immigrants. Less documentation exists regarding other relevant policy areas, such as housing access, the formation and impact of CDCs, or the linkages of skills development programs to expanding industrial sectors. The Cuban enclave of Miami is a well-documented example of an ethnic economy. Like the Chinese restaurant and garment businesses of New York City or the Korean import and distribution businesses of Los Angeles, the Miami ethnic-enclave economy serves as evidence of how ethnic solidarity translates into economic advancement opportunities.

Alejandro Portes and Robert Bach (1985:203; see also Portes 1981) have defined the ethnic enclave as an economic formation "characterized by the spatial concentration of immigrants who organize a variety of enterprises to serve their own ethnic market and the general population." An enclave has two critical and interrelated characteristics.

First, the ethnic enclave has a large number of interconnected, small, and, in some instances, medium-size businesses that provide employment opportunities to a growing and continuous flow of immigrants. Between 1967 and 1976, Cuban-owned businesses in Miami grew in number from less than a thousand to more than eight thousand (Wilson and Portes 1980). Most of them were concentrated in the textile, leather, furniture, cigar, construction, and finance industries. Cubans owned 40% of construction firms, 30% of local banks, and most restaurants, supermarkets, clinics, and other service businesses in the area (Pedraza-Bailey

1985). The high density of businesses owned by individuals with the same ethnicity in a particular industry and region offers economies of agglomeration. Business contacts and information, access to capital, and sharing of other resources provide an advantage to the ethnic entrepreneur over other competitors in the area. And, as Waldinger (1993) has pointed out, the benefits of ethnic solidarity are reaped whether businesses are heavily concentrated in one area (as in the Cuban or Chinese cases) or spread over a broader geographical demarcation (as in the Korean case). Thus, from an economic development policy perspective, ethnic economies could be regarded as a special case of business and industry support programs.

A second characteristic of the ethnic enclave is the continuous influx of immigrants to work and purchase ethnic goods in the area. Jobs in ethnic-owned businesses offer unique employment opportunities for immigrants with limited English skills and little access to the social networks that would facilitate their adaptation to a new social environment. Indeed, one of the most controversial aspects of the ethnic enclave argument is that immigrants in this protected labor market may actually have better earnings and employment outcomes than immigrants with similar characteristics working outside of the enclave economy. There is little dispute, however, about the fact that immigrants must work long hours for many years before they can either seek employment outside ethnic-owned businesses or start their own businesses. The attractiveness of the ethnic economy to immigrants is that employment is steady and allows them to adapt to new labor-market requirements and eventually to move to better employment outside the enclave.

The success of Cuban-owned businesses in Miami is explained by the interaction of a number of factors. Immigrants' social networks and ethnic solidarity have played a critical role in fostering business development. According to Portes and Stepick (1993), access to start-up capital through "character loans" was a common practice among Cuban entrepreneurs. But the Federal Cuban Refugee Program also provided tremendous assistance to Cuban immigrants to acquire businesses. It provided student loans, retraining for professional positions and other educational opportunities, as well as welfare and housing assistance. Pedraza-Bailey (1985) estimates that the United States government spent nearly $1 billion for assistance within a short period of time. Another important factor was the high educational and entrepreneurial level of the first waves of political refugees from Cuba. Despite the hardship of employment in the secondary labor market, the enclave economy offered

Cubans the opportunity for upward social mobility and political advancement. Today, Miami is largely a Cuban city. Anglos have changed their negative view of Cubans and have accepted their contributions (Portes and Stepick 1993).

SMALL BUSINESS DEVELOPMENT

There is no comparable experience among Mexicans and Puerto Ricans (the two largest Latino groups in the United States) or among other recent immigrant groups from Latin America. Although there are large concentrations of Mexican–owned businesses in the Southwest and Puerto Rican–owned businesses in New York, Chicago, and other Northeast cities, the Mexican and Puerto Rican business classes have not gained economic and political power comparable to that of the Cubans in Miami. According to Fratoe (1986), Mexicans (18.6%), Dominicans (14.6%), and Puerto Ricans (10.6%) have among the lowest business participation rates (per 1,000 persons) of all ethnic groups (48.9% national average). On the other hand, Mexicans and Puerto Ricans have a more prominent participation in antipoverty programs and have developed a vast institutional base of CDCs and CBOs (community-based organizations) that conduct a variety of housing, job training, and educational programs.

There is no study that documents and explains the differences in levels of entrepreneurship among Cubans, Puerto Ricans, Mexicans, and other Latino groups. But, based on studies of other ethnic groups, one could hypothesize that groups with more class and ethnic resources tend to outperform groups with a lower endowment of resources (Light 1984). Cubans have a higher share of professionals and managers, higher educational levels (Meléndez, Rodriguez and Barry-Figueroa 1991), and greater access to capital (Portes 1987) than other groups. However, the experience of the African American community suggests the presence of other factors. Waldinger and Aldrich (1990) propose that the underdevelopment of Black-owned businesses is due to the lack of a business tradition, the failure to create a protected market, a fragmented social structure, and discrimination. These are important factors to consider when explaining differences in business formation among ethnic and racial groups.

The evidence regarding the role of public programs in assisting minority-owned businesses points to the difficulty of overcoming the above-mentioned barriers. For the most part, state and city set-aside programs are unsuccessful because minority-owned businesses remain undercapitalized and unable to compete in the open market. Equal opportunity loans, perhaps the most important minority business assistance program, have had historically high rates of delinquency (Waldinger and Aldrich 1990). Public policy regarding small business assistance for disadvantaged urban communities seems to face a critical dilemma: if public assistance to foster business development focuses on the most disadvantaged groups, high loan-default and business-failure rates should be expected, but if assistance is targeted to more established firms, then there is less chance of achieving the desired impact on targeted groups.

This discussion suggests that conventional small business development programs are insufficient to promote economic development in distressed minority communities. The Cuban experience in Miami seems to be an exception. The development of the enclave economy was made feasible by a combination of factors (including the geopolitical context that rationalized support for Cuban immigrants to the U.S.) that is unlikely to be replicated. It is doubtful that the promotion of small business will produce the volume of employment and capital formation that is necessary for sustained economic development in impoverished urban communities. Nonetheless, the enclave economy offers a valuable example of how ethnic solidarity can be important for economic development, particularly as it pertains to disadvantaged populations. Indeed, the Cuban enclave experience in Miami constitutes a special case of how ethnic identity and social networks among immigrant communities provide a basis for successful urban economic development strategies.

The Mexican and Puerto Rican experiences in small business and neighborhood revitalization illustrate the potential impact of best-practice programs that seem to overcome the public policy dilemma posed by traditional business assistance programs in minority communities. What these strategies have in common are the dual objectives of building effective capacity within Latino organizations, based upon ethnic identity and solidarity, and deploying this organizational capacity to link neighborhood residents to the larger economy. These two objectives are clearly interrelated: the development of ethnic leadership ultimately facilitates access to jobs and financial and other resources.

The Regional Alliance for Small Contractors in New York and New Jersey, a multiethnic organization created by the Port Authority of New York, is extremely effective in promoting linkages of minority-owned businesses to corporate America (Harrison, Weiss and Gant 1995).

Latino-owned firms constitute approximately 23% of the participating small businesses, while the vast majority of participants are minority- or women-owned firms. Social networks among these communities play a critical role in the success of the program. Although there are no data available to indicate the ethnic composition of the Latino population in the program, Puerto Ricans are the largest Latino group in the New York-New Jersey region, followed by Dominicans. Even in the New York region, Cubans are the dominant small business group among Latinos. The alliance has grown from twelve to sixty-two corporate partners since its inception in 1989 and currently serves more than nine hundred firms. It provides a variety of technical, educational, and financial services, with the objective of building the capacity of all participating small firms.

The alliance benefits both the small contractor, by facilitating access to regular subcontracting for large construction projects, and the major construction companies, by providing access to a reliable pool of subcontractors. The program is based on mutually beneficial business transactions, not on set-asides. However, it directly benefits the targeted ethnic business community. As a multiethnic coalition, the alliance relies on cultural ties and shared ethnic identity to improve the quality of subcontractors available for major development projects. It connects small businesses to mainstream economic actors. Technical assistance to participating businesses, which builds capacity in Latino and other communities, is provided without the public perception that the alliance is a poverty-alleviation program. Ultimately, the alliance provides a unique mechanism to link ethnic and women entrepreneurs to the key actors in the construction industry and the regional economy, as a whole.

HOUSING AND COMMUNITY DEVELOPMENT

Mexican and Puerto Rican populations have had more active participation in housing and community revitalization. Most of their CDCs in these areas started during the late 1960s or 1970s, during the Model Cities Program.

Gittel and Wilder (1995) provide two examples of successful CDCs in predominantly Mexican communities that illustrate how ethnic identity and solidarity can be translated into effective multiethnic alliances for economic development. Mission Housing Development is a CDC that evolved from a Mexican-led multiethnic coalition blocking urban renewal plans for the Mission neighborhood in San Francisco. Since its inception in 1971 under the Model Cities Program, Mission Housing

Development has developed more than three hundred new housing units and rehabilitated more than one thousand units. Caritas Management Corporation, its for-profit subsidiary owns more than 450 units and oversees more than one thousand units for the CDCs and other private and nonprofit organizations in the area. Their housing programs provide integrated social services to the residents and are part of a neighborhood collaboration that provides housing units for individuals who are homeless, disabled, HIV-infected, and alcoholic, as well as other needy and hard-to-serve populations. Perhaps as important as the direct service to the neighborhood, Mission Housing Development has engaged in a host of economic and neighborhood planning activities ranging from child care, tenant organizing, and educational programs to the development of "Centro del Pueblo"—a combined housing and commercial facility that also provides space for many of the area's nonprofit organizations.

The Coalition for a Better Acre (CBA) was founded in 1982 in Lowell, Massachusetts as a community response to the implementation of an economic revitalization plan that emphasized downtown and high-tech industrial development and excluded low-income neighborhoods. The Acre neighborhood historically has served as an entry port for French Canadians, Irish, and other immigrants. More recently, the neighborhood has become predominantly Puerto Rican, with an increasing Asian immigrant population. CBA's programs have focused on affordable housing and community development—including small business assistance, revolving loan funds, and training for mothers with children on public assistance (AFDC). However, CBA also supports youth programs and other social services. CBA is known in Lowell for its political activism. It has participated in changing the composition of the City Council, has influenced key government appointments in its area, and has supported the election of state-level representatives.

The East Los Angeles Community Union (TELACU), the largest Latino CDC in the country, was founded in 1968 by Mexican activists to promote socioeconomic development in the distressed East Los Angeles area. TELACU has owned and developed seventeen affordable housing projects with more than twelve hundred units valued at more than $80 million. This alone would make them one of the largest CDCs in the country, but their economic development activities go well beyond housing to include creation of industrial and commercial space, banking, construction, and many other businesses. For instance, their industrial park was founded in 1977 to redevelop a vacant forty-eight-acre former B.F. Goodrich tire plant—a facility with nine thousand square feet of industrial space that since then has served dozens of businesses. It currently houses twenty-seven businesses, most of which are minority-owned. TELACU's commercial building program rents space to more than fifty firms, employing more than two thousand workers. In addition to these housing and business activities, TELACU provides a wide range of educational and social services.

Like other Latino CDCs, Los Sures was established in 1972 to promote the social and economic development of the south side of Williamsburg, one of the poorest Puerto Rican communities in New York City. Although originally focused on housing, completing more than two thousand units over the years, Los Sures has engaged in numerous economic development projects and has provided a wide variety of social services to residents. In addition to these traditional CDC activities, Los Sures is involved in a variety of community planning and coalition building activities. Most notable, Los Sures is working with the United Jewish Organization to improve relations between the Hasidic Jewish community and Latino residents in Williamsburg who have a history of contentious and sometimes violent relations. The hope is that such collaborative efforts in economic-development and job-creation provide the best means to improve inter-ethnic relations. The first project involves the rehabilitation of a six-story building in the Hasidic neighborhood that will eventually be occupied by both Latino and Jewish tenants.

Like most successful CDCs, these Latino-led CDCs are truly representative of community interests and are governed and staffed by local leaders and longtime residents. Funding for their operation comes from multiple city, county, state, and federal government agencies as well as charitable foundations and private corporations. Long-term partnerships and networks are intrinsic parts of their operations.

The key to the success of such community organizations, whether they focus on small business assistance or housing and real estate development, has been the articulation of a dual mission of community leadership/institutional development and the effective use of external relations to attract resources to the neighborhood. Like Coastal Enterprises (Maine), Bethel New Life (Chicago), New Community Corporation (Newark), and many other successful CDCs in the country, these Latino CDCs represent a new type of community institution that focuses on community revitalization strategies that profit from long-range trends in regional economic development. Ethnic identity and solidarity, in this context, are translated into effective grassroots civic participation (Fisher 1993).

CONCLUSIONS

The formulation of effective urban development strategies and public policy initiatives must recognize that ethnic and racial identity constitutes the basis for community mobilization and the institutionalization of participatory processes that engage low-income populations in neighborhood revitalization and economic development programs. One of the obvious challenges of urban economic development initiatives is to engage the effective participation of CDCs and CBOs in program governance and development. The historical record shows, however, that local politics often interfere with the access that ethnic communities have to CDBG (Community Development Block Grants) and other federal funds targeting distressed urban communities. As Kaplan (1995) has proposed, policy makers must understand that effective economic development strategies involve the engagement of a broad set of actors from the government and private sector, as well as the community.

In this chapter we have argued that racial and ethnic identity can be successfully used as the basis for community development. Based on the general literature on community development, we have argued that spatially-based people policies seem to offer the most potential to promote and support small business and CDC activities. In many ways, the Cuban experience in Miami is unique and there might be few places where lessons from this example are directly applicable. However, one lesson from the Miami experience that does lend itself to generalization is that ethnicity and national identity can play a critical role in the economic development of a region. Small businesses in Miami have relied on the support of social networks to succeed in the marketplace. In a clearly different context, Black and Latino owned businesses in the greater New York City region have been able to take advantage of business opportunities in the construction industry supported by a model program that facilitates access to main contractors. Once again, the success of the program is in part explained by the connections established to the Black and Latino business communities through already existing social networks.

In contrast to small business support programs that target broad metropolitan areas, CDCs often concentrate their activities in specific neighborhoods. However, as the cases of Latino-led CDCs illustrate, they can have a broader community development mission than just improving a physical infrastructure and housing. The comprehensive approach to their activities is related to the dual focus on place and people, wherein servicing the needs of people and human development is as critical as improving the area's infrastructure. There are also similarities of these activities to small business support programs in terms of the potential to build coalitions with other ethnic and racial groups through community economic development activities. Both Coalition for a Better Acre and Los Sures are in areas where the composition of local residents has changed significantly in recent years. In response, they have undertaken direct action to create programs to combat racial tensions. They have provided a vehicle for neighbors to focus on common problems and to emphasize how, by combining resources, they can solve them.

Defending the role of community organizations, public policies, and programs that are both people- and place-oriented is of foremost importance in the current policy debate. Cities and urban areas continue to provide the social context in which many cultures interact. In this context, race and ethnicity continue to be powerful forces shaping social organization and opportunities. Community economic development strategies are beneficial to coalition building among groups and are useful in closing the gap between policies oriented to promote economic growth and those designed primarily for poverty alleviation.

NOTES

[1] Another antipoverty urban policy that is increasingly being debated concerns people dispersal policies such as the Department of Housing and Urban Development's "Moving to Opportunity" program. The goal of this policy is to provide incentives for people to move from, or implement programs that move people from, distressed communities to more prosperous ones (e.g., from central cities to suburbs).

[2] This is not to suggest that we advocate spatially-based people policies in place of race–based policies, but rather in combination with them.

[3] For instance, CDCs make housing rehabilitation loans, run training and employment programs, assist new minority–owned firms by providing management counseling and direct loans, and provide a variety of other nonprofit, community economic development services.

[4] A recent survey of over two thousand CDCs reports that 88 percent were developing affordable housing, while only 25% were developing commercial real estate or "business enterprises." In fact, CDCs have helped develop over 320,000 units of affordable housing, including 87,000 units in the last three years. In contrast, CDCs have created or retained approximately 90,000 jobs (National Council for Community Economic Development 1991).

CHAPTER 12

Understanding the Future
Toward a Strategy for Black and Latino Survival and Liberation in the Twenty-First Century

JAMES B. STEWART

This paper examines the future prospects for Blacks and Latinos in response to professional "futurists," who, for the most part, are dismissive of the potential of both groups to be major actors in the twenty-first century. From this vantage point, the paper is also a call to action, advocating the development of Black–Latino coalitions to oppose the ominous fate that could await both groups in the absence of a massive counter initiative.

This chapter begins with an overview of the analytical frameworks used by futurists who represent either the "optimistic" or "pessimistic" schools of thought. Writers associated with the first school tend to focus their principal attention on what might be described as the "new potential for human liberation," presumably associated with ongoing social and technological changes. Those more pessimistic emphasize potentially dehumanizing consequences of ongoing global economic transformation. This view focuses on global corporations' growing dominance of human lives and the destruction of traditional work culture and employment bases.

The analysis juxtaposes the perspectives of representative futurists with the historical and contemporary realities of Blacks and Latinos in three areas: (1) current and future employment prospects; (2) access to public goods; and (3) linkage to the emerging international economic order. It examines each topic to rectify the lack of specific attention to the circumstances of Blacks and Latinos found in futurists' writings and identifies a variety of bases and strategies for increased Black–Latino collaboration. It argues that domestic and international initiatives must be pursued simultaneously, with Blacks and Latinos situated in the United States serving as the hub of a transnational linkage that connects Africa, South America, and the Caribbean.

The concluding section summarizes the main recommendations and suggests establishing the groundwork for broader collaborative efforts to involve other populations highly vulnerable to the process of global transformation because of race and historical patterns of exploitation.

ALTERNATIVE VIEWS OF THE FUTURE

> *"The same battle in the clouds will be known to the deaf only as lightning and to the blind only as thunder."*
>
> GEORGE SANTAYANA

The "optimistic" school of future studies is aptly represented by the work of John Naisbitt and associates. Naisbitt's group presents future scenarios in the form of so-called "megatrends," i.e. "directions transforming our lives" (Nesbitt 1982). The group emphasizes the declining significance of traditional patterns of association, for example racial/ethnic and national identity. In the world envisioned by the optimistic futurists, disembodied technological change is the driving force shaping the future. The new possibilities created by these technologies are seen as liberating, especially at the individual level.

In his 1982 bestseller, Naisbitt identifies ten megatrends. His analysis focuses principally on those megatrends that relate directly to the ongoing global economic transformation. They include the (1) transition from an industrial to an information society; (2) transformation of the national economy to a world economy; (3) de-emphasis of centralized institutions in favor of decentralized solutions; (4) movement away from traditional institutions in favor of self-help programs; (5) transition from representative to participatory democratic processes; and (6) de-emphasis of hierarchial structures in favor of increased networking and flatter (i.e., less hierarchical) organizations.

For present purposes, it is important to highlight that the positive developments foreseen by Naisbitt are generated from a mind set that restricts attention to a small, relatively affluent, segment of American society. In addition, his analysis treats the United States as an isolated island unconnected to global developments. To illustrate, Blacks and Latinos are mentioned specifically only in the discussion of his last megatrend in the context of population growth of other identifiable populations that will shift the traditional focus of domestic social policy away from Black–White relations, thereby increasing the marginalization of Blacks and creating greater potential for intergroup conflict.

Writers who use changes in the economic arena as their point of departure to forecast the future produce significantly fewer optimistic scenarios than scholars such as Naisbitt. For example, Alvin and Heidi Toffler (1995) have received widespread media attention, in part because their latest book, *Creating a New Civilization, The Politics of the Third Wave*, contains a foreword written by Newt Gingrich, former Speaker of the U.S. House of Representatives. Their central argument is that three major waves of technological advance have been and are continuing to shape major transitions in global civilization. They employ what is described as "social wavefront analysis" to examine the patterns of transformation. According to the Tofflers (1995:21-22), social wavefront analysis

> Looks at history as a succession of rolling waves of change and asks where the leading edge of each wave is carrying us. It focuses our attention not so much on the continuities of history (important as they are) as on the discontinuities, on innovation and break points. It identifies key change patterns as they emerge so that we can influence them.
>
> It begins with the very simple idea that the rise of agriculture was the first turning point in human social development and that the industrial revolution was the second great breakthrough. It views each of these not as a discrete, one-time event but as a wave of change moving at a certain velocity.

For the Tofflers, a critical force shaping the future is the emergence of a global "Third Wave" economic system based on the accumulation and manipulation of information. One consequence of this development is the increasing marginalization of societies with economies heavily dependent on industrial and/or agricultural production.

> We are speeding toward a totally different structure of power that will create not a world cut in two but sharply divided into three contrasting and competing civilizations—the first still symbolized by the hoe, the second by the assembly line, and the third by the computer (Toffler and Toffler 1995:30).

This chapter considers what such global changes might mean for Blacks and Latinos in the United States. It first examines trends in employment levels and occupational patterns.

BLACKS, LATINOS, AND THE WORLD OF WORK

Despite quantitative differences in employment status, occupational distributions and earnings, the qualitative dimensions of the employment picture facing Blacks and Latinos in the future are similar. This parallel trajectory results from comparable contemporary labor market experiences discussed throughout this book. This section adds a few indicators in support of these claims while advancing some general hypotheses suggested by the information.

The precipitous decline in manufacturing has been a major factor affecting the employment status of Blacks. Several studies indicate that while manufacturing accounted for only about 20% of total jobs in the mid-1980s, about 50% of all workers displaced as a result of plant closings/relocations had been employed in manufacturing. Blacks have been significantly over represented among displaced workers (see Jacobson, LaLonde and Sullivan 1993).

Latinos have also been adversely affected by the "skills mismatch" created by the ongoing economic transformation. To illustrate, Ortiz's study of Latino employment patterns in New York and Los Angeles (1991) found that African Americans, continental Puerto Ricans and even Mexican Americans, to some extent, had experienced similar patterns of job loss as a result of the decline of manufacturing and the growth in the service sector. Although the service sector far outstrips manufacturing as an employment base in the American economy now, it is important to recognize that it, too, is vulnerable to international competition. Both Black and Latino men in the service sector are much more likely to be employed in those industries with the largest employment losses (Armah 1994). Despite the significant growth in service-sector employment, Blacks and Latinos continue to be under represented in white-collar occupations and over represented in blue-collar and farming occupations.

On the other hand, Blacks tend to be over represented among union members. Although Black union members earn less than their white counterparts, the earnings gap is less than for non-union workers. In contrast, the most powerful industrial unions historically have excluded Puerto Ricans from important positions and civil service unions have also been a barrier to Puerto Rican economic mobility (Gonzalez and Gray 1984).

Although Latinos have been active in farm unions, the status and visibility of the United Farm Workers, founded by Cesar Chavez, began to decline in the 1980s with the increasing urbanization of Mexican Americans (Skerry 1993). The over representation of Latinos in farming is almost totally accounted for by the employment patterns of Mexican Americans. In 1992, approximately 12% of Mexican American males were employed in farming, forestry and fishing. The comparable figures for Puerto Rican and Cuban males were 1.8% and 2.7%, respectively (Montgomery 1994). Blacks in rural areas are also experiencing high levels of impoverishment (Stewart and Allen 1995). These points suggest that the projections of futurists that unions will be less influential in the decades to come do not portend well for Blacks and Latinos.

Futurists such as Aburdene and Naisbitt (1992) predict that opportunities for women will be expanding. This, however, does not guarantee that all racial/national groups will benefit in equal proportions. Non-Cuban Latinas have been more successful than Latino men in making gains in professional, managerial and technical occupations. A similar pattern occurs among Blacks (Montgomery 1994). However, Black and Latina women continue to share the burden of the dual barriers of race/ethnicity and gender (Simms and Malveaux 1986; Sokoloff 1992; Morales and Bonilla 1993). More generally, Latina women have a lower labor force participation rate than Black women (Segura 1992). Experience suggests that Black and Latina women will lag in benefiting from the developments forecasted by futurists. Consequently, Blacks and Latinos would seem to have a shared interest in developing strategies to reduce this lag.

Another pattern predicted by futurists is that the Federal government will continue to decline in significance as a direct employer, although it is unclear whether these job losses will be offset by gains at the state and local levels. Presently, Blacks are more likely than Latinos to be employed in the public sector at all levels (Edwards, Thomas and Burch 1992; Reimers and Chernick 1991; Stafford 1991). Some exceptions to this pattern do exist, for example, in San Antonio, Texas, where Mexican Americans have had employment parity in local government since the 1960s (Skerry 1993). In general, Blacks and Latinos tend to be concentrated in low-paying agencies and occupations (Reimers and Chernick 1991; Idson and Price 1992).

Present and future changes in the U.S. industrial base also shape the prospects for Black and Latino workers. According to Mar and Ong (1994), two years after the 1985 sectoral recession in Silicon Valley's semiconductor industry, only 43% of Black workers had been rehired compared to 60% of white and 65% of Latino workers (Mar and Ong 1994). Using 1989 and 1992 data, Ong and Lawrence (1995) found that Black and Latino workers bore a disproportionate share of the employment losses associated with defense cuts in California's aerospace industry. In addition, much of the employment growth in the last decade has occurred in small to medium-sized firms associated with high-tech and service—many not covered by existing anti-discrimination legislation.

In addition to losses in high-tech and aerospace industries, Williams (1994) projected that Blacks would lose nearly 158,000 military and defense-related jobs between 1991 and 1996. According to the author, this would represent 12% of anticipated defense-related job losses resulting from military downsizing—compared to an approximate 9% representation of Blacks in the civilian labor force. Although specific estimates were not generated for Latinos, it is likely that they are experiencing disproportionate effects in some states, specifically California and Texas, where Blacks also experienced disproportionate losses. Yet, since Latinos, unlike Blacks, are under represented in the armed forces (Rosenfeld and Culbertson 1992), they will not feel the impact of ongoing military downsizing as directly as will Blacks.

The preceding discussion has identified several issues that could form the basis for a Black–Latino coalition inspired by the bleak forecasts of future employment patterns.

The future prospects for Blacks and Latinos in labor markets suggest many areas in which they could benefit from coalition politics, despite some differences in their job experiences:

- Both are more likely than Whites to be employed in unstable industries with possibilities for continuing employment losses.
- Union membership, which has had some success in improving working conditions, is declining (both in numbers and in influence).
- In the highly unstable, high-tech industries that seem to represent the wave of the future, employment cuts have disproportionately affected Latinos and Blacks.
- Both groups often miss opportunities for jobs in high-tech industries because of the large number of small-and medium-sized

firms that are not required to consider anti-discrimination guidelines.

• They will be disproportionately affected by continuing military and arms related cuts.

A strategy for reducing potential conflicts between workers in both communities needs to consider the international patterns of capital movements that devalue the contributions of laborers on both sides of the U.S.-Mexican border. Perhaps this devalorization is as significant as actual jobs losses because of the suppression of the hourly wage on both sides of the border

Other reasons exist, however, to develop such a coalition. In some cases, it can arise from shared heritage and similar legacies of struggle against oppression. It can also arise from the shared recognition that skin color matters. Studies examining the factors affecting the employment and earnings of Puerto Ricans in the USA are particularly instructive. Comparing the determinants of wage differences between African Americans and Puerto Ricans in New York City on the basis of 1960, 1970 and 1980 census data, Torres (1991) found that Puerto Ricans have had more success in generating wage improvements through investments in human capital and labor market experience than non-Latino Blacks. In contrast, non-Latino Blacks have benefited more from patterns of labor market segmentation.

Cotton's (1993) comparison of the earnings of Latino Black, Latino White, non-Latino Black and non-Latino White males revealed that significant differences existed between Latino Blacks and Latino Whites. Latino Whites with fewer years of schooling and work experience earned higher wages and experienced less discrimination in labor markets than Latino Blacks. Non-Latino Blacks had more education and work experience than Black Latinos and earned more. Similar results are reported by Rodriguez (1991) for males, but she found no significant differences between Latino Black and Latino White females.

There are, of course, substantial barriers to developing coalitions. One is the perception that there is substantial competition between Black and Latino workers. The principal evidence relates to the impact of immigrant workers on the employment of domestic minority groups. Some research suggests that, prior to the mid-1970s, Black male workers suffered from competition from women and recent immigrants (Hyclak and Stewart 1986). However, evidence based on 1980 data suggests that Black native-born men have in fact benefited from the increase in immigration, while the major impacts of immigration have fallen on other immigrant groups. To illustrate, Borjas (1986:15) reports that "increases in the supply of the various Latino groups—Mexicans, Puerto Ricans, Cubans and other Latinos—have small effects in [sic] the earnings of non-Latinos, but sizable effects on the earnings of the groups themselves" (see Herring, Bennett and Gills, Chapter 7, for a related finding).

Irrespective of the extent to which intergroup competition exists, the shared vulnerability of Blacks and Latinos mandates the development of a coalition. The fundamental dynamic that underlies the commonalties discussed previously has been aptly described by Jeremy Rifkin (1995). In *The End of Work,* he argues that "We are entering a new phase in world history—one in which fewer and fewer workers will be needed to produce the goods and services for the global population—moving toward a near workerless world" (Rifkin 1995:xvi). It is predicted, for example, that 35% of the workforce will comprise contingent workers by the year 2000. Aside from the fact that contingent workers do not receive benefits, these predictions are troubling because part-time workers earn 20 to 40% less than full-time workers. Blacks and Latinos are the most vulnerable to this continuing erosion of full time employment.

At present, there is no mechanism to monitor how a changing economy will affect Black and Latino populations. At a minimum, a coalition could set up mechanisms to monitor the effects of economic transitions and downsizing of government on Latinos and Blacks in the following areas identified in this chapter as potentially troubling: (1) accessibility to quality jobs; (2) labor union membership and strength; (3) income disparities, both between Whites and Latinos/Blacks and between the sexes; (4) real and perceived competition between resident groups and immigrants; (5) the trend toward contingent workers; and (6) actual declines in relative earnings of workers resulting from international competition between workers and the actions of capital, exploiting differences in the standards of living of workers in different countries.

Recent attacks on affirmative action clearly can provide a rallying point for the development of a coalition of Blacks and Latinos, since they are the principal targets of efforts to curtail such programs in employment. This and the other bases for a Black–Latino coalition discussed in this section are buttressed further by emergent patterns in the provision and consumption of public goods.

BLACKS, LATINOS, AND ACCESS TO PUBLIC GOODS

Futurists predict that highly bureaucratic approaches to solving social problems will continue to decline in importance relative to sources of support provided through voluntary organizations in closer proximity to the constituents served, characterized as the "third sector." Rifkin (1995:249) argues that "In the coming century, the market and public sectors are going to play an ever-reduced role in the day-to-day lives of human beings around the world. The power vacuum will likely be taken up either by the growth of an increasing outlaw subculture or by greater participation in the third sector." The discussion of employment trends in the previous section suggests that the need for income assistance and other forms of support traditionally provided through the federal government will increase substantially. This anticipated escalation in need obviously collides headlong with reductions in federal "welfare" outlays. These trends invite serious questions regarding the capacity of the "third sector" to provide alternative sources of support in the necessary magnitudes. Given our concern with the future prospects for Blacks and Latinos, it is useful to focus the discussion of public goods access to developments that principally affect children.

Poverty Rates and Income Assistance

Proposed cutbacks in income assistance programs, such as Aid to Families with Dependent Children (AFDC), are layered on top of previous large scale reductions implemented during the Reagan and Bush administrations. To illustrate, the welfare reductions that were implemented in Reagan's 1981 budget led to an increase of more than 135,000 in the number of persons in poverty (Storey 1982). These reductions further exacerbated an already deleterious situation for Blacks and Latinos as demonstrated below in Table 12-1.

The data indicate that the "War on Poverty" succeeded in reducing poverty significantly among Black children from the late 1960s to the mid-1970s at the same time that the poverty rate for Whites increased slightly. During the Carter administration, Latino children experienced significant reductions in poverty rates, with fewer dramatic declines occurring for Whites and Blacks. The policies of Reagan and Bush produced a dramatic upturn in the poverty rate for Latinos and significant, but smaller increases for Whites and Blacks. Throughout all three periods, Blacks experienced dramatically higher poverty rates than Whites. Black poverty rates were also higher than those of Latinos. As a final

Table 12-1 Poverty Status —Children in Related Families, Whites, Blacks and Latinos—Selected Years

	White		Black		Latino	
Year	Number*	Pct.	Number	Pct.	Number	Pct.
1991	8,316	16.1	4,637	45.6	2,977	39.8
1979	5,909	11.4	3,745	40.8	1,505	27.7
1975	6,748	12.5	3,884	41.4	1,619	33.1
1966	7,204	12.1	4,774	50.6	NA	NA

Source: U.S. Department of Commerce. 1992. *Poverty in the United States: 1991.* Current Population Reports, Consumer Income, Series P-60, No. 181, Table 3.

*in thousands (000).

note, the poverty rate for Whites is significantly higher now than before the War on Poverty was announced and the reduction that has occurred for Blacks is small relative to the initial magnitude. These data strongly suggest that any future cutbacks in income assistance are likely to increase the vulnerability of Latino and Black children disproportionately. In addition, the workfare schemes that are being designed and implemented will further reduce parental contact with children. Such schemes also beg at least two important questions. The first, raised in the previous section, regards employment prospects for Blacks and Latinos; the second asks whether the level of compensation from available employment is sufficient to escape poverty status. Expectations that welfare recipients will work themselves out of poverty are naively optimistic or intentionally dishonest, given the relatively limited success of job training programs in enabling participants to escape poverty status (Romero 1994).

The modest accomplishments of formal training programs indicate the need to explore the implications of plans to reduce federal support for preschool programs and public elementary and secondary education in the context of the future school-to-work transition of Black and Latino students. It is likely that these cuts will further erode the already limited likelihood that human capital acquisition through traditional venues will be a viable strategy for escaping poverty in the future.

Segregation, Under-Funding and the School-to-Work Transition

Useful evidence regarding the potentially disastrous implications of proposed cutbacks in federal support for elementary and secondary education can be distilled from the record associated with budget cutbacks during the Reagan administration. In fiscal year 1986, federal funding for elementary, secondary and vocational programs was approximately 30% lower than in 1981 (O'Neill and Simms 1982). These reductions dramatically worsened the existing funding inequities between urban and suburban school districts. Black students, in particular, have been disproportionately affected because, in 26 of the 50 states, more than 40% of Black students were attending segregated schools (Hacker 1992).

The result of the pattern of segregation and under-funding described above is that Black and Latino children are disproportionately attending schools with substantial resource deficits. These deficits derive from the manner in which public education is currently funded, which penalizes areas that have eroding property tax bases. Kozol (1991) poignantly documents the disastrous consequences of under funding public education in selected cities, including East St. Louis, New York City, and San Antonio.

The deterioration of public education also reflects the fact that urban school improvement programs targeted at the "disadvantaged" are no longer a national priority. As Jones-Wilson (1991) observes, funding for some of these programs has been reduced or eliminated. The direct result is a service reduction, further taxing a school's ability to provide compensatory education for students in need. For example, a House appropriation's committee approved a bill that would eliminate 43 education programs and reduce spending in more than a dozen others for fiscal 1995. Included in this plan was the rescission of $105 million from the Title I compensatory education program (Pitsch 1995). The amount of local/state dollars that would be needed to replace the federal money for Title I alone is $6.3 billion (Facts on File 1995).

Rather than confronting these structural inequities directly, one current public policy thrust is to provide public subsidies for private alternatives to public education. The subsidy would take the form of "vouchers" that presumably provide parents and students with the opportunity to choose alternatives to public schools. The most likely outcome, however, is to increase the segregation of Black and Latino students as a result of selective enrollment practices of private schools. While some independent Black and Latino schools and their students would, of course, benefit directly from such policies (Slaughter and Johnson 1988), the situation for the majority of Black and Latino students would deteriorate as public schools are left with those students who need the most supplemental support.

Moreover, there is no evidence that independent, not-for-profit schools are better at facilitating the school-to-work transition of students. Black- and Latino-run schools are certainly more successful in cultivating a positive self-image and indigenous cultural orientations than most public schools, but the critical question in the context of creating a viable economic future is whether they can improve the school-to-work transition of students. If we take the results of preliminary experiments in which private, for-profit corporations have been contracted to operate public schools as a guide, the answer may well be "no." These initiatives have not generated long-term improvements in student outcomes.

All this is not to deny the need for drastic reform in public education, but to caution against assuming that market and "third-sector" alternatives are panaceas. Experimentation with such alternatives should continue, but the principal agenda item for a Black–Latino coalition must be structural reform of public education. Another aspect of the educational agenda must be to encourage greater cooperation between historically Black- and Latino-serving institutions of higher education in cultivating a stronger emphasis on community-oriented education.

A Black–Latino coalition to create the type of educational delivery system that will meet the needs of both communities in the future has, of course, difficult barriers to overcome. As an example, geographic segregation limits the potential for cross-cultural interaction. Skerry (1993) reports that Mexican Americans in Los Angeles have been willing to endure double and summer sessions to alleviate crowding in their schools rather than participate in busing schemes designed to promote desegregation. Skerry (1993) also suggests that Latino concerns with bilingual education have been pursued in a manner that creates potential conflicts with the agendas sought by Blacks. Finally, to the extent that Black and Latino "third sector" alternative educational initiatives are organized around overly narrow and exclusive conceptions of cultural authenticity, opportunities for constructive cross fertilization will be limited. Despite the intransigence of these and other barriers to Black–Latino collaboration, a focused effort to overcome them must be undertaken if the foundation for a viable future is to be constructed.

Health Care and Other Social Services

The existing scope of nonprofit organizations' involvement in providing goods and services to vulnerable populations in U.S. society is very extensive. Palmer and Sawhill (1982:13) note that "There are more than 100,000 private, nonprofit service organizations in the United States. They deliver most of the country's hospital care, much of the higher education, and a considerable portion of the social services (such as foster care and family counseling). They are also the principal channels for a host of cultural, civic, and community-organization activities."

However, many of these nonprofit service providers are highly dependent upon federal government subsidies and, thus, will not be able to expand significantly the services provided in the future. In 1981, nonprofit organizations received about 40% of their budgets from the federal government. The Reagan budget entailed an approximate $35 billion reduction in support to nonprofits between FY 1981 and FY 1985. In addition, Salamon (1990) observes that tax cuts implemented as part of the Reagan economic plan reduced incentives for charitable giving that could have partially offset the budget reductions.

Various statistics illustrate the challenge facing "third sector" organizations attempting to provide services directly or lobby local and state governments for support. Ries (1991) reported that in 1989, whereas 18.9% of Black persons under age 18 had no health coverage, only 14% of Whites were in a similar situation. The comparable figures for persons between 18 and 24 were 34.3% and 26.3%, respectively. Similar statistics were not available for Latinos. Blacks have been forced to use emergency room facilities in hospitals disproportionately as an alternative source of primary medical care. The situation facing Latinos is not very different.

However, even the hospital options have been increasingly curtailed. Although the advent of the Medicare and Medicaid programs provided the previously denied access to White hospitals, one result was a precipitous decline in the number of Black hospitals, to the point that there are only about 30 still in existence (Rice 1990). This decline means that it will be difficult to organize community-based health care alternatives that reflect the documented preference of Blacks for same-race health care providers. Access to quality health care for Blacks is further endangered by threats of continuing reductions in Medicaid and the growing movement toward health maintenance organizations (HMOs).

The problem of promoting improved health among Blacks and Latinos is compounded by poor nutrition. Data collected by the National

Center for Health Statistics indicate that, although large gaps do not exist in the intake of minerals, vitamins and dietary fibers across racial/ethnic groups, the intakes are generally lower for Blacks, with the exception of sodium (Alaimo, McDowell, Briefel et.al. 1994). Women and children are the most likely to suffer nutritional deficiencies. Nutritional gaps between Blacks and Whites are likely to increase if planned social support reductions include the Food Stamp and Women, Infants and Children (WIC) programs.

Increasing health improvement challenges are also posed by self-inflicted and externally imposed environmental hazards. Black children less than five years old are much more likely than White or Latino children to have been exposed to smoke after birth (Overpeck and Moss 1991). Continuing public health problems, including exposure to environmental hazards like lead and air pollution, are related to the cutbacks in funding for public housing programs during the Reagan and Bush administrations (see Leigh 1992 for a discussion of public housing policies). Finally, efforts to locate hazardous chemical dumps and other environmental hazards in close proximity to Black and Latino communities have been documented by Bullard (1990).

These health-related issues adversely affect future patterns of human capital accumulation by Blacks and Latinos in ways that will worsen their prospects for stable employment. Faced with such challenges, Blacks and Latinos need to develop strategies to maximize access to the social services necessary to support stable communities in the next century. Such a strategy must have at least three components: (a) organizing and funding self-provision of social services, (b) lobbying local government agencies to provide services equitably, and (c) undertaking political action and community education to increase the priority assigned to social services.

One strategy Blacks have employed to mobilize additional funding and target the delivery of social services was to create an alternative to the United Way to channel donations directly to service providers operating in predominantly Black communities. The National Black United Fund (NBUF) was established in 1974 with the mission to "raise and distribute funds exclusively for charitable purposes, with particular emphasis on those which include eliminating prejudice, discrimination, reducing neighborhood tension, relieving the poor and underprivileged, and combating deterioration" (Davis 1975:150). The NBUF has waged a continuing struggle to gain the same visibility and access to payroll deductions as the United Way.

One of the most successful examples of such self-funded provision of social services was initiated by Rev. Leon Sullivan in Philadelphia. In 1962, he originated what was called the 10-36 plan in his Philadelphia church. Congregation members were asked to contribute $10 for 36 months to undertake community economic development efforts. Ten of the 36 payments were used to fund nonprofit social services through the Zion Non-Profit Charitable Trust. From this start, the number of churches participating in Sullivan's 10-36 program reached a maximum of 400 (Stewart 1984). This voluntary donation arrangement was closely linked to Sullivan's community-based vocational training enterprise, Opportunities Industrialization Centers, increasing its effect and significance. A strong community-based voluntary giving program is highly preferable to excessive dependence on external donations.

Barnet's (1994) critique of the type of goods and services that are marketed and sold in Black and Latino communities raises the question of whether self-provision efforts can be extended from the provision of social services to the production of goods. Leon Sullivan's program addressed this issue by channeling most of the monies raised through the 10-36 program into the purchase of shares in Zion Investment Associates—a for-profit holding company or community development corporation. This company generated Progress Enterprises, a subsidiary that undertook construction of Progress Plaza Shopping Center and an apartment building. Other ventures included a garment manufacturing plant and a chain of convenience stores.

Thus, the emergent strategy incorporated provisions for growth-enhancing activities alongside vehicles to accomplish redistribution, becoming one model for federally supported Community Development Corporations that now operate in many Black and Latino communities (Stewart 1984). As noted by Handy (1993:50) "Some CDCs may act as, work closely with, or actually become quasi-public economic development corporations in local jurisdictions. CDCs, now numbering more than 1,000 throughout the country and located in nearly every state, have gained increasing sophistication in organizing communities and supervising local development." It is important to distinguish these collective economic development efforts from the expansion of self-employment or sole-proprietorships touted by some futurists as the wave of the future. The characteristics of Black businesses limit the extent to which they constitute vehicles for upward mobility of large numbers of people. To illustrate, approximately 94% of Black-owned firms are sole proprietorships and two-thirds operate in the service or retail trade areas. Only 10% have paid employees and only about 340 have 100 or more employees (U.S. Department of Commerce 1995).

Community-based initiatives among Mexican Americans in San Antonio and Los Angeles provide an interesting contrast to the model described previously. Skerry (1993) has described the emergence in the 1970s of Communities Organized for Public Service (COPS) in San Antonio and the United Neighborhoods Organization (UNO) in Los Angeles, spearheaded by community organizer, Ernesto Cortes, using the principles advanced by Saul Alinsky. Some of COPS' struggles in San Antonio have focused on drainage systems, street pavements, better housing, improved police protection and education reform. UNO has focused on similar issues and has also been involved in efforts to increase the minimum wage in California (Skerry 1993). However, the linkage to the Alinsky philosophy has meant that neither organization has focused on national and international issues of special concern to Latinos such as U.S. foreign policy toward South and Central America, bilingual education and immigration (see Chapter 8).

The Sullivan and Cortes initiatives suggest the outlines for a large-scale collaborative Black–Latino self-help initiative organized at the local level. But broader public policy issues must also be addressed. Such engagement will require collaboration between other types of organizations, such as the NAACP Legal Defense Fund and the Mexican American Legal Defense Fund, which has not occurred to any significant degree to date.

One of the areas where such collaboration is crucial is the protection of the rights of incarcerated Blacks and Latinos. The over representation of Black males in correctional institutions and under other types of criminal justice system control is well documented (see, for example, Mauer 1994). A large proportion of Latino males are in similar circumstances. This phenomenon reflects, in part, the marginalization of Black and Latino males from emerging labor markets. Moreover, it can call attention to another policy inequity: the thinly disguised pattern of constructing correctional institutions in rural, impoverished White communities to provide alternative employment to that lost by the decline in manufacturing, mining and agriculture.

This pattern of social warehousing of redundant labor should signal to Blacks and Latinos that self-help efforts alone will be insufficient to meet the growing demand for public goods. Thus, Blacks and Latinos must become part of broader coalitions to seek greater governmental commitments for the provision of public goods to those populations that are most vulnerable to the ongoing global transformation. The Tofflers (1995:53) argue, for example, that:

The jobless desperately need money if they and their families are to survive, and it is both necessary and morally right to provide them with decent levels of public assistance . . .

As . . . new jobs are not likely to be found in what we still think of as manufacture, we will need to prepare people through schooling apprenticeships and on-the-job learning for work in such fields as the human services.

They maintain further that:

if . . . wages are low in the service sector, then the solution is to increase service productivity and to invent new forms of workforce organization and collective bargaining. Unions, primarily designed for the crafts or for mass manufacturing, need to be totally transformed or else replaced by new-style organizations more appropriate to the supersymbolic economy (Toffler and Toffler 1995:53).

In a similar vein, Aronowitz and DiFazio (1994) claim there is a need for society to provide subsidies in the form of tax deductions for shadow wages for voluntary community service work.

In the absence of an expanded commitment to the provision of public goods, the forces of international migration associated with the global economic transformation will continue to increase social tension in those areas where the previously marginalized and the new immigrants interact. One manifestation of this phenomenon is the effort in California to deny social services to so-called "undocumented" immigrants. Another manifestation that poses a significant barrier to Black–Latino cooperation is the rising level of inter-group conflicts.

Kotkin (1993:254) argues that "The border boom . . . places the Third World on the doorstep of advanced First World Societies, with enormous environmental and social costs. In many of the most intense points of contact, the conflicts between assertive ethnic groups—Muslims, Koreans, Latinos and Africans—have been marred by urban disturbances, most spectacularly in the racial conflagration that consumed Los Angeles in the spring of 1992." More generally, he maintains that "Many older, more established communities—both African-American and Anglo—will feel themselves overwhelmed and in some sense displaced by the energetic newcomers, both in the marketplace and, over time, in the political arena" (Kotkin 1993:254). In a similar vein, Toffler

(1970:249) argues that "in addition to traditional conflict between majority and minorities, democratic governments must now cope with open
warfare *between* rival minority groups, as happened in Miami, for example, between Cuban and Haitian immigrants, and elsewhere in the United
States between African-Americans and Latinos."

This growing potential for inter-group conflict means that efforts to
build Black–Latino coalitions must conceptualize the project in global,
rather than simply national or local, terms. It is a project that has the potential to shape the near and intermediate future of the new international
order. In the Tofflers' (1995:34) terms, "the globally competitive race
will be won by the countries that complete their Third Wave transformation with the least amount of domestic disruption and unrest."

The Tofflers' (1995:24) insist that the current transformation gener-
ates possibilities for new political formations and alliances:

> In the United States—and in many other countries—the collision of
> Second and Third Waves creates social tensions, dangerous conflicts
> and strange new political wave fronts that cut across the usual divisions
> of class, race, sex or party. This collision makes a shambles of tradi-
> tional political vocabularies and makes it very difficult to separate pro-
> gressives from reactionaries, friends from enemies. All the old
> polarizations and coalitions break up.

This perspective suggests that Blacks and Latinos can overcome the
tendency toward fragmentation and the conceptualization of distinct
struggles if the similarity of their linkage to the international economic
order is fully comprehended.

BLACKS, LATINOS, AND THE NEW INTERNATIONAL ECO-
NOMIC ORDER

The potential human tragedies associated with the ongoing global transformation have been cogently described by Aronowitz and DiFazio
(1994:425-426):

> An astonishingly large and increasing number of people are not needed
> or wanted to make the goods or to provide the services that the paying
> customers of the world can afford. The gathering pressures of global
> competition to cut costs threaten the vast majority of the 8 billion
> human beings expected to be living on earth in the first quarter of the

next century with the prospect that they will be neither producers nor consumers.

From this vantage point, it is no accident that the *World Development Report* (1995) focuses on the theme "Workers in an Integrating World." The report (1995:2) observes that "Workers in low-income countries dominate the world's agricultural work force and also, by their sheer numbers, account for nearly half of the world's industrial workers and about a third of its unemployed." The domestic manifestations of this pattern for Blacks and Latinos have been described in the preceding sections. But both groups must be cognizant of the vulnerability of their regions of origin to the ongoing global economic transformation and understand how the various types of actors are integrated. To illustrate, the Tofflers (1995:30-32) observe:

> In this trisected world the First Wave sector supplies agricultural and mineral resources, the Second Wave sector provides cheap labor and does mass production, and a rapidly expanding Third Wave sector rises to dominance based on the new ways in which it creates and exploits knowledge.
>
> Third Wave nations sell information and innovation, management, culture and pop culture, advanced technology, software, education, training, medical care and financial and other services to the world. One of those services might well also turn out to be military protection based on its command of superior Third Wave forces . . .
>
> {T}hese changes threaten to slash many of the existing economic links between the rich economies and the poor.

The implications of the trends described by the Tofflers for Africa and South and Central America are not promising. In general, Africa is presented by futurists as a terminal patient, and the recent round of GATT negotiations demonstrates that it is not yet a major player in the emerging global economy. The projections of economic benefits resulting from the new trade agreement indicated that every continent would gain as a result of the agreement—except Africa. Kennedy (1993:217) argues that "As Africa struggles to stay connected with the rest of the world, the inclinations—declining amounts of aid, shrinking trade and investment flows, reduction in media coverage, diminished superpower involvement—are that it is becoming more peripheral."

In contrast, South America is portrayed as an emerging economic force, buttressed by the recent passage of NAFTA. To illustrate, Kotkin (1993:253) argues that the border region "between Mexico and the United States by the 1980s had grown as rapidly as virtually anyplace in North America, with nearly 30% population growth along the border during the decade. Ethnic ties, and particularly growing economic links, were creating transnational cities, with culture and families as well as cash and commerce flowing both ways."

Although the prospects for South America were initially more promising than for Africa, recently, the Mexican economy has stagnated and the projections of benefits have been reduced. Consistent with the Tofflers' assessment, both South America and Africa can only aspire to the status of Second Wave enclaves in a world dominated by Third Wave interests, if the present drama is allowed to play itself out. One critical question is whether Blacks and Latinos in the U.S.A. will establish linkages with their regions of origin that can alter the current trajectory.

The above patterns of cross-national economic activity, involving Mexicans in the United States and in Mexico, constitute one example of a pattern associated with what Kotkin (1993) describes as "global tribes" that have been, and will be, major actors in the world order. These global tribes, which he argues (1993:4-5) include the British, Jews, Japanese, Chinese and Asian Indians, are said to have three critical characteristics:

1. A strong ethnic identity and sense of mutual dependence that helps the group adjust to changes in the global economy and political order without losing its essential unity;
2. A global network based on mutual trust that allows the tribe to function collectively beyond the confines of national or regional borders; and
3. A passion for technical and other knowledge from all possible sources, combined with an essential open-mindedness that fosters rapid cultural and scientific development critical for success in the late-twentieth-century world economy.

According to Kotkin (1993:16), "The power of global tribes derives from their successful coalescing of two principles that, in classic liberal thought, have been separated: an intrinsic "tribal" sense of unique historical and ethnic identity and the ability to adapt to a cosmopolitan global economy."

Consistent with the treatment of the Black experience in most other futuristic studies, peoples of African descent are not considered to be one of these "global tribes" by Kotkin. Latinos are treated as a potential global tribe of the future, not yet having the sophistication and organizational nexus of existing global tribes. However, despite Kotkin's failure to recognize similar developments among peoples of African descent and Latinos, there have been historical efforts to create the type of linkage ascribed to other groups and there are growing contemporary efforts to build on the historical foundations.

To illustrate, the efforts of Rev. Leon Sullivan described in the previous section are now focused in the international arena through the International Foundation for Education and Self-Help (IFESH). IFESH is operating in a number of African countries, but it is also establishing programs in South America. IFESH currently operates "Teachers for Africa" and "Schools for Africa" programs in African countries, which can be seen as an internationalization of the thrust for improved domestic education. In a similar vein, IFESH has established a partnership with the World Health Organization, in a sense internationalizing domestic development.

IFESH is also actively involved in the "Debt for Development" program in both Africa and South America, a program that contributes directly to improved economic development prospects. Although IFESH has, to this point in time, focused most of its energies on Africa, it is clear that it views Central and South Americans as part of its constituency. It provides a paradigm of the type of Black–Latino national–international structures that must be created. In a similar vein, the aggressive and successful lobbying activities of TransAfrica on behalf of Africa and the Caribbean could be extended with little additional resource requirements to include Central and South America, if appropriate dialogues are pursued. The shared interests of Africa, the Caribbean, and Central and South America make such a linkage both attractive and necessary.

Rev. Leon Sullivan is also the principal sponsor of the three African-African American Summits that were held in West African countries in early 1990s. These summits involved large delegations, made up principally of African Americans, journeying to the motherland to explore issues of common concern to the continent and the Diaspora. One initiative that has emerged from these summits is the effort to establish opportunities for African Americans to obtain dual citizenship. Interestingly, officials in Mexico are considering a similar proposal for Mexican Americans (Dillon 1995).

The African-African American summits offer a prototype for a comparable African-South American Summit, with Blacks and Latinos in the

United States serving as a major organizing vanguard. In addition to exploring issues related to shared cultural heritage that link many Blacks and Latinos, such a Summit could both disseminate information about existing initiatives that are operating to promote synergies of interests and develop strategies to increase economic and cultural exchange among Africa, South America, Central America, and the Caribbean, and their Diasporas in the United States.

Initially such linkages would allow only limited disengagement from the pattern of exploitative trade described by the Tofflers. If successful, however, they could be the keys to survival and development for Blacks and Latinos worldwide in the twenty-first century.

CONCLUSION

This analysis explored various bases for Black–Latino collaboration in support of a viable economic future, using as its platform the writings of futurists, who generally relegate both groups to the backwaters of the massive changes that are sweeping global society. The analysis focused principally on prospective employment trends, likely patterns of access to public goods and the implications of the structure and functioning of the emergent global economic order, and found that Blacks and Latinos are disproportionately at risk in similar ways in all three areas.

The analysis also suggested strategies and organizational initiatives that can alter the current trajectory, concluding that those organizations that focus on the interplay of domestic and international forces will be the most useful in the future. As these new types of domestic and international formations emerge, we should not be surprised to see the demise or marginalization of some traditional organizations that have been critical to Black and Latino liberation struggles during the "Second Wave."

Advancing a Third Wave agenda for Blacks and Latinos will not be an easy task. As the Tofflers (1995:79) observe, "Unlike the 'masses' during the industrial age, the rising Third Wave constituency is highly diverse. It is demassified. It is composed of individuals who prize their differences. Its very heterogeneity contributes to its lack of political awareness. It is far harder to unify than the masses of the past."

However, those working to create the type of coalition advocated here should not be daunted by setbacks; for as W.E.B. Du Bois so cogently observed at the turn of the last century: the problem of the twentieth century is the problem of the color line. This color line remains a powerful tool for forging a sense of unity among oppressed people of color. It may also provide the basis for expanding the proposed coalition to include Asian populations. For example, in response to conflicts between Koreans and Blacks, the Korea Society, headquartered in Washington and New York, has initiated cultural exchange programs whereby Black teenagers have the opportunity to visit Korea and learn about its rich cultural heritage and establish networks. Another notable example is the formation of the KAUR Group, a consulting firm specializing in multi-cultural issues and the problems of women in development. The organizer is a Sikh woman who has linked the organization's agenda to the historical struggles of Blacks.

These examples and the various prototypes described in the analysis are a cause for hope for the future even in the face of a juggernaut that threatens to marginalize much of the world's population. Efforts to forge a winning strategy for the twenty-first century can draw inspiration from the unswerving historical struggle for unity between Black and White Cubans waged by Jose Marti in the fight against imperialism. Marti envisioned a future Cuban republic in which the interests of all people were harmonious and justice was color-blind, a vision very similar to that propagated by Du Bois. Marti (1889:24) insisted that "The coloured man has the right to be treated for his human qualities, without reference being made to his colour."

But the vision of Du Bois and Marti with respect to equal treatment of all peoples is very different from that promoted by contemporary opponents of affirmative action, whose proposed policies would have the singular effect of institutionalizing existing inequities into the next millennium. Honoring the legacy of Du Bois and Marti requires a full-scale assault on the forces that would turn back the clock of history and restore historical forms of oppression. Perhaps one positive outcome that may emerge from the struggle to forestall retrenchment in the quest for social justice is the establishment of a foundation for a sustainable and effective coalition between Blacks and Latinos. Such a coalition could well play a vanguard role in synthesizing and operationalizing the visions of Du Bois and Marti in the twenty-first century.

CHAPTER 13

The Possibilities of Collaboration and the Challenges of Contention
Concluding Remarks

JOHN J. BETANCUR

This book examines objective and subjective as well as internal and external factors of collaboration and contention between and within the African American and Latino communities and between them and other groups in the urban United States. Most objective factors examined point to the need for and possibility of unity to secure a viable socioeconomic and political future for both communities. Conditions, risks, and prospects, in fact, are so similar that it seems natural for Latinos and Blacks to coalesce. Many external and subjective factors, however, keep them separated and, often, in contention. Although historical and circumstantial developments have facilitated unity, collaboration, however, must be carefully constructed and maintained. Similarities or shared conditions do not create unity by themselves.

Through the analysis of multiple examples of joint Black and Latino action, the book explores the sources of success and the pitfalls resulting from these initiatives. Each chapter provides important insights from past and ongoing experiences, while identifying new challenges posed by recent changes in the political economy. A few points from this discussion are worth highlighting.

First, the fact that collaboration between African Americans and Latinos operates within a dynamic and creative tension can be construed as an asset. Rather than assuming that unity implies the merging (or assimilation) of two groups into a single community, the challenge can be one of developing forms of cooperation that maintain the identities of each within a democratic framework. Although tensions will always threaten any joint action, ways should be explored to bring them into the picture as elements of diversity. Bilingual education is a case in point. Instead of assuming that bilingual and Afrocentric education compete with each other, African Americans and Latinos could unite around a struggle for approaches to education that build on the cultural identities of all groups in the U.S. Different conjunctures and issues call for different interventions and forms of cooperation. They could be best worked out if they were informed by a discourse of inclusiveness—applicable to society at large.

Second, Latinos and Blacks must seriously reexamine the nature and possibilities of electoral coalitions as part of their strategy of collective development. Chapters 3 and 4 show the high risks associated with excessive or exclusive reliance on the electoral process. Combinations of grassroots movements and interventions with electoral initiatives seem to be a condition for solutions to the collective needs of Latinos and Blacks. Only through their association with popular action will coalitions and elected representatives remain accountable to the masses of their communities/constituents. Individual ambition and political careerism, party loyalties (particularly with parties of the dominant elites), class affiliations, and other dynamics of the political process often coopt the best intentioned politicians, especially when their constituencies are not holding them accountable to policies in their interest.

Various chapters suggest that cooperation has been more effective at the grassroots level than between elites in both the Latino and the African American communities. The authors see the need for strategies of direct, grassroots action for achieving real gains. They suggest building unity up from the bottom around the daily realities that challenge the vast majority of African Americans and Latinos in their neighborhoods and work places. This conscientious work can help people learn and feel comfortable about each other, confront mutual prejudices and become aware of common problems and common enemies. Such relationships can, then, become the basis for larger undertakings and lasting collaborations.

Third, the state continues to be the most powerful arena for the struggle of African Americans and Latinos. The claim that there is no government surplus for investment in the development of the urban centers and communities in which Latinos and Blacks live is highly misleading. The surplus exists but is being diverted to corporate welfare (corpfare). By engaging in cutthroat competition for decreasing allocations, Blacks and Latinos play into the hands of the corporate state. Latino and Black communities need to work intensely to increase the electoral participation of their majority low-income sectors behind their collective interests and needs. They should join forces with the low-income and displaced members of other groups to demand a socially responsible public sector with adequate levels of quality services. This requires a movement to hold the state accountable to its citizens. It is ironic that our government can find financial resources to bail out Asian markets while failing to assist its own citizens trapped in cities.

Fourth, urban concentration of Blacks and Latinos can be an advantage in the building of coalition power (electoral and non electoral) around the collective needs of national minority communities and many other populations at risk in the global political economy. Its emergence has produced opportunities for building collaboration from the bottom up; for combining place- and people-based strategies of collective advancement; for development of trust through positive and continuous interactions (around education, housing, environmental and other community- based interventions); and for experimenting with new forms of social organization and struggle. Increasingly concentrated in cities, Blacks and Latinos can join forces with other urban low-income groups to improve their lives, while promoting new policies and politics of change.

Fifth, middle and upper class Latinos and Blacks (and whites and others) have often manipulated movements and initiatives of their communities for their own class gains, at the expense of the collective developmental needs of their majority low-income populations (see Chapters 3 through 5). Although racism and race-related underdevelopment continue uniting these communities along the color line, the interests and needs of low-income Black and Latino masses run in contradiction with those of elites from their middle and upper classes. Grassroots movements and initiatives of development of the majority in these communities need to focus on their collective class interests and needs. They need to hold their leadership accountable and work to stave off middle class opportunism and domination. Blacks and Latinos need to be aware that many class interests can never be conciliated. Since the majority of Latinos and African Americans are low-income, their coalitions for development must focus on the masses of the poor and their collective needs. They, in fact, should seek to involve low-income populations from other groups (Asians, American Indians).

Sixth, the obsessive denial of racism in U.S. society has become a new tool of racism. The attribution of national minority underdevelopment to cultural traits and individual behavior legitimizes racism as it ignores the racial path that produced many of those traits and behaviors in the first place (see Chapter 6 in particular). While preaching a model of open competition and opportunity, our society relies on mechanisms such as racism to secure privilege along racial lines. African Americans and Latinos confront entrenched power structures that keep them subjugated. To the extent that racism continues to be reproduced, the color line remains a universal focus of the Back and Latino struggle. While making the Black–Latino struggle for advancement particularly complex, the deep association between poverty and race remains a powerful basis for forging a sense of unity between them.

Seventh, community building should proceed on the basis of highly democratic approaches. The model of centralized formations, in which the agenda is set from the top, invites elitism, class manipulation and outside cooptation. It works to empower the few in the leadership at the expense of the masses. Experiences around environmental and economic justice and progressive local administrations demonstrate, again and again, that collective interests are best represented when movements are led by those who bear the problems. While middle class leadership can bring crucial resources to these initiatives, agendas are more difficult to thwart, and individual interests less likely to prevail through democratic practice than through conventional, closed door, small group arrangements and negotiations that make the concerns of the majority secondary or ignore them altogether.

Eighth, organizations with outside linkages can be most successful and, in fact, most powerful if they allow for broad undertakings through networking (see Chapters 9 and 12). Increasingly, the issues affecting local communities call for interventions beyond the local scene. Interorganizational cooperation allows for larger and larger levels of unity; it brings more resources to the effort; it prevents outside forces from playing community against community; it helps with information gathering; and it allows for synchronized action in multiple fronts (see Chapter 9). International linkages are becoming particularly important (see Chapter 12) as the forces of oppression increase their networking and reach far beyond the local scene.

Ninth, globalization has added a new dimension to the struggle. While pitting the U.S. working class against working classes elsewhere, particularly in the Third World, it acts to deny the legitimacy of the Black and Latino causes. On the one hand, it is working to redefine the role of the state away from redress and social equity—and, hence, reduce the ability of marginalized groups to address equity issues through the state. On the other hand, it pits Blacks against Latinos, Blacks against Blacks, and Latinos against Latinos in unique ways. Immigration is a case in point. By resorting to increasingly selective forms of immigration, the U.S.A. is creating categories of citizens with different rights and opportunities. A discourse of *model* minorities is being crafted to discredit the struggles of traditional nationality or racial minorities. Meanwhile, as immigration from Latin America becomes a wage-reducing substitute, it undermines the gains that domestic minorities may have achieved through their struggles. Selective investment in a few communities is forcing Blacks and Latinos to compete against each other for a reduced social budget. This competition turns them into involuntary allies of policies of exclusion. Moreover, Haitians and other Blacks are being denied entry into the U.S.A. seemingly because they are poor and Black. Latinos and African Americans can confront such challenges through increased awareness and solidarity against practices that divert them from their legitimate, collective causes. They should certainly intensify international efforts to link up with their peers in the diaspora and to encourage their governments of origin to support their cause.

Tenth, by necessity or choice, African Americans and Latinos face many common issues in cities. Confrontation can cancel each other's efforts. Coalition with majority elite machines has proven to benefit only a few. Cooperation with each other will likely increase their negotiating power and the ability to advance the agendas of their majority low-income populations.

Finally, increased diversification of the Black and Latino communities calls for each of them to engage in efforts of internal cooperation and community building similar to those that need to take place between the two communities. Composed of multiple nationalities, Latinos have already the experience of community building between different nationals. As part of this, they are aware of the difficulties posed by middle- and upper-class nationality elites competing for position, at the expense of each other or of their majority low-income members.

These points are not necessarily raised by each of the chapters in this volume. All of them, however, agree on the critical impacts of globalization and the urgency of action. They see different levels of hope. All authors view racism as central an issue as ever before. The fates of the Black and Latino communities seem so tied together that the gains of one at the expense of the other are the losses of both. Meanwhile, class and intracommunity diversification emerge as elements that require special attention. All authors insist on the opportunity and potential of Black and Latino collaboration. This may be the new agenda of both communities.

Certainly, the relationship between minorities is one of the main issues in central cities today.

Cities provide a unique opportunity and arena for Black and Latino collaboration—as well as contention. What Latinos and Blacks do in cities will determine their future in this society in a very significant way. Current and past experiences can inform new initiatives and approaches for joint local efforts. Analyses in this book call for special efforts to break through the recurrent circles that work to reproduce their condition of underdevelopment. The chapters identify the limitations of past efforts both within and between the two communities and point to systemic and political factors producing and maintaining their underdevelopment.

While new and renewed initiatives and approaches to development are required, power emerges as the single element pushing such approaches and changes to the fore. Race-based struggles have helped Blacks and Latinos achieve some political power. Community-based power has made significant strides. It has certainly resulted in important collective gains.

A sustained process of building and maintenance of power is more crucial every day, as economic power claims its space beyond the political realm and as states line up even more intensely behind it. As some authors suggest, Latinos and Backs need to gain more strength for their struggle for advancement through coalition with each other, with other national minorities, and with the increasing number of displaced and low-income members of the majority populations. As the new model of capital accumulation intensifies, it produces persistent marginalization and the politics of exclusion. With the growing divide between the haves and the have nots, collaboration becomes an increasing necessity and possibility. Only together can Latinos and African Americans confront the formidable forces of the state and racism in association with global capital against the masses. It is time to put the wealth and power of the United States where its mouth is and to build a society of real equal opportunity for all.

References

Abramson, Harold. 1973. *Ethnic Diversity in Catholic America*. New York: Wiley.

Aburdene, P. and Naisbitt, J. 1992. *Megatrends for Women*. New York: Villard Books.

Acuña, Robert. 1984. *A Community Under Siege: A Chronicle of Chicanos in East of the Los Angeles River, 1945-1975*. Los Angeles: Chicano Studies Research Center, University of California at Los Angeles.

Acuña, Rodolfo. 1988. *Occupied America. A History of Chicanos*. 3rd Edition. New York: Harper and Row.

Adams, Carolyn, David Bartelt, David Elesh, Ira Goldstein, Nancy Kleniewski and William Yancey. 1991. *Philadelphia: Neighborhoods, Division, and Conflict in a Postindustrial City*. Philadelphia: Temple University Press.

Adams, Carolyn Teich. 1990. "Philadelphia: The Private City in the Post-Industrial Era." Pp. 209–226 in *Snowbelt Cities: Metropolitan Politics in the Northeast and Midwest since World War II*, edited by Richard M. Bernard. Bloomington: Indiana University Press.

Alabama Blackbelt Defense Committee. n.d. *The Accused Speak*. Gainesville: Alabama Blackbelt Defense Committee.

Alaimo, Katherine, Margaret McDowell, Ronette Briefel, et al. 1994. "Dietary Intake of Vitamins, Minerals, and Fiber of Persons Ages 2 Months and Over in the United States: Third National Health and Nutrition Examination Survey, Phase 1, 1988–91," Advance Data from Vital and Health Statistics; No. 258. Hyattsville, MD: National Center for Health Statistics.

Alexander, Stephen J. and Nikolas C. Theodore. 1994. *Capacity Building for Neighborhood Development: An Analysis of the Chicago Approach*. Chicago: Chicago Urban League.

Alexander, Stephen. J. 1994. *Industrial Policy and Local Development Strategies*. Chicago: Chicago Urban League.

Alexander, Stephen J. 1995. "Public Resource Allocation and Disribution Among African American, Latino and Low-Income Communities." Paper presented at the Urban Challenges for Blacks and Latinos in the 1990s and Beyond Conference. Chicago: University of Illinois Center for Urban Economic Development (September 7–9).

Alkalimat, Abdul. 1995. "Comments for Workshop 7 of the Conference Urban Challenges for Blacks and Latinos in the 1990s: Strategies of Contention and Collaboration." Chicago: Center for Urban Economic Development, University of Illinois at Chicago (September 7–9).

Alkalimat, Abdul and Associates. 1984, 1989 revised. *Introduction to African American Studies: A Peoples College Primer*. Chicago: Twenty-first Century Books and Publications.

Alkalimat, Abdul and Douglas Gills. 1989. *Harold Washington and the Crisis of Black Power in Chicago*. Chicago: Twenty-First Century Books and Publications.

Alkalimat, Abdul, Douglas Gills and Kate Williams. 1995. *Job Tech: the Technological Revolution and Its Impacts on Society*. Chicago: Twenty-first Century Books.

Alkalimat, Abdul, and Doug Gills. 1984. "Black Power vs. Racism: Harold Washington Becomes Mayor." Pp. 53–180 in *The New Black Vote, Politics and Power in Four American Cities*, edited by Rod Bush. San Francisco: Synthesis.

All Chicago City News. Chicago: *All Chicago City News, Inc.* (Selected articles on the state of Chicago social and political movement activities and developments, 1982–1991). Author's files.

Allport, Gordon. 1954. *The Nature of Prejudice*. Cambridge, MA: Addison-Wesley.

Amin, Ash. Ed.1995. *Post-Fordism, A Reader.* Cambridge, MA: Blackwell.

Anderson, Elijah. 1990. *Streetwise: Race, Class, and Change in an Urban Community.* Chicago: University of Chicago Press.

Año Nuevo Kerr, Louise. 1976. "The Chicano Experience in Chicago, 1920–1970." Ph.D. Dissertation. Chicago: University of Illinois at Chicago.

Archer, Kate. 1987. *The Politics of Privatization: Contracting Out Public Services.* New York, NY: St. Martin Press.

Armah, Bartholomew. 1994. "Implications of Trade on Service Employment: Implications for Women and Minorities." *Contemporary Economic Policy*, 12: 67–78.

Aronowirtz, Stanley and William DiFazio. 1994. *A Jobless Future: Sci-Tech and the Dogma of Work.* Minneapolis: University of Minnesota Press.

Arrighi, Giovanni, Terence K. Hopkins and Immanuel Wallerstein. 1989. *Antisystemic Movements*. New York, NY: Verso.

Baca Zinn, M. 1989. "Family, Race and Poverty in the Eighties." *Signs: Journal of Woman in Culture and Society* 14: 856–874.

Banfield, E. 1970. *The Unheavenly City*. 2nd Edition. Boston: Little and Brown.

Barnet, Richard. 1994. *Global Dreams: Imperial Corporations and the New World Order*. New York: Simon and Schuster.

Barnet, Richard and John Cavanah. 1995. *Global Dreams. Imperial Corporations and the New World Order*. New York: Touchstone, Simon and Schuster.

Barrera, Mario. 1979. *Race and Class in the Southwest: A Theory of Racial Inequality*. South Bend, IN: Notre Dame University Press.

Bartelt, David W. 1993. "Housing the 'Underclass.'" Pp. 118-157 in *The "Underclass" Debate: Views from History,* edited by Michael Katz. Princeton, NJ: Princeton University Press.

Beal, Frances. 1995. "Slave of a Slave No More: Black Women in Struggle." *The Black Scholar* 4: 2–10.

Bean, Frank D. and Marta Tienda. 1987. *The Hispanic Population of the U.S.* New York: Russell Sage Foundation.

Bell, Brenda, John Gaventa and John Peters. eds. 1990. *We Make the Road by Walking: Conversations on Education and Social Change: Miles Horton and Paulo Freire*. Philadelphia: Temple University Press.

Berry, Thompson and Portney. 1993. *The Rebirth of Urban Democracy*. Washington, DC: The Brookings Institute.

Betancur, John J. and Douglas C. Gills. 1993. "Race and Class in Local Economic Development." Pp. 191–212 in *Theories of Local Economic Development. Perspectives from Across the Disciplines,* edited by Richard D. Bingham and Robert Mier. Newbury Park, CA: Sage Publications.

Betancur, John J. and Douglas C. Gills. 1997. "Understanding Black/Latino Conflict and Concerns." Pp. 83-100 in *Race and Politics in the United States: New Challenges and Responses for Black Activism* edited by James Jennings. New York: Verso.

Betancur, John J., Teresa Cordova and Maria Torres. 1993. "Economic Restructuring and the Process of Incorporation of Latinos into the Chicago Economy." Pp. 109-132 in *Latinos in a Changing U.S. Economy,* edited by Rebecca Morales and Frank Bonilla. Newbury Park, CA: Sage Publications.

Bethell, Thomas. 1982. *Sumter County Blues: The Ordeal of the Federation of Southern Cooperatives*. Washington, DC: National Committee in Support of Community Based Organizations.

Blalock, Hubert. 1967. *Toward a Theory of Minority Group Relations*. New York: Wiley.

Blauner, Robert. 1972. *Racial Oppression in America*. New York: Harper & Row.

Blaustein, Albert and Robert Zangrando. eds. 1968. *Civil Rights and the American Negro*. New York: Washington Square Publishers.

Bloch, Herman D. 1969. *The Circle of Discrimination*. New York: New York University Press.

Bluestone, Barry and Bennett Harrison. 1982. *The Deindustrialization of America: Plant Closings, Community Abandonment, and the Dismantling of Basic Industry*. New York, NY: Basic Books.

Bonacich, Edna. 1972. "A Theory of Ethnic Antagonism: The Split Labor Market." *American Sociological Review* 37: 547–559.

Bonacich, Edna and John Modell. 1980. *The Economic Basis of Ethnic Solidarity: Small Business in the Japanese American Community*. Berkeley: University of California Press.

Bonilla, Frank. 1988. "From Racial Justice to Economic Rights: the New American Dilemma." Dr. Martin Luther King, Jr., Birthday Celebration. Washington, DC: Smithsonian Institution.

Bonilla, Frank and Ricardo Campos. 1981. "A Wealth of Poor: Puerto Ricans in the New Economic Order." *Daedalus* 110, 2: 133-134.

Bonilla, Frank and Richard Campos. 1982. "Bootstraps and Enterprize Zones: The Underside of Late Capitalism in Puerto Rico and the United States." *National Review* 4 (Spring).

Borjas, George. 1986. *Immigrants, Minorities, and Labor Market Competition*. Working Paper No. 2028. Cambridge: National Bureau of Economic Research.

Bowles, Samuel and Herbert Gintis. 1976. *Schooling in Capitalist America: Educational Reform and the Contradictions of Economic Life*. New York: Basic Books.

Brecher, Jeremy and Jim Costello. 1996. *Global Village or Global Pillage: Economic Restructuring from the Bottom- up*. Boston: South End Press.

Brecher, Jeremy and Tim Costello. eds. 1990. *Building Bridges: the Emerging Grassroots Coalition of Labor and Community*. New York: Monthly Review Press.

Brehm, Robert. 1991. "The City and the Neighborhoods: Was it Really a Two-Way Street?" Pp. 238–269 in *Harold Washington and the Neighborhoods: Progressive City Government in Chicago, 1983–1987*, edited by Pierre Clavel and Wim Wiewel. New Brunswick, NJ: Rutgers University Press.

Browning, Rufus P., Dale Rogers Marshall, and David Tabb, eds. 1982. *Protest is Not Enough: The Struggle of Blacks and Hispanics for Equality in Urban Politics.* Los Angeles: University of California Press.

Browning, Rufus. ed. 1990. *Racial Politics in American Cities.* New York: Longman.

Browning, Rufus. ed. 1996. *Racial Politics in American Cities.* Second Edition. New York: Longman.

Brune, Tom. 1994. "Residents Disagree on Race as Factor." *Chicago Sun Times,* (May 1): 1.

Bryan, Bunyan and Paul Mohair. 1992. *Race and the Incidence of Environmental Hazards.* Boulder, CO: Westview Press.

Buenker, John. 1973. *Urban Liberalism and Progressive Reform.* New York: Scribner.

Bullard, Robert. 1990. *Dumping in Dixie: Race, Class, and Environmental Quality.* Boulder, CO: Westview Press.

Bullard, Robert, ed. 1993. *Confronting Environmental Racism: Voices from the Grassroots.* Boston: South End Press.

Bullard, Robert, ed. 1994. *Unequal Protection.* San Francisco: Sierra Club Books.

Carnoy, Martin, Manuel Castells, Stephen S. Cohen and Fernando E. Cardoso. 1993. *The New Global Economy in the Information Age. Reflections on Our Changing World.* University Park, PA: The Pennsylvania State University Press.

Castells, Manuel. 1989. *The Informational City: Information Technology, Economic Restructuring and the Urban-Regional Process.* Oxford: Basil Blackwell Press.

Chavez, John R. 1984. *The Lost Land: The Chicano Image of the Southwest.* Albuquerque: University of New Mexico Press.

Chicago Rehab Network. 1993. *The Chicago Affordable Housing Fact Book: Visions for Change.* Chicago: Chicago Rehab Network.

Chicago Sun Times. 1987. "Special Commercial Real Estate Report." *Chicago Sun Times* (Spring).

Chicago Tribune. 1988. "Chicago Schools: Worst in America. An Examination of Two Public Schools that Fail Chicago." Chicago: Chicago Tribune.

Chicago Tribune. 1988. "Office Uprising. Chicago's Latest Boom in Commercial Real Estate." *Chicago Tribune.* Section 8 (Sept 28).

Chicago Urban League, Latino Institute and Northern Illinois University. 1993. *Working Poor Families in Chicago and the Chicago Metropolitan Area.* Chicago: Chicago Urban League, Latino Institute and Northern Illinois University.

Chicago Urban League, Latino Institute, and Northern Illinois University. 1994. *The Changing Economic Standing of Minorities and Women in the Chicago Metro Area, 1970–1990*. Chicago: Northern Illinois University.

City of Chicago. 1995. *Remarks of Mayor Richard M. Daley, 1995 Budget Speech*. Chicago: City of Chicago: Office of the City Council Clerk (October 13).

City of Chicago Department of Planning. 1983.*Chicago Statistical Abstract. Community Area Profiles*. Chicago: City of Chicago Department of Planning.

City of Chicago Department of Planning and Development. 1992. *Social and Economic Characteristics of Chicago's Population. Community Area Profiles*. Chicago: City of Chicago Department of Planning and Development.

Clark, Dave. 1996. *Urban World/Global City*. New York: Routledge.

Clark, Terry N., and Lorna C. Ferguson. 1983. *City Money, Political Processes, Fiscal Strain and Retrenchment*. New York: Columbia University Press. Pp.33–36.

Clark, Terry N. ed. 1994. *Urban Innovation, Creative Strategies for Turbulent Times*. Thousand Oaks, CA: Sage Publications.

Clavel, Pierre. 1986. *The Progressive City: Planning and Participation, 1969-1984*. New Brunswick, NJ: Rutgers University Press.

Clavel, Pierre and Wim Wiewel, eds. 1991. *Harold Washington and the Neighborhoods: Progressive City Government in Chicago, 1983–1987*. New Brunswick, NJ: Rutgers University Press.

Coalition of Neighborhood Developers (CND). 1994. *From the Ground Up: Neighbors Planning Neighborhoods*. Los Angeles: Coalition of Neighborhood Developers.

Cole, Leonard. 1976. *Blacks in Power: a Comparative Study of Black and White Elected Officials*. Princeton, NJ: Princeton University Press.

Coleman, (Walter) Slim and George Atkins. 1989. *Fair Share: the Struggle for the Rights of The People*. Chicago: Fair Share Coalition/Justice Graphics.

Colon-Warren, Alice. 1996. "The Impact of Job Losses on Puerto Rican Women in the Middle Atlantic Region, 1970-1980." Pp. 105-138 in *Puerto Rican Women and Work: Bridges in Transnational Labor*, edited by Altagracia Ortiz. Philadelphia: Temple University Press.

Commission on the Future of the South. 1986. "Shadows in the Sunbelt" Report. Chapel Hill, NC: MDC, Inc.

Community Service Society. 1995. *Updated poverty Tables for New York City with March 1994 Current Population Survey Estimates*. New York: Community Service Society.

Congress of Community Organizations (COCO). Undated. *Mission Statement*. East Palo Alto, CA.

Córdova, Teresa. "Global Forces and Local Communities: Processes of Interaction in the Conflict over Urban Meaning." Forthcoming.

Cortes, Ernesto Jr. 1993. "Reweaving the Fabric: The Iron Rule and the IAF Strategy for Power and Politics." Pp. 294–319 in *Interwoven Destinies: Cities and the Nation,* editd by Henry G. Cisneros. New York: W.W. Norton.

Cotton, Jeremiah. 1992. "Toward a Theory and Strategy for Black Economic Development." Pp. 11-31 in *Race, Politics and Economic Development,* edited by James Jennings. New York: Verso.

Cotton, Jeremiah. 1993. "Color or Culture?: Wage Differences Among Non-Hispanic Black Males, Hispanic Black Males and Hispanic White Males." *The Review of Black Political Economy* 21, 4:53-67.

Couto, Richard. 1991. *Ain't Gonna Let Nobody Turn Me Round: The Pursuit of Racial Justice in the Rural South.* Philadelphia: Temple University.

Craig, Gary and Majorie Mayo. 1995. *Community Empowerment: A Reader in Citizen Participation.* New York: Zed Books.

Dalto, Guy V. 1987. "Economic Segmentation, Human Capital, and Tax-Favored Fringe Benefits." *Social Science Quarterly* 68:583-597.

Davis, James A. and Tom W. Smith. 1992. *General Social Surveys, Cumulative Codebook.* Chicago: NORC.

Davis, King. 1975. *Fund Raising in the Black Community: History, Feasibility, and Conflict.* Metuchen, NJ: The Scarecrow Press.

Davis, Mike. 1992. *City of Quartz.* New York: Vintage Books

Dawson, Michael C. 1994. *Behind the Mule: Race and Class in African American Politics.* Princeton, NJ: Princeton University Press.

Dawson, Michael C. 1996. "Empowerment Zones and Implications for Citizen Participation and Poverty Alleviation." Presentation at the University of Illinois at Chicago Working Conference on Empowerment Zones. Chicago: University of Illinois at Chicago (June 19).

De la Garza, Rodolfo, ed. 1992. *Latino Voices: Mexican, Puerto Rican, and Cuban Perspectives on American Politics.* Boulder, CO: Westview Press.

DeFreitas, Gregory. 1991. *Inequality at Work: Hispanics in the U.S. Labor Force.* New York: Oxford University Press.

Delgado, Gary. 1994. *Beyond the Politics of Place. New Directions in Community Organizing in the 1990s.* Oakland, CA: Applied Research Center.

Dennis, Denise. 1984. *Black History for Beginners.* New York, NY: Writers and Readers.

Department of Commerce. 1994. *County and City Data Book.* Washington, DC: U.S. Department of Commerce.

Dillon, Sam. 1995. "Mexico Woos U.S. Mexicans, Proposing Dual Nationality." *The New York Times* (December 10): 16.

Doeringer, Peter and Michael Piore. 1971. *Internal Labor Markets and Manpower Analysis.* Lexington: D.C. Heath.

Dowie, Mark. 1995. *Losing Ground: American Environmentalism at the Close of the Twentieth Century.* Cambridge, MA: MIT Press.

Du Bois, W.E.B. 1990. *The Souls of Black Folk.* New York: Penguin/Signet Group.

Edwards, Jack, Marie Thomas and Regina Burch. 1992. "Hispanic Representation in the Federal Government: Lessons From the Navy's Equal Employment Opportunity Enhancement Research Program." Pp. 231-245 in *Hispanics in the Workplace,* edited by Stephen Knouse, Paul Rosenfeld, and Amy Culbertson. Newbury Park, CA: Sage Publications.

Eisenger, Peter. 1980a. *The Politics of Displacement: Racial and Ethnic Transition in Three American Cities.* New York, NY: Academic Press.

Eisenger, Peter.1980b. "Black Mayors and the Politics of Racial Economic Advancement" a paper originally presented at the Western Political Science Association meeting (March 26–29).

Eisenger, Peter.1983a. *Black Employment in City Government, 1973-1980.* Washington, DC: Joint Center for Political Studies.

Eisenger, Peter.1983b. "Black Mayors: Who Gets Elected, How and What Difference Does it Make?" a speech to the National Conference on Black Mayoral Politics. Chicago: University of Illinois (January 28).

Environmental Health Coalition. 1993. *Toxic-Free Neighborhood Community Planning Guide.* San Diego, CA: Environmental Health Coalition (January).

Fact File 1995. *Leadership News* (April 15): 5.

Falcon, Angelo. 1985. *Black and Latino Politics in New York City: Race and Ethnicity in a Changing Urban Context.* New York: Institute for Puerto Rican Policy.

Falcon, Angelo. 1988. "Black and Latino Politics in New York City: Race and Ethnicity in a Changing Urban Context." Pp. 171–194 in *Latinos and the Political System,* edited by F. Chris Garcia. Notre Dame, IN: Notre Dame University Press.

Falk, William and Thomas Lyson. 1988. *High Tech, Low Tech, No Tech.* Albany, NY: SUNY Press.

Farley R. and W. Allen. 1989. *The Color Line and the Quality of Life in America.* New York: Oxford University Press.

Ferman, Barbara. 1996. *Challenging the Growth Machine: Neighborhood Politics in Chicago and Pittsburgh.* Lawrence, KS: University of Kansas Press.

Finley, Lawrence K., ed. 1989. *Public Sector Privatization.* New York: Quorum Books.

Fletcher, William and Eugene Newport. 1992. "Race and Economic Development:The Need for a Black Agenda." Pp. 117-130 in *Race, Politics, and Economic Development*, edited by James Jennings. New York: Verso.

Franklin, Raymond S. 1991. *Shadows of Race and Class*. Minneapolis: University of Minnesota Press.

Frazier, E. Franklin. 1957. *Race and Cultural Contacts in the Modern World*. New York: Knopf.

Friedman, John and Goetz Wolf. 1982. "World City Formation." *International Journal of Urban and Regional Research* 6,3 (Sept): 309-344.

Friese, Elfriede. 1949. "Report of Visit to Farm Labor Camp, Glassboro, New Jersey," February 4. *Friends Neighborhood Guild Collection*. Philadelphia: Urban Archives, Temple University.

Fuchs, Esther R. 1992. *Mayors and Money: Fiscal Policy in New York and Chicago*. Chicago: University of Chicago Press.

Fuentes, Luis. 1995. "The Community Control Movement: Excerpts from an Interview with Luis Fuentes." *Critica* 15: 1, 6–8.

Gaither, Gerald. 1977. *Blacks and the Populist Movement*. Tuscaloosa: University of Alabama Press.

Galster, George C. and Edward W. Hill. eds. 1992. *The Metropolis in Black and White. Place, Power and Polarization*. New Brunswick, NJ: Center for Urban Policy Research, Rutgers State University.

Gaventa, John, Barbara Ellen Smith and Alex Willingham. 1990. *Communities in Economic Crisis: Appalachia and the South*. Philadelphia: Temple University.

Gecas, Victor. 1979. "The Influence of Social Class on Socialization." Pp. 365-404 in *Contemporary Theories about the Family*, edited by W. Burr, R. Hill, F. Nye, and I. Reiss. Vol. I. New York, NY: Free Press.

Gecas, Victor. 1980. "Family and Social structural Influences on the Career Orientation of Rural Mexican Youth." *Rural Sociology* 45:272-289.

Gills, Douglas. 1991. "Chicago Politics and Community Development: A Social Movement Perspective." Pp. 34-63 in *Harold Washington and the Neighborhoods: Progressive City Government in Chicago, 1983-1987*, edited by Pierre Clavel and Wim Wiewel. New Brunswick, NJ: Rutgers University Press.

Gills, Douglas. 1993. "The Politics of Community Development in Chicago." Pp. 146-54 in *Chicago's Future in a Time of Change*, edited by Dick Simpson. Champaign, IL: Stipes Publishing.

Gills, Douglas and Wim Wiewel. 1995. "Community Development Organizational Capacity Building and U.S. Urban Policy: Lessons from the Chicago Experience,1983-93." Pp.127-39 in *Community Empowerment: A Reader in*

Participation and Development, edited by Gasry Craig and Majorie Mayo. New York: Zed Books.

Glazer, Nathan and Daniel Patrick Moynihan. 1963. *Beyond the Melting Pot: The Negroes, Puerto Ricans, Jews, Italians, and Irish of New York City*. Cambridge, MA: MIT Press.

Glazer, Nathan and Daniel Patrick Moynihan. 1970. *Beyond the Melting Pot*. Second Edition. Cambridge, MA: MIT Press.

Glenn, Norvall. 1962. "The Negro Population in the American System of Social Stratification: An Analysis of Recent Trends." Ph.D Dissertation, Austin: University of Texas.

Goldsmith, William and Edward J. Blakely, eds. 1992. *Separate Societies: Poverty and Inequality in U.S. Cities*. Philadelphia: Temple University Press.

Gomes, Ralph and Linda Faye Williams. eds. 1992. *From Exclusion to Inclusion: The Long Struggle for African American Political Power*. New York: Greenwood.

Gonzalez, Eddie and Louis Gray. 1984. "Puerto Ricans, Politics and Labor Activism." Pp. 117–126 in *Puerto Rican Politics in Urban America*, edited by J. Jennings and M. Rivera. Westport, CT: Greenwood Press.

Goode, Judith. 1994. "Polishing the Rustbelt: Immigrants Enter a Restructuring Philadelphia." Pp. 199–230 in *Newcomers in the Workplace: Immigrants and the Restructuring of the U.S. Economy*, edited by Louise Lamphere, Alex Stepick, and Guillermo Grenier. Philadelphia: Temple University Press.

Goode, Judith and Jo Anne Schneider. 1994. *Reshaping Ethnic and Racial Relations in Philadelphia: Immigrants in a Divided City*. Philadelphia: Temple University Press.

Gordon, Milton M. 1964. *Assimilation in American Life*. New York, NY: Oxford University Press.

Gordon, Milton M. 1981. "Models of Pluralism, The New American Dilemma." *Annals of the American Academy of Political and Social Sciences* 454:178-188.

Gove, Samuel K., and Louis H. Masotti, eds. 1982. *After Daley: Chicago Politics in Transition*. Urbana: University of Illinois Press.

Greeley, Andrew. 1974. *Ethnicity in the United States: A Preliminary Reconnaissance*. New York, NY: Wiley.

Green, Paul. 1990 Revised. "The Chicago Political Tradition: A Mayoral Retrospective." Pp. 214-224 in *The Mayors: The Chicago Political Tradition*, edited by Paul Green and Melvin Holli. Carbondale: Southern Illinois University Press.

Green, Charles and Basil Wilson. 1989. *The Struggle for Black Empowerment in New York City.* New York: Praeger.

Green, Paul M. and Melvin G. Holli. eds. 1987, 1990 revised. *The Mayors: The Chicago Political Tradition.* Carbondale, IL: Southern Illinois University Press.

Green, Paul M.and Melvin G. Holli. eds. 1991. *Restoration 1989: Chicago Elects Another Daley.* Chicago: Lyceum Books.

Greer, James and Lawrence B. Joseph. 1989. *Public and Private Investment in Chicago. A Report of the Neighborhood Information System Project.* Chicago: The Center for Urban Research and Policy Studies, The University of Chicago.

Grimshaw, William. 1982. "The Daley Legacy: A Declining Politics of Party, Race and Unions." Pp. 57–87 in *After Daley: Chicago Politics in Transition,* edited by S. Gove and Louis Massotti. Urbana: University of Illinois Press.

Grimshaw, William. 1992. *Bitter Fruit: Black Politics and the Chicago Machine, 1931-1991.* Chicago, IL: University of Chicago Press.

Gugliotta, Guy. 1993. "Number of Poor Americans Rises for 3rd Year." *The Washington Post* (October 5): A6.

Gupte, Parnay. 1978. "New York Urban League Sees Growing Racial Unrest." *New York Times,* Section 11 (January 20): 3:1

Hacker, Andrew. 1992. *Two Nations: Black and White, Separate, Hostile, Unequal.* New York, NY: Charles Scribner's Sons.

Haines, Pamela. 1982. "Clothing and Textiles: The Departure of an Industry." Pp. 211-219 in *Community and Capital in Conflict: Plant Closings and Job Loss,* edited by John C. Raines, Lenora E. Berson and David Gracie. Philadelphia, PA: Temple University Press.

Handsaker, Morrison. 1953. *Seasonal Farm Labor in Pennsylvania.* Easton, PA: Lafayette College.

Handy, John. 1993. "Community Economic Development: Some Critical Issues." *The Review of Black Political Economy* 21, 3: 41-64.

Hanks, Lawrence J. 1987. *The Struggle for Black Political Empowerment in Three Georgia Counties.* Knoxville, TN: University of Tennessee Press.

Harris, Theresa L. 1994. "White Supremacy and the Political Structure of the South: A Historical Materialist Analysis of the Post-Reconstruction Era from 1877 to 1900." Ph.D. Dissertation. Washington, D.C.: Howard University.

Harrison, Bennett. 1995. "Racial and Ethnic Diversity." Pp. 141-210 in *State of the Union—America in the 1990s, Volume Two: Social Trends,* edited by Reynolds Farley. New York, NY: Russell Sage.

Harrison, Bennett and Barry Bluestone. 1988. *The Great U-Turn: Corporate Restructuring and Polarization of America.* New York, NY: Basic Books.

Harvey, David. 1989. *The Condition of Post-Modernity.* Oxford, UK: Blackwell.

Hayes Bautista, David E. and Jorge Chapas. 1987. "Latino Terminology: Conceptual Bases for Standardized Terminology." *American Journal of Public Health* 77, 1: 61-68.

Hechter, Michael. 1975. *Internal Colonialism.* Berkeley, CA: University of California Press.

Henderson, Julia. 1945. "Foreign Labour in the United States during the War." *International Labor Review* (December): 609-631.

Henwood, Doug. 1993a. "Old Party, New Bottle." *Left Business Observer* 58 (April).

Henwood, Doug. 1993b. "New Party Revisited." *Left Business Observer* 59 (July).

Hero, Rodney E. 1992. *Latinos and the U.S. Political System: Two-Tiered Pluralism.* Philadelphia: Temple University Press.

Herring, Cedric. 1993. "Ethnic Notions About Alien Nations: American Ethnic Groups' Changing Sentiments Toward Foreign Countries." *Sociological Focus* 26: 315-332.

Herring, Cedric, Michael Bennett, Doug Gills and Noah Temaner-Jenkins, eds. 1998. *Empowerment in Chicago: Grassroots Participation in Economic Developmentand Poverty Alleviation.* Chicago, IL: Great Cities Institute / University of Illinois Press.

Hershberg, Theodore, Alan Burnstein, Eugene Erickson, Stephanie Greenberg, and William Yancey. 1981. "A Tale of Three Cities: Blacks, Immigrants, and Opportunity in Philadelphia, 1850-1880, 1970." Pp. 461-491 in *Philadelphia: Work, Space, Family, and Group in the Nineteenth Century*, edited by Theodore Hershberg. New York, NY: Oxford University Press.

Hess, G. Alfred Jr. 1991. *School Restructuring, Chicago Style.* Newbury Park, CA: Corwin Press.

History Task Force, Centro de Estudios Puertorriquenos. 1979. *Labor Migration under Capitalism: the Puerto Rican Experience.* New York: Monthly Review Press.

Hochner, Arthur and Daniel Zibman. 1982. "Capital Flight and Job Loss: A Statistical Analysis." Pp. 198-210 in *Community and Capital in Conflict.* Philadelphia, PA: Temple University Press.

Hollander, Elizabeth. 1991. "The Department of Planning under Harold Washington." Pp. 121-145 in *Harold Washington and the Neighborhoods: Progressive City Government in Chicago 1983-1987,* edited by Pierre Clavel and Wim Wiewel. New Brunswick, NJ: Rutgers University Press.

Holli, Melvin. 1987. "Ranking Chicago's Mayors: Mirror, Mirror on the Wall, Who is the Greatest of them All?" Pp. 202-211 in *The Mayors: The Chicago*

Political Tradition edited by Paul Green, and Melvin Holli. Carbondale: Southern Illinois University Press.

Holli, Melvin. 1991. "Daley to Daley." Pp. 193–207 in *Restoration: Chicago Elects Another Daley* edited by Paul M. Green and Melvin G. Holli. Chicago: Lyceum Books.

Horowitz, Craig. 1994. "New Struggle for Post-Dinkins leadership in the Black Community." *New York* 27, 14: 36-45.

Hyclak, Thomas and James Stewart. J. 1986. "The Effects of Immigrants, Women, and Teenagers on the Relative Earnings of Black Males." *The Review of Black Political Economy* 15, 1: 93-101.

IDES. 1970. *Where Workers Work. Chicago Metropolitan Area 1970.* Chicago: State of Illinois, Illinois Department of Employment Security.

IDES. 1980. *Where Workers Work. Chicago Metropolitan Area 1990.* Chicago: State of Illinois, Illinois Department of Employment Security.

IDES. 1990. *Where Workers Work. Chicago Metropolitan Area 1990.* Chicago: State of Illinois, Illinois Department of Employment Security.

Idson, Todd and Hollis Price. 1992. "An Analysis of Wage Differentials by Gender and Ethnicity in the Public Sector." *The Review of Black Political Economy* 20, 3: 75–98.

Industrial Areas Foundation Network of Southern California. 1988. "A Win for the Working Poor: The Moral Minimum Wage Campaign." Los Angeles: Industrial Areas Foundation.

Jackson, Bryan O., and Michael B. Preston. 1994. "Race and Ethnicity in Los Angeles Politics." Pp. 85-104 in *Big City Politics, Governance, and Fiscal Constraints,* editd by George E. Peterson. Washington, D.C.: The Urban Institute Press.

Jackson, Thomas F. 1993. "The State, the Movement, and the Urban Poor: The War on Poverty and Political Mobilization in the 1960s." Pp. 403–439 in *The "Underclass" Debate: Views from History* edited by Michael Katz. Princeton, NJ: Princeton University Press.

Jacobson, Louis, Robert LaLonde and Daniel Sullivan, D. 1993. *The Costs of Worker Dislocation.* Kalamazoo, MI: W.E. Upjohn Institute for Employment Research.

Jaynes, G. and R. Williams. 1989. *A Common Destiny: Blacks and American Society.* Washington, DC: National Academy Press..

Jennings, James. 1988. "The Puerto Rican Community: Its Political Background." Pp. 65-80 in *Latinos and the Political System,* edited by F. Chris Garcia. South Bend, IN: Notre Dame University Press.

Jennings, James. 1992a. *The Politics of Black Empowerment. The Transformation of Black Activism in Urban America.* Detroit, MI: Wayne State University Press.

Jennings, James, ed. 1992b. *Race, Politics, and Economic Development.* New York: Verso.

Jennings, James. 1994a. *Understanding the Nature of Poverty In Urban America.* Westport, CT: Praeger.

Jennings, James, ed. 1994b. *Blacks, Latinos and Asians in Urban America: Status and Prospects for Politics and Activism.* Westport, CT: Praeger.

Jennings, James, ed. 1997. *Race and Politics.* New York Verso.

Johnson, James H. Jr., Cloyzelle K. Jones, Walter C. Farrell, Jr., and Melvin L. Oliver. 1992a. "The Los Angeles Rebellion, 1992: A Preliminary Assessment From Ground Zero." Working Paper. Los Angeles: Center for the Study of Urban Poverty, UCLA.

Johnson, James H. Jr., Cloyzelle K. Jones, Walter C. Farrell, Jr., and Melvin L. Oliver. 1992b. "The Los Angeles Rebellion: A Retrospective View." *Economic Development Quarterly* 6, 4: 356-372.

Jones, Jacqueline. 1993. "Southern Diaspora: Origins of the Northern 'Underclass." Pp. 27-54 in *The "Underclass" Debate: Views from History,* edited by Michael Katz. Princeton, NJ: Princeton University Press.

Jones, Mack. 1992. "The Black Underclass as Systemic Phenomenon." Pp. 53-66 in *Race, Politics and Economic Development.Community Perspectives,* edited by James Jennings. New York: Verso.

Jones-Wilson, Faustine. 1991. "School Improvement Among Blacks: Implications for Excellence and Equity." Pp. 72-78 in *The Education of African Americans,* edited by W. Willie, A. Garibaldi, and W. Reed. Westport, CT: Auburn House.

Karnig, Albert K. and Susan Welch. 1980. *Black Representation and Urban Policy.* Chicago: University of Chicago Press.

Katz, Michael. 1993. "The Urban 'Underclass' as a Metaphor of Social Transformation." Pp. 3-23 in *The "Underclass" Debate: Views from History,* edited by Michael Katz. Princeton, NJ: Princeton University Press.

Katz, William Loren. 1986. *Black Indians: A Hidden Heritage.* New York: Atheneum.

Katz-Fishman, Walda and Jerome Scott. 1986. "Electoral Politics and Class Struggle: Democracy Under Attack in West Alabama." *Humanity & Society* (November):469-478.

Katz-Fishman, Walda and Jerome Scott. 1994. "Diversity and Equality: Race and Class in America." *Sociological Forum* 9, 4:569-581.

Keil, Roger, Gerda R. Wekerle and David V.J. Bell. 1996. *Local Places in the Age of the Global City.* New York: Blackwell.

Keller, John. 1983. *Power in America: The Southern Question and the Control of Labor.* Chicago: Vanguard Books.

Kelley, Robin. 1990. *Hammer and Hoe: Alabama Communists During the Great Depression.* Chapel Hill: University of North Carolina Press.

Kelley, Robin D. G. 1994. " 'Check the Technique': Black Urban Culture and the Predicament of Social Science." W.E.B. Du Bois Distinguished Visiting Lecturer Series. New York: City University of New York.

Kennedy, Paul. 1993. *Preparing for the Twenty-First Century.* New York: Random House.

Kilson, Martin. 1981. "Black Social Classes and Intergenerational Poverty." *The Public Interest* 54:58–78.

Kirkpatrick, Sale. 1991. *The Conquest of Paradise: Christopher Columbus and the Columbian Legacy.* New York: Dutton.

Kleinberg, Benjamin. 1995. *Urban America in Transformation . . . Perspectives on Urban Policy and Development.* Thousand Oaks, CA: Sage.

Kleppner, Paul. 1985. *Chicago Divided: The Making of a Black Mayor.* DeKalb: Northern Illinois University Press.

Korten, David C. 1995. *When Corporations Rule the World.* West Hartford, CN: Kumarian Press and San Francisco: Berett-Koeler.

Kotkin, Joel. 1993. *Tribes: How Race, Religion, and Identity Determine Success in the New Global Economy.* New York: Random House.

Kozol, Jonathan. 1991. *Savage Inequalities: Children in America's Schools.* New York: Crown Books.

Landry, Bart. 1987. *The New Black Middle Class.* Berkeley: University of California Press.

Lane, Roger. 1991. *William Dorsey's Philadelphia and Ours: On the Past and Future of the Black City in America.* New York: Oxford University Press.

Leadership Council for Metropolitan Open Communities. 1991. *Jobs, Housing and Race in the Chicago Metropolitan Area. A Geographic Imbalance.* Chicago: Leadership Council for Metropolitan Open Communities.

Leid, Utrice. 1995. "Interview with Beatrice Leid, Former Managing Editor of the New York City Sun." (August 27).

Leigh, Wilhemina. 1992. "Civil Rights Legislation and the Housing Status of Black Americans: An Overview." Pp. 5-28 in *The Housing Status of Black Americans,* edited by W. Leigh and J. Stewart. New Brunswick, NJ: Transaction Publishers.

Lewis, Oscar. 1965. *La Vida: A Puerto Rican Family in the Culture of Poverty-San Juan and New York.* New York: Random House.

Lewis, Oscar. 1973. "The Culture of Poverty." Pp. 469-479 in *Contemporary Cultures and Societies of Latin America,* edited by Dwight B. Heath. New York: Random House.

Lieberson, Stanley. 1980. *A Piece of the Pie.* Berkeley: University of California Press.

Lindemeyer, Otto J., Ernest Kaiser, and Harry Ploski. 1971. *Reference Library of Black America*. New York, NY: Bellwether Publication Company.

Lipietz, Alan. 1993. "The Local and Global: Background, Individuality or Inter-regionalism?" *Transactions Institute of British Geographers* 18: 8–18.

Logan, Andy. 1993. "Two Percent Solutions." *The New Yorker* 69, 32: 52-59.

Long, Larry. 1988. *Migration and Residential Mobility in the United States*. New York, NY: Sage Publications.

Lowi, Theodore. 1981. *Incomplete Conquest: Governing America*. New York, NY: Holt, Rinehart and Winston.

Ludgin, Mary K. 1989. *Downtown Development: Chicago 1987-1990*. Chicago, IL: City of Chicago, Department of Planning.

Ludgin Mary K. and Louis Massotti. 1985. *Downtown Development: Chicago 1979-1984*. Evanston, IL: Center for Urban Affairs and Policy Research, Northwestern University.

Mabee, Carleton. 1979. *Black Education in New York State*. Syracuse, NY: Syracuse University Press.

Madden, Janice Fanning and William J. Stull. 1991. *Work, Wages, and Poverty: Income Distribution in Post-Industrial Philadelphia*. Philadelphia: University of Pennsylvania Press.

Mahtesian, Charles. 1995. "Chicago Goes Private." *Governing* (May):26–29.

Mansfield, Harvey C. 1995. "Real Change in the USA." *Government and Opposition* 30, 1. London: London School of Economics and Science.

Mar, Don and Paul Ong. 1994. "Race and Rehiring in the High-Tech Industry." *The Review of Black Political Economy* 22, 3: 43-54.

Marable, Manning.1985. *Black American Politics. From the March on Washington to Jesse Jackson*. London: Thedford Press.

Marti, Jose. 1889. "Letter to Serafin Bello." 16 November, *Obras Completas*, Vol. 1 (Havana: Editora Nacional de Cuba, 1963-5, 27 vols., p. 48); cited in P. Turton, *Jose Marti: Architect of Cuba's Freedom*. London: Zed Books.

Mason, Maryann and Wendy Siegel. 1997. *Does privatization Pay? A Case Study of Privatization in Chicago. Analysis of Its Effect on Workers and Cost Saving Estimates*. Chicago, Il: The Chicago Institute of Urban Poverty.

Massey, Douglas S. 1990. "American Apartheid: Segregation and the Making of the Underclass." *American Journal of Sociology* (September):329-357.

Massey, Douglas S. and Nancy A. Denton. 1993. *American Apartheid: Segregation and the Making Of the Underclass*. Cambridge, MA: Harvard University Press.

Mauer, M. 1994. "A Generation Behind Bars: Black Males and the Criminal Justice System." Pp. 81-94 in *The American Black Male, His Present Status and His Future*. Chicago: Nelson-Hall Publishers.

Mayor LaGuardia's Commission on the Harlem Riot. 1969. *The Complete Report of Mayor LaGuardia's Commission on the Harlem Riot of March 19,1935*. New York: Arno Press.

McAdams, Doug. 1982. *Political Process and the Development of Black Insurgency, 1930-1970*. Chicago: University of Chicago Press.

Medoff, Peter and Holly Sklar. 1994. *Streets of Hope: The Fall and Rise of an Urban Neighborhood*. Boston: South End Press.

Meier, August and Elliot Rudwick. 1993. *From Plantation to Ghetto*. New York: Hill and Wang.

Meier, Kenneth J., Joseph Stewart, Jr.and Robert E. England. 1989. *Race, Class and Education: the Politics of Second Generation Discrimination*. Madison: University of Wisconsin Press.

Melendez, Edwin. 1993. "Understanding Latino Poverty." *Sage Race Relations Abstracts* 18,2:3-42.

Mier, Robert. 1994. "Some Observations on Race in Planning." *Journal of American Planning Association* 60, 2 (Spring).

Mier, Robert. 1993. *Social Justice and Local Development Policy*. Newbury Park, CA: Sage Publications.

Mier, Robert and Kari Moe. 1991. "Decentralized Development: From Theory to Practice." Pp. 64-99 in *Harold Washington and the Neighborhoods: Progressive City Government in Chicago, 1983-1987*, edited by Pierre Clavel and Wim Wiewel. New Brunswick, NJ: Rutgers University Press.

Miles, Jack. 1992. "Blacks vs. Browns." *Atlantic Monthly.* 270,4:41-68.

Miller, Alton B. 1989. *Harold Washington: The Mayor, The Man*. Chicago: Bonus Books

Mollenkopf, John H. and Manuel Castells, Eds. 1992. Dual City: *Restructuring in New York*. New York: Russell Sage Foundation.

Monkkonen, Eric H. 1995. *The Local State: Public Money and American Cities*. Stanford CA: Stanford, University Press.

Montgomery, Patricia. 1994. *The Hispanic Population in the United States: March 1993*. Current Population Reports, Population Characteristics, Series P20-475. Washington, DC: U.S. Government Printing Office.

Moore, Joan and Raquel Pinderhughes. 1993. "Introduction." Pp. xi-xxxix in *In the Barrios: Latinos and the Underclass Debate*, edited by Joan Moore and Raquel Pinderhughes. New York, NY: Russell Sage Foundation.

Morales, Rebecca. 1996. "Project QUEST: An Embedded Network ET (Employment Training) Organization." Report 421. Chicago: University of Illinois Center for Urban Economic Development.

Morales, Rebecca and Frank Bonilla, eds. 1993. *Latinos in a Changing U.S. Economy: Comparative Perspectives on Growing Inequality*. Newbury Park, CA: Sage Foundation.

Morales, Rebecca and Paul Ong. 1993. "The Illusion of Progress—Latinos in Los Angeles." Pp. in *Latinos in a Changing U.S. Economy: Comparative Perspectives on Growing Inequality* edited by Rebecca Morales and Frank Bonilla. Newbury Park, CA: Sage Publications.

Morales-Nadal, Milga. 1995. "Interview with Milga Morales Nadal, Office of the President, Brooklyn College." (August 29).

Morris, Aldon D. 1984. *The Origins of the Civil Rights Movement: Black Community Organizing for Change*. New York: Free Press.

Morris, Aldon D. and Carol McClurg-Mueller. eds. 1982. *Frontiers in Social Movement Theory*. New Haven, CT: Yale University Press.

Moses, Robert, et.al. 1989. "The Algebra Project. Organizing in the Spirit of Ella." *Harvard Educational Review* 59, 4: 423–44.

Muller, Peter O., Kenneth C. Meyer, and Roman A. Cybriwsky. 1976. *Metropolitan Philadelphia: A Study of Conflicts and Social Cleavages*. Cambridge, MA: Ballinger.

Naisbitt, John. 1982. *Megatrends: Ten New Directions Transforming Our Lives*. New York: Warner Books.

National Archives, Record Group 211-269. 1944a. File: War Manpower Commission Collection, January 19. "Memo on Preliminary Draft of 1944 Program for Recruiting Workers for Food Processing Industry," written by Frank L. McNamee, Regional Director of the War Manpower Commission.

National Archives, Record Group 211-269. 1944b. File: War Manpower Commission Collection, April 6. "Memo from Frank L. McNamee on the Shortage of Labor for Food Processors, Region III."

National Archives, Record Group 211-269. 1944. File: War Manpower Commission Collection, July 12. "Food Processing Employer's Agreement."

National Archives, Record Group 211-269. 1944. File: War Manpower Commission Collection, July 31. "Special E.S. Bulletin No. 244: Immigration of Puerto Rican Workers."

National Archives, Record Group 211-269. 1944. File: War and Manpower Commission Collection, May 25. Cross Reference Sheet to Costello, written by W.T. Doe.

National Archives, Record Group 211-269. 1944. File: War Manpower Commission Collection. Letter from Thomas Costello to Frank L. McNamee.

New York Times. 1978. "New York Urban League Report." *New York Times,* Section 11 (January 20): 3:1.

New York Times. 1979. "Poverty is Said to affect a fourth of City's Youth." *New York Times*, Section 11 (March 5): 4:2

Newman, Katherine S. 1993. *Declining Fortunes. The Withering of the American Dream*. New York: Basic Books.

Nyden, Phillip and Wim Wiewel. eds. 1991. *Challenging Uneven Development.* New Brunswick, NJ: Rutgers University Press.

Oberman, Joseph and Stephen Kozakowski. 1976. *History of Development in the Delaware Valley Region.* Philadelphia: Delaware Valley Regional Planning Commission (September).

Oliver, Melvin and Thomas Shapiro. 1995. *Black Wealth, White Wealth: A New Perspective on Racial Inequality.* New York: Routledge.

Omi, Michael and Willen Winant. 1986. *Racial Formation in the United States.* New York: Routledge and Kegan Paul.

Ong, Paul, et al. 1989. *The Widening Divide: Income Inequality and Poverty in Los Angeles.* Los Angeles: Graduate School of Architecture and Urban Planning, UCLA.

Ong, Paul and Abel Valenzuela, Jr. 1995. "Job Competition Between Immigrants and African Americans." *Poverty & Race* 4:9-10,12.

Ong, Paul and Janette Lawrence. 1995. "Race and Employment Dislocation in California's Aerospace Industry." *The Review of Black Political Economy* 23, 3: 91–102.

Orfield, Gary and Ken Gaebler. 1991. *Residential Segregation and the 1990 Census. Metropolitan Chicago Census Analysis Project.* Chicago, IL: Leadership Council for Metropolitan Open Communities.

Ortiz, Victoria. 1988. "The Legacy of Arthur Alfonso Schomburg." *Centro Boletin* (Centro de Estudios Puertorriquenos, Hunter College, CUNY) II, 4 (Fall).

Ortiz, Vilma. 1991. "Latinos and Industrial Change in New York and Los Angeles." Pp. 119-134 in *Hispanics in the Labor Force: Issues and Policies,* edited by E. Melendez, C. Rodriguez and J. Figueroa. New York: Plenum Press.

Overpeck, Mary and Abigail Moss. 1991. "Children's Exposure to Environmental Cigarette Smoke Before and After Birth: United States, 1988." Advance Data from Vital and Health Statistics No. 202. Hyattsville, MD: National Center for Health Statistics.

O'Connell, Mary. 1991. *School Reform Chicago Style: How Citizens Organized To Change Public Policy.* Special Issue of the *Neighborhood Works.* Chicago, IL: Center For Neighborhood Technology (Spring).

O'Connor, James. 1973. *The Fiscal Crisis of the State.* New York: St. Martin Press.

O'Connor, James. 1987. *The Meaning of Crisis: A Theoretical Introduction.* New York: Basil Blackwell.

O'Laughlin. 1983. "How Black Mayors are elected: A Comparative Assessment." Speech to the National Black Mayoral Politics Conference. Chicago, IL: University of Illinois (January 30–February 3).

O'Neill, June and Margaret Simms. 1982. "Education." Pp. 329–359 in *The Reagan Experiment,* edited by J. Palmer and I. Sawhill. Washington, DC: The Urban Institute Press.

Padilla, Felix. 1987. *Puerto Rican Chicago*. South Bend, IN: University of Notre Dame Press.

Palmer, John and Isabel Sawhill. 1982. "Perspectives on the Reagan Experiment." Pp. 1-28 in *The Reagan Experiment*, edited by John Palmer and Isabel Sawhill. Washington, DC: The Urban Institute Press.

Park, Robert E. and Ernest W. Burgess. 1921. *Introduction to the Science of Sociology*. Chicago: University of Chicago Press.

Park, Robert E., Ernest W. Burgess and Robert D. McKenzie. 1925. *The City*. Chicago: University of Chicago Press.

Pastor, Manuel Jr. 1993. *Latinos and the Los Angeles Uprising: The Economic Context*. Claremont, CA: The Tomas Rivera Center.

Peery, Nelson. 1992. *African American Liberation and Revolution in the United States*. Chicago: Workers Press.

Peery, Nelson. 1994. *Black Fire: The Making of an American Revolutionary*. New York: New Press.

Pennsylvania Bureau of Employment Security. 1953. *Annual Report*. Philadelphia: Pennsylvania Report of Employment Security.

Pennsylvania Bureau of Employment Security. 1954-1970. *Annual Report*. Philadelphia: Pennsylvania Bureau of Employment Security.

Pennsylvania Bureau of Employment Security. 1958. *Annual Report*. Philadelphia: Pennsylvania Report of Employment Security.

Pennsylvania Bureau of Employment Security. 1968. "Manpower Planning Report for the Philadelphia, Pennsylvania Area." Philadelphia: Pennsylvania Report of Employment Security (June).

Pennsylvania Economy League (Eastern Division) in association with the Bureau of Municipal Research. 1962. *Special Assimilation Problems of Underprivileged In-Migrants to Philadelphia*. Philadelphia: Pennsylvania Economy League.

Peoples College Collective. 1977. *Introduction to Afro-American Studies*. 2 Volumes. Chicago: Peoples College Press.

Peterson, Paul E. 1976. *School Politics Chicago Style*. Chicago: University of Chicago.

Philadelphia Commission on Human Relations. 1961. *Philadelphia's Non-White Population: Report No. 1, Demographic Data*, prepared by Martha Lavall.

Philadelphia District Health and Welfare Council, Inc. 1960. *Community Assessment East of Ninth Street*. Philadelphia,: Philadelphia District Health and Welfare Council, Inc.

Pinderhughes, Diane M. 1987. *Race and Ethnicity in Chicago Politics. A Reexamination of Pluralist Theory*. Urbana: University of Illinois Press.

Pinderhughes, Diane M. 1994. "Racial and Ethnic Politics in Chicago Mayoral Elections." Pp. 37-62 in *Big City Politics: Governance and Fiscal Con-

straints, edited by George E. Peterson. Washington, DC: Urban Institute Press.

Pitsch, Mark. 1995. "House Panel Approves $1.7 Billion in Cuts to 1995 Education Program." *Education Week* xiv, 23:21.

Podair, Jerald. 1994. "White Values, Black Values: The Ocean Hill-Brownsville Controversy and New York City Culture." *Radical History Review* 59:36–59.

Pohlmann, Marcus. 1992. *Black Politics in Conservative America.* New York: Longman.

Pooley, Eric, "Dave's Latin Test." *New York* 26, 44: 14.

Putnam, Robert D. 1991. *Making Democracy Work: Civic Traditions in Modern Italy.* Princeton, NJ: Princeton University Press.

Putterman, Julie. 1985. *Chicago Steelworkers: The Cost of Unemployment.* Chicago: Steel-workers Research Project, Hull House Association and Local 65 of United Steelworkers of America.

Quadagno, Jill. 1994. *The Color of Welfare: How Racism Undermined the War on Poverty.* Boston: South End Press.

Race, Poverty, and the Environment. 1995. "Burning Fires: Nuclear Technology and Communities of Color." *Race, Poverty and the Evironment* (Spring–Summer).

Ranney, David C. 1992. *Transnational Investment and Job Loss: The Case of Chicago.* Chicago, IL: Center for Urban Economic Development, University of Illinois at Chicago.

Ranney, David C. and William Cecil. 1993. *Transnational Investment and Job Loss in Chicago: Impacts on Women, African-Americans and Latinos.* Chicago: Center for Urban Economic Development, University of Illinois at Chicago.

Reed, H.C. 1982. "Appraising Corporate Investment Policy: A Financial Center Theory of Foreign Direct Investment." Pp.219-243 in *The Multinational Corporation in the 1980s,* edited by Charles P. Kindleberger and David B. Audretsch. London: MIT Press.

Regalado, Jaime. 1994. "Community Coalition-Building." Pp. 205-235 in *The Los Angeles Riots: Lessons for the Urban Future,* edited by Mark Baldassare. San Francisco: Westview Press.

Regalado, James. 1994. "Review of Rodney Eltero."*American Political Science Review* 88, 3:765-766.

Regalado, James and Gloria Martinez. 1991. "Reapportionment and Coalition Building: A Case Study of Barriers to Latino Empowerment in Los Angeles County." Pp. 126-143 in *Latinos and Political Coalitions: Political Empowerment in the 1990s,* edited by Roberto Villarreal and Norma Hernandez. New York: Praeger.

Reimers, Cordelia and Howard Chernick. 1991. "Hispanic Employment in the Public Sector: Why Is It Lower Than Blacks?" Pp. 135-158 in *Hispanics in the Labor Force, Issues and Policies*, edited by Edwin Melendez, Clara Rodriguez and Janis Figueroa. New York: Plenum Press.

Rice, Mitchell. 1990. "Black Hospitals: Institutional Impacts on Black Families." Pp. 49-68 in *Black Families: Interdisciplinary Perspectives*, edited by Harold Cheatham and James Stewart. New Brunswick, NJ: Transaction.

Ries, Peter. 1991. "Characteristics of Persons With and Without Health Coverage: United States, 1989." Advance Data from Vital and Health Statistics No. 201. Hyattsville, MD: National Center for Health Statistics.

Rifkin, Jeremy. 1995. *The End of Work: the Decline of the Global Labor Force and the Dawn of the Post-Market Era*. New York: Tarcher/Putnam Books.

Ringer, Benjamin. 1983. *We the People and Others*. New York: Tavistock Publications.

Rivlin, Gary. 1987. "The Blacks and the Browns: Is the Coalition Coming Apart?" *Chicago Reader* 17, 7 (November).

Rivlin, Gary. 1992. *Fire on the Prairie: Chicago's Harold Washington and the Politics of Race*. New York: H. Holt.

Rodriguez, Clara. 1991. "The Effect of Race on Puerto Rican Wages." Pp. 77-100 in *Hispanics in the Labor Force: Issues and Policies*, edited by Edwin Melendez, Clara Rodriguez and Janis Figueroa. New York: Plenum Press.

Romero, Carol. 1994. *JTPA Programs and Adult Women on Welfare: Using Training to Raise AFDC Recipients Above Poverty*. Research Report No. 93-01. Washington, DC: National Commission for Employment Policy.

Roper Organization. 1992. *New York City Intergroup Relations Survey*. New York: The American Jewish Committee (July 27-August 10).

Rosenfeld, Paul and Amy Culbertson. 1992. "Hispanics in the Military." Pp. 211-230 in *Hispanics in the Workplace*, edited by Stephen Knouse, Paul Rosenfeld, and Amy Culbertson. Newbury Park, CA: Sage Publications.

Roth, Byron M. 1994. *Prescription for Failure. Race Relations in the Age of Social Science*. New Brunswick and London: Transaction Publishers.

Rothenberg, Paula S., ed. 1995. *Race, Class and Gender in the United States: An Itegrated Study*. New York: St. Martins Press.

Rowan, Dan. 1996. *The Coming Race War in America*. New York: Alfred Knopf.

Saint Clair, Drake and Horace B. Cayton. 1945. *Black Metropolis*. Chicago: University of Chicago Press.

Salamon, Lester. 1990. "The Nonprofit Sector and Government: The American Experience in Theory and Practice." Pp. 219-267 in *The Third Sector: Comparative Studies of Nonprofit Organizations*, edited by Helmut Anheir and Wolfgang Seibel. New York, NY: Walter de Gruyter.

Saltzstein, Alan L., and Raphael J. Sonenshein. 1991. "Los Angeles: Transformation of a Governing Coalition." Pp. 189-201 in *Big City Politics in Transition*, Urban Affairs Annual Reviews. Newbury Park, CA: Sage Publications.

Sanchez-Korrol, Virginia. 1983. *From Colonia to America: The History of Puerto Ricans in New York*. Westport, CT: Greenwood.

Sassen, Saskia. 1992. *The Global City: New York, London, Tokyo*. Princeton, NJ: Princeton University Press.

Segura, Denise. 1992. "Walking on Eggshells: Chicanas in the Labor Force." Pp. 194-210 in *Hispanics in the Workplace*, edited by Stephen Knouse, Paul Rosenfeld and Amy Culbertson. Newbury Park, CA: Sage Publications.

SEJ-Southerners for Economic Justice. 1993. *Building Just Relationships for the Next 500 Years: Gathering #3 Report*. Durham, NC: Southeast Regional Economic Justice Network.

Semyonov, Moshe. 1988. "Bi-Ethnic Labor Markets, Mono-Ethnic Labor Markets, and Socioeconomic Inequality." *American Sociological Review* 53:256–266.

Semyonov, Moshe and Noah Lewin-Epstein. 1994. "Ethnic Labor Markets, Gender and Socioeconomic Inequality: A Study of Arabs in the Israeli Labor Force." *Sociological Quarterly* 35:51–68.

Semyonov, Moshe, Danny R. Hoyt, and Richard Ira Scott. 1984. "Place, Race, and Differential Occupational Opportunities." *Demography* 21:259–270.

Simms, Margaret and Julianne Malveaux. 1986. *Slipping Through the Cracks, The Status of Black Women*. New Brunswick, NJ: Transaction.

Simpson, Dick, ed. 1993. *Chicago's Future*. 3rd edition. Chicago: Snipes Press.

Skerry, Peter. 1993. *Mexican Americans: The Ambivalent Minority*. Cambridge, MA: Harvard University Press.

Sklar, Holly. 1995. *Chaos or Community? Seeking Scapegoats for Bad Economics*. Boston: South End Press.

Slaughter, Diana and Deborah Johnson, eds. 1988. *Visible Now: Blacks in Private Schools*. New York: Greenwood Press.

Slaughter, John. 1992. *New Battles over Dixie: The Campaign for a New South*. Dix Hills, NY: General Hall.

Smith, Michael Peter. 1992. *After Modernism: Global Restructuring and the Changing Boundaries of City Life*. Comparative Urban and Community Research, 4. New Brunswick: Transaction Publishers.

Smith, Michael Peter and Joe R. Feagin. 1987. *The Capitalist City: Global Restructuring and Community Politics*. New York: Blackwell.

Smith, Neil. 1996. *New Urban Frontier. Gentrification and the Revanchist City*. New York: Routledge.

Sokoloff, Natalie. 1992. *Black Women and White Women in the Professions*. New York: Routledge.

Sonenshein, Raphael J. 1993. *Politics in Black and White: Race and Power in Los Angeles*. Princeton, NJ: Princeton University Press.

Southern Region Up & Out of Poverty Now. n.d. *Street Heat*. Atlanta, GA: Georgia Citizens Coalition on Hunger.

Southwest Network for Environmental and Economic Justice. 1993. "Statement on the North American Free Trade Agreement." Albuquerque, NM: Southwest Network for Environmental and Economic Justice.

Southwest Network for Environmental and Economic Justice. 1994. "Border Justice Hearings." Albuquerque, NM: Southwest Network for Environmental and Economic Justice.

SouthWest Organizing Project. 1990. "Letter to Group of Ten." Albuquerque, NM: SouthWest Organizing Project.

SouthWest Organizing Project. 1993. *Report on the Interfaith Hearings on Toxic Poisoning in Communities of Color*. Albuquerque, NM: SouthWest Organizing Project.

SouthWest Organizing Project. 1995a. *Voces Unidas Newsletter*. Albuquerque, NM: SouthWest Organizing Project.

SouthWest Organizing Project. 1995b. *Intel Inside*. Albuquerque, NM: SouthWest Organizing Project.

Sowell, Thomas. 1981. *Ethnic America: A History*. New York: Basic Books.

Squires, Gregory D. 1994. *Capital and Communities in Black and White: the Intersection of Race and Class and Uneven Development*. Albany: State University of New York Press.

Squires, Gregory D., Larry Bennett, Kathleen McCourt and Phillip Nyden. 1987. *Chicago: Race, Class and the Response to Urban Decline*. Philadelphia: Temple University Press.

Stafford, Walter. 1986. *Closed Labor Market*. New York: Community Service Society

Stafford, Walter. 1991. "Racial, Ethnic, and Gender Employment Segmentation in New York City Agencies." Pp. 159-182 in *Hispanics in the Labor Force: Issues and Policies*, edited by Edwin Melendez, Clara Rodriguez and Janis Figueroa. New York: Plenum Press.

Stanfield, John H. II and Rutledge M. Dennis. 1993. *Race and ethnicity in Research Methods*. Newbury Park, CA: Sage Publications.

Starks, Robert T. and Michael B. Preston. 1990. "Harold Washington and The Politics of Reform in Chicago." Pp. 88–107 in *Racial Politics in American Cities* edited by Rufus Browning, Dale Marshall and David Tabb. New York: Longman .

Steinberg, S. 1989. *The Ethnic Myth: Race, Ethnicity, and Class in America.* Boston: Beacon Press.

Stevens-Arrogo, Anthony M. and Ana Maria Diaz Stevens. 1995. *An Enduring Flame: Studies in Latino Popular Religiosity.* New York: Paral.

Stewart, James. 1984. "Building a Cooperative Economy: Lessons from the Black Experience." *Review of Social Economy* 42: 360–368.

Stewart, James and Joyce Allen. 1995. *Blacks in Rural America.* New Brunswick, NJ: Transaction Consortium.

Stone, Clarence. 1989. *Regime Politics: Governing Atlanta.* Lawrence: University of Kansas Press.

Stone, Clarence and Heywood Saunders, eds. 1987. *The Politics of Urban Development.* Lawrence: University of Kansas Press.

Storey, James. 1982. "Income Security." Chapter 12, Pp. 361-392 in *The Reagan Experiment*, edited by John Palmer and Isabel Sawhill. Washington, DC: The Urban Institute Press.

Tate, Katherine. 1993. *From Protest to Politics: The New Black Voters in American Elections.* New York: Russell Sage Foundation.

Taylor, John B. 1995. "Changes in American Economic Policy in the 1980s: Watershed or Pendulum Swing?" *Journal of Economic Literature* XXXIII (June).

Taylor, Paul S. 1932. *Mexican Labor in the United States: Chicago and the Calumet Region.* Berkeley: University of California Press.

The Chicago Reporter. *Annual Report of Minority Employment and Contracting in City Gvernment 1980-1995.* Chicago: Archives of *The Chicago Reporter,* Community Renewal Society.

The Chicago Reporter. *Chicago Reporter.* Chicago: The Community Renewal Society. (A monthly news magazine of race, and class assessment of politics and government in Chicago, 1980–85.) Authors' files.

The Chicago Reporter. 1992. Twenty Years Later . . . A City Still Divided. *Chicago Reporter* 21, 7 (July).

The Civic Federation. 1996. *From Privatization to Innovation.* Chicago: The Civic Federation.

The Nation. 1993. "Rainbow's End." *The Nation* 257, 17: 607-608.

The National Law Journal. 1992. "Unequal Protection: The Racial Divide in Environmental Law" (September 21).

The New York Times. 1978. *New York Times.* Section 11 (January 20): 3:1.

The New York Times. 1979. *New York Times.* Section 11 (March 5): 4:2.

The New York Times. 1995. 144, 50, 41. Author's files.

Thrift, N.J. 1989. "The Geography of International Economic Disorder." Pp. 16-78 in *A World in Crises: Geographical Perspectives*, edited by Ronald John Johnson and Peter James Taylor. Oxford: Basil Blackwell.

Tidwell, Billy with Monica Kuumba, Dionne Jones and Betty Watson. 1993. "Fast Facts: African Americans in the 1990s." Pp. 243-266 in *The State of Black America*, edited by B. Tidwell. New York: National Urban League.

Tienda, Marta and D. T. Lii. 1987. "Minority Concentration and Earnings Inequality: Blacks, Hispanics and Asians Compared." *American Journal of Sociology* 93:141-165.

Tilly, Charles. 1978. *From Mobilization to Revolution*. Reading, MA: Addison-Wesley.

Tobias, Ruth Anne and Chandrima Roy. 1993. *The Future of Diversity in the Northwest Suburbs*. Chicago: The Leadership Council for Open Communities.

Toffler, Alvin. 1970. *Future Shock*. New York, NY: Random House.

Toffler, Alvin and Heidi Toffler. 1995.*Creating a New Civilization, The Politics of the Third Wave*. Atlanta, GA: Turner.

Tomasky, Michael. 1993. "The Tawdry Mosaic: Identity Politics in New York City." *The Nation* 256,24: 860-864.

Torres, Andres. 1991. "Labor Market Segmentation: African American and Puerto Rican Labor in New York City, 1960-1980." *The Review of Black Political Economy* 20, 1:59-77.

Torres, Andres. 1995. *Between Melting Pot and Mosaic: African Americans and Puerto Ricans in the New York Political Economy*. Philadelphia: Temple University Press.

Torres, Maria de Los Angeles. 1991. "The Commission on Latino Affairs: A Case Study of Community Empowerment." Pp. 165-187 in *Harold Washington and the Neighborhoods: Progressive City Government in Chicago, 1983-1987* edited by Pierre Clavel and Wim Wiewel. New Brunswick, NJ: Rutgers University Press.

Travis, Dempsey J. 1987. *The Autobiography of Black Politics*. Chicago, IL: Urban Research Institute Press.

Travis, Dempsey J. 1989. *"Harold," The Peoples Mayor: The Authorized Biography of Mayor Harold Washington*. Chicago: Urban Research Institute Press.

Trotter, Joe William, Jr. 1991. "Black Migration in Historical Perspective: A Review of the Literature." Pp. 1-21 in *The Great Migration in Historical Perspective: New Dimensions of Race, Class, and Gender*, edited by Joe William Trotter, Jr. Bloomington: Indiana University Press.

Trotter, Joe William, Jr. 1993. "Blacks in the Urban North: The 'Underclass Question' in Historical Perspective." Pp. 55-81 in *The "Underclass" Debate: Views from History*, edited by Michael Katz. Princeton, NJ: Princeton University Press.

U.S. Bureau of the Census. 1940-1970. *U.S. Census of Population*. Washington, DC: U.S. Government Printing Office.

U.S. Bureau of the Census. 1960. *US Census of Population and Housing: 1960 PHC (1)-104, Part 1, New York, New York.* Washington, DC: Government Printing Office.

U.S. Bureau of the Census. 1990. *U.S. Census of Population.* Washington, DC: Government Printing Office.

U.S. Bureau of the Census. 1993a. *We, the American Hispanics.* Washington, DC: U.S. Government Printing Office.

U.S. Bureau of the Census. 1993b. *We, the American Blacks.* Washington, DC: U.S. Government Printing Office.

U.S. Bureau of the Census. 1994. *Statistical Abstract of the United States: 1994.* Washington, D.C.: Government Printing Office.

U.S. Department of Commerce. 1992. *Poverty in the United States: 1991.* Current Population Reports, Consumer Income, Series P-60, No. 181. Washington, D.C.: U.S. Government Printing Office.

U.S. Department of Commerce. 1995. *Black-Owned Businesses.* Report MB92-1. Washington, D.C.: U.S. Government Printing Office.

U.S. Department of Labor. 1994. *Geographic Profile of Employment and Unemployment* Bulletin 2446. Washington, D.C.: U.S. Government Printing Office.

U.S. Department of Labor, Employment Service, Bureau of Employment Security. 1952. *Employment Security Review,* 19 (March).

U.S. Department of Labor, Employment Service, Farm Placement Service. 1950. *Handbook for Farm Placement Service.* Washington, D.C.: Bureau of Labor Statistics.

U.S. General Accounting Office. 1983. *Siting of Hazardous Waste Landfills and Their Correlation with Racial and Economic Status of Surrounding Communities.* Washington, DC: U.S. Government Printing Office.

Uhfelder, Eric. 1996. "Rethinking Privatization." *Urban Land* (July): 67-71 and 89-90.

United Way of Chicago. 1990. Revised. *Assessing Chicago's Needs in Community Development and Human Services.* Chicago: United Way of Metropolitan Chicago.

United Church of Christ Commission for Racial Justice. 1987. *Toxic Waste and Race in the United States, a National Report on the Racial and Socioeconomic Characteristics of Communities with Hazardous Waste Sites.* New York: United Church of Christ.

United Church of Christ Commission for Racial Justice. 1992. *The First National People of Color Environmental Leadership Summit: Proceedings.* New York: United Church of Christ.

Van Sertima, Ivan. 1976. *The African Presence in Ancient America: They Came Before Columbus.* New York, NY: Random House.

Vander Weele, Maribeth. 1994. *Reclaiming Our Schools: the Struggle For Chicago School Reform.* Chicago: Loyola University/Campion Books.

Vigil, Maurilio E. 1994. "Latinos in American Politics." Pp. 80-109 in *Handbook of Hispanic Cultures in the United States: Sociology,* edited by Felix M. Padilla. Houston, TX: Arte Publico Press.

Villareal, Roberto E. and Norma G. Hernandez. 1991. *Latinos and Political Coalitions: Political Empowerment in the 1990s.* Westport, CT: Praeger Books.

Wallerstein, Immanuel. 1979. *The Capitalist World-Economy.* New York: Cambridge University Press.

Walton, Hanes. 1985. *Invisible Politics: Black Political Behavior.* Albany, NY: SUNY Press.

Washington Post. 1944. "Puerto Ricans Recruited." *Washington Post,* 19 April, clipping, Record Group 126, File 9-8-116, Population, Emigration, General, National Archives, Washington, DC.

Webster, Yehudi. 1992. *The Racialization of America.* New York: St. Martins.

Weisberg, Berry. 1983. "Harold Washington and the Peoples Movement for Reform." Unpublished manuscript.

Whalen, Carmen Teresa. 1994. "Puerto Rican Migration to Philadelphia, Pennsylvania 1945-1970: A Historical Perspective on a Migrant Group." Ph.D. Dissertation, Philadelphia: Rutgers University.

Wiewel, Wim. 1986. *The State of the Economy and Economic Development in the Chicago Metropolitan Region.* Chicago: Center for Urban Economic Development, University of Illinois at Chicago.

Wildavsky, Aaron. 1986. *Budgeting: A Comparative Theory of the Budgetary Process.* New Brunswick, NJ: Transactions Books.

Williams, Eric. 1971. *The History of the Caribbean: From Columbus to Castro.* New York: Harper & Row.

Williams, John Alexander. 1992. "Prism of Columbus." *Tulanian* (Summer):19-23. New Orleans, LA: Tulane University Office of University Relations.

Williams, Roger. 1994. "An Estimate of Black Gross Job Losses Due to Reduced Defense Expenditures." *The Review of Black Political Economy* 22, 3:31-42.

Wilson, Kenneth and Alejandro Portes. 1980. "Immigrant: An Analysis of the Labor Market Experience of Cubans in Miami." *American Journal of Sociology* 86:295-319.

Wilson, William Julius. 1978. *The Declining Significance of Race: Blacks and Changing American Institutions.* Chicago: University of Chicago Press.

Wilson, William Julius. 1987. *The Truly Disadvantaged: The Inner City, The Underclass and Public Policy.* Chicago: University of Chicago Press.

Wilson, William Julius. 1996. *When Work Disappears: The World of the New Urban Poor*. New York: Alfred Knopf.

Winant, Howard. 1994. *Racial Conditions: Politics, Theory, Comparisons*. Minneapolis: University of Minnesota Press.

Wolff, Goetz. 1992. "The Making of a Third World City? Latino Labor and the Restructuring of the L.A. Economy." Draft Paper for the XVII International Congress of the Latin American Studies Association. Los Angeles. (September).

Woodward, C. Vann. 1951. *Reunion and Reaction: The Compromise of 1877 and the End of Reconstruction*. Boston, MA: Little, Brown.

Workers Press. n.d. *Power in the Black Belt*. Chicago: Workers Press.

World Development Report. 1995. *Workers in an Integrating World*. New York: Oxford University Press.

Yeoman, Anne. 1992. "Viewed from the Shores." *Tulanian* (Summer):15–17. New Orleans: Tulane University Office of University Relations.

Zhou, M. and John Logan. 1989. "Returns on Human Capital in Ethnic Enclaves: New York City Chinatown." *American Sociological Review* 54:809-820.

Zinn, Howard. 1965. *Student Nonviolent Coordinating Committee: The New Abolitionists*. Boston: Beacon Press.

Zinn, Howard. 1980. *A People's History of the United States*. New York: Harper and Row.

Zinn, Howard. 1995. *A People's History of the United States 1492–Present* (revised and updated). New York: Harper & Row.

About the Authors

Stephen Alexander holds a Ph.D. in Urban Planning and Policy from the University of Illinois at Chicago. He is currently the Public Policy Analyst for the Chicago Urban League (CUL), involved in a variety of advocacy and policy-based economic development and empowerment related activities. His research activities include an analysis of the capacity of the City of Chicago's budget to address priorities of the city's low and moderate-income communities for the Policy Research Action Group, of which he is a Core Group member.

John J. Betancur is associate professor at the Urban Planning and Policy Program of the College of Urban Planning and Public Affairs of the University of Illinois at Chicago. He received his Ph.D. in Urban Planning and Policy from the University of Illinois. He has published multiple articles on housing and economic development, which include analyses of the impact of socioeconomic restructuring on Latinos and Blacks, critical assessments of community development, theories of economic development and analyses of squatter settlements.

Frank Bonilla is Thomas Hunter Professor Emeritus of Sociology, at Hunter College of the City University of New York. His current research, writing, and advocacy efforts are focused on promoting a vitalizing of Latino academic and policy research capabilities, a reconnection of these resources to their counterparts in the countries of origin of the principal Latino communities in the U.S.A., and especially bringing Latino voices and perspectives into the U.S. foreign policy arena.

Jose T. Bravo has been a community organizer in the San Diego/Tijuana border since 1981. For several years, Jose was the coordinator of the Environmental Health Coalition's Border Environmental Justice Campaign. He is currently a field organizer with the Southwest Network for Environmental and Economic Justice.

Teresa Cordova is Associate Professor of Community and Regional Planning at the University of New Mexico. She works closely with the environmental Justice Movement and is a member of the Southwest Organizing Project. She publishes on the topic of global/local relations and issues of community development, as well as in the area of Chicano Studies. She sits on numerous advisory boards and steering committees of community development corporations, planning organizations, and campus committees.

Douglas C. Gills is an Assistant Professor of Community Development in the Urban Planning and Policy Program and at the Center for Urban Economic Development in the College of Urban Planning and Rublic Affairs at the University of Illinois at Chicago. A Political Science Ph.D. from Northwestern University, he has written extensively on African American mayoral politics, community development and coalition politics.

Jeanne Guana is a founding member and current Director of the Southwest Organizing Project. She has a Bachelor of University Studies from the University of New Mexico, and has over twenty years of experience as a community and student activist and organizer. Her work has involved organizing welfare recipients, the disabled, and undocumented people.

Cedric Herring is Professor in the Department of Sociology at the University of Illinois at Chicago and in the Institute of Government and Pubic Affairs at the University of Illinois. In addition, he is a Faculty Associate at the Irving B.Harris Graduate School of Public Policy Studies at the University of Chicago. He received his Ph.D. from the University of Michigan in 1985. Professor Herring has published widely on such topics as social policy, political sociology, and stratification and inequality.

Walda Katz-Fishman received her Ph.D. in Sociology from Wayne State University in 1978 and is a professor of sociology at Howard University, where she has taught since 1970. Walda is a scholar activist who combines her research interests in class, race, and gender inequality and political economy with political activism in struggles to transform society. She is currently working on a book examining the social history of America, the high technology revolution, and the process of societal transformation.

Edwin Melendez is the director of the Mauricio Gaston Institute for Latino Community Development and Public Policy at the University of Massachusetts, Boston, as well as a faculty member in the Department of Economics. He earned his Ph.D. in economics from the University of Massachusetts, Amherst in 1985. Dr. Melendez has conducted considerable research in the areas of economic development, labor and poverty. His volume entitled Latinos, Poverty, and Public Policy: A Case Study of Massachusetts, co-edited with Miren Uriarte, is being published By the Gaston Institute this fall.

Richard Moore is a key national leader of the environmental justice movement, currently holding the position of Coordinator for the Southwest Network. He has worked with a variety of community-based organizations around such issues as welfare rights, police brutality, street gang activities, drug abuse, low cost healthcare, child nutrition, and the fight against racism including the struggle for environmental and economic justice.

Rebecca Morales holds a Ph.D. from MIT's Department of Urban Studies and Planning in Urban and Regional Planning. Her fields of expertise are urban and regional development, international industrialization, and community development. Among her publications is the co-edited volume *Borderless Borders: U.S. Latinos, Latin Americans, and the Paradox of Interdependence,* along with numerous articles and reports.

Manuel Pastor is Chair of Latin American and Latino Studies at UC Santa Cruz. An economics Ph.D. from the University of Massachusetts, Amherst, his research on urban issues has been published in *Economic Development Quarterly, Review of Regional Studies, Social Science Quarterly*, and elsewhere. He is co-author of *Growing Together: Linking Regional and Community Development* (forthcoming, University of Minnesota Press).

Jerome Scott is Executive Director and past-Board Chair of Project South: Institute for the Elimination of Poverty & Genocide, southern regional organizer for Up & Out of Poverty Now!, co-editor of Street Heat the magazine of the Southern Region Up & Out of Poverty Now!, and a steering committee member of the Regional Economic Justice Network. He works with activists and scholars to conduct action research and popular economic and political education for grassroots groups throughout the country.

Walter Stafford is a professor of urban planning and public policy at the Robert F. Wagner School of Public Policy at New York University. He is currently writing about human rights and multiculturalism, public policy, public administration and racism. Recent publications include, "International Human Rights Instruments and Racial Discrimination in the United States" in the *International Policy Review,* 1996.

James Stewart is Vice Provost for Educational Equity and Professor of Labor Studies and Industrial Relations and African American Studies at Penn State. He holds a Ph.D. in Economics from the University of Notre Dame. Dr. Stewart has published over twenty articles and book chapters on topics directly connected to Black/African Studies. He has also published extensively in economics journals and served as editor of *The Review of Black Political Economy* from 1987 to 1995.

Michael A. Stoll received his Ph.D. in Urban Planning from MIT. He is currently an Assistant Professor in Policy Studies at UCLA, where his chief areas of study are the interplay of race/ethnicity, labor markets, urban poverty, and community economic development.

Carmen Teresa Whalen is an assistant professor in the Puerto Rican and Hispanic Caribbean Studies Department and the History Department at Rutgers University in New Brunswick, New Jersey. She received her Ph.D. in U.S. History from Rutgers University in 1994. She is currently completing a book on Puerto Rican migration to Philadelphia in the post-World War II era, and conducting research on Latinas and the garment industry.

Name Index

Subject Index